Playing by Their Rules

Playing by Their Rules

coastal teenage girls in Kenya on life, love and football

Sarah Forde

Ipas Resource Center

Moving the Goalposts
Box 605, Kiliï 80108, Kenya
T: +254 722 823834, +254 20 350 9411
E: mtgkiliï@yahoo.com
E: playingbytheirrules@gmail.com
W: http://mtgk.org

Contents

Prologue:
Warming up

I hadn't bought the newspaper that day but a colleague who was an avid reader of the papers had spotted it—a full-page article on Kilifi, on teenage girls in Kilifi. She'd ripped the page out and put it on my desk. There, staring out at me were six, maybe seven, young girls in brightly coloured dresses under a headline lamenting, 'Village teenagers learn bitterly not to experiment with love affairs'.

The former Minister of Health, Charity Ngilu, had been visiting Kilifi to meet 40 young single mothers who all lined up for her, singing and ululating, with their babies strapped to their backs. 'This problem is massive,' Ngilu is quoted as saying. 'It will completely destroy the girls in this province.'[1]

Moving the Goalposts (MTG), a community-based organisation (CBO), works in Kilifi District, which is in Coast Province in Kenya. One of the poorest in the country, it's a large rural district that stretches from the east coast far inland to the edge of Tsavo National Park, with an economy that relies on agriculture and tourism. Kilifi town, where MTG has its offices, is the main centre of the district, a small but growing town of around 40,000 people, with one main road, the usual scattering of district government buildings, a police station and a football pitch just off the coast road from Mombasa to Malindi. Going inland, one dirt road snakes towards Bamba, Ganze and Vitengeni, all sparsely populated rural outposts, while another takes you to Kaloleni, a town much smaller than Kilifi but relatively close to Mombasa and its urban influence.

MTG aims to tackle some of the issues around the lack of opportunities that affect young women and girls in Kilifi District. But it doesn't do so in a particularly conventional way. Football for girls is the cornerstone of MTG's programmes. Initiated in 2001, MTG now has close to 3,000 girls and young women who regularly play in its girls' football leagues and tournaments. Girls take part as players, field committee members, football coaches, referees, first aiders, peer educators and counsellors, organising their own activities and showing people that 'Tunaweza!'—'We can do it', the MTG slogan.

MTG has used football as an entry point for a vibrant, peer-led, reproductive health, HIV and AIDS programme, in which trained peer educators and counsellors provide much-needed information, social support and advice to teenage rural girls. Through a leadership award scheme, MTG also encourages girls to stay in school and helps them develop many others skills, such as business skills, public speaking, planning and evaluation.

Three girls from MTG, trained in photography, took the photos in this book, telling stories of Kilifi through their lens.

❖ ❖ ❖

In Kenya it's made clear to me every day what I am; foremost I'm *mzungu* (a white person). Children sing it to me on my way to the bus stop—'mzungu, mzungu, jambo (hello), mzungu'—as I go for my lunch, people in meetings point me out, people in the health clinic, in restaurants, in cafes—always reminding me, just in case I may have forgotten.

I am white; nothing is going to change that. Who am I, then, to delve into the lives of teenage rural girls in Kenya? What right did I have to have spent so long talking with teenage girls about their lives? What right do I have to use my voice, to tell their stories, in my words?

I'd been working as a youth football coach and a radio journalist in Norwich, UK. I came to Kenya in 2001 to set up Moving the Goalposts, which at that time seemed like a radical development programme with football for girls at its core. There were a few girls' football teams in Kilifi but the link between girls' sport, development and empowerment was regarded as a tenuous one. In the early days we had a small committee of football coaches, researchers and teachers who supported me in Kilifi to get the project up and running. But it wasn't easy. People would tell us that girls don't need football; they have much more pressing concerns. Their families need water, they need health care. Others were perplexed by the choice of football. Can't girls just play more netball, or volleyball? Why football? The doubt cast on its appropriateness made implementation both more difficult and more exciting. By 2005 MTG was an established CBO and had contributed towards football becoming a mainstream sport for girls in schools. It gained national recognition in 2007 when the Coast Province Girls' Primary Schools football team, which included ten players from MTG, won the national championships in Nairobi—the first time Coast Province had ever become the champions. MTG's health peer education and other add-on activities had opened the eyes of many people who were not interested in sport to the potential benefits of being involved in MTG's programmes.

By the time I began this book I'd been in Kilifi for five years, working and playing football with girls. As the project developed I learnt Kiswahili, the language that the girls used most of the time, and by the time I started talking to the girls I was virtually fluent. We had our conversations in Kiswahili, a language we all felt comfortable with.

This book is about what I learnt. I was certainly different from the girls, but I could speak the same language and had built up trust with them. What I heard, what the girls told me, what we discussed, was determined to a great extent by who I am. What I was told would be different from what someone else would have been told. A middle-class Kenyan woman from Nairobi, a grandmother from Mombasa, a man, someone straight from Europe—we would all ask different questions, get varied stories, pick up on different parts of the stories and interpret them from our own positions. That is why this is my story and the girls' stories—a unique telling that contains stories that, I hope, will give others a better understanding of rural girls' lives.

❖ ❖ ❖

Sitting in dusty school classrooms, libraries, under trees, at the side of football pitches, I interviewed nine girls over two years. I met each of the girls separately seven times and we met three times as a group. This project became known in MTG as 'Life Stories' as in 'Sarah's doing Life Stories this week'. A bit like how the health peer-education programme is known as 'Peer' and the business skills and saving scheme is called 'Economic'. It seems we don't like unnecessarily long names for projects in MTG. The nine girls, Asya, Carol, Janet, Juliet, Kadzo, Kanze, Mariam, Mercy and Salma (all their names have been changed) shared their teenage lives with me and have now become a part of my life.

Janet once told me that she wanted to talk to me so that other girls could read her story and understand that they were not the only ones going through what they were going through. As Tolman writes: 'Girls can easily misdiagnose their problems as theirs and theirs alone, and then attempt to devise individualized solutions, which are neither answers nor routes to changing the social circumstances that produce the dilemma in the first place.'[2]

This book brings rural teenage girls' stories into the public. Our original objective was 'to contribute to the improvement of the general understanding of the sexual and reproductive health experiences and needs of rural girls'. Our target audience was policy makers, donors and development practitioners. The book is funded by the Ford Foundation.

Through the openness of the girls interviewed we are offered insight into their complex lives and the decisions they make as they navigate through adolescence. Their stories expose us not only to their actual experiences but to the many social pressures they are under, their understanding of what they should and shouldn't do, the myths, rumours and misinformation they hear and help spread, and their place in their society as rural teenage girls.

1

A whole new ball game: Girls' football and teenage stories from Kilifi

It was the first time we'd got to the quarter finals and we were excited. When we went to Mwaraba we didn't think we would win, we didn't think we'd make it, to get to go to Kilifi. We knew Mwaraba was a good team, but we struggled and we won, one-nil. It was me who scored the goal. I felt so happy. Our number 8, Janet, she had the ball, and I was up ahead of her, I'm number 9. She passed the ball to me. I was in space, then I dribbled past the defender and there was no one there, just the goalkeeper, and I scored. We were delighted. Our teacher couldn't stop himself and he ran on to the pitch to celebrate with us, and we knew that now, we'd be going to Kilifi.

Juliet, July 2007

I first met Juliet at her school on a dry, hot and windy day in October 2005. She was one of a group of girls that play football I'd travelled to meet to discuss this 'life stories' project. Her school, not one of the most remote I'd visited, was just an hour's journey by matatu, a public transport minibus, from Kilifi town. The road wasn't tarmacked; it was a dirt road and at this time of year, during the dry season, a route where any passing vehicle leaves anyone in a cloud of dust that settles onto your clothes and hair to let people know where you've been in the district: red for Chonyi and Kaloleni, sandy grey for Ganze and Bamba.

As Juliet was to sing later, I had travelled through the gentle valleys and hills from Kilifi to her school. I got out at the stop for her school, a school like most others in Kilifi District: three or four long classroom blocks with concrete walls and roofed with iron sheets, each housing two classes, a small office for the head teacher, one for the deputy and a staff room. Many schools were set in large compounds with a space for sports, be it a football pitch or a patch of bare earth, and were fenced with barbed wire and thin sticks and twigs to keep out goats, cows and any other passing livestock.

Walking into the school grounds I could see that the head teacher's development plan was well on track. A huge metal gate, attached to concrete walls, was being erected at the entrance. I knew Mrs Karissa well and made my way to her office for the obligatory courtesy call, which with her was normally much more than that. She'd welcome me in like an old friend, we'd chat about her school, its academic performance, and how the girls playing football were getting on. I'd been to many head teacher's offices in the district, which ranged from sparse, dusty, dark, neglected affairs with outdated calendars and timetables with curling corners peeling off the walls to the immaculate one that Mrs Karissa had nurtured. She had a big solid, wooden desk, with a bright flowery plastic tablecloth tacked on to the desk with drawing pins. Her pens, pencils, paper clips and stapler were all neatly kept in a varnished wooden stationery box with her name engraved on it. She had an overbearing metal cupboard to the right behind her desk, firmly padlocked. There were colourful hand-written charts on the walls behind her desk, a list of all the teachers and school prefects and the school timetable.

The largest and most striking was the table of exam results, the ups (mainly ups in this school) and downs, compared to last term, to last year and the school's position in the division and the district, the key criterion in measuring school performance. This woman was thoroughly committed to the school despite, or maybe because of, the hostility she encountered when she was first appointed. The school board hadn't wanted a woman head teacher and the parents were less than happy about her appointment. But she had been deployed there by the Ministry of Education and there was little they could do about it. She was a slight woman, in her forties, with a friendly smile that masked her steely determination to succeed in a rural Kenyan school. Her number one agenda was improving academic performance, which is exactly what she did.

As we chatted I asked her about the new gate. To me, it had seemed an odd investment when the rest of the school fence was made of wire and sticks. I mean, it looked good, painted in the school colours, but it wasn't going to help with security. She told me, 'Ah yes, the gate. I've been wanting to put one up since coming to this school. Do you know that this is the only school in the division with a school gate?' To her the gate was a symbol of development, status, a sign that this school was moving forward, was a step ahead of other schools. I wasn't the sort of person she was trying to impress. She was more interested in what parents, teachers and people from the Ministry of Education thought and she gave me the impression that her development agenda was winning her many friends in all of these quarters.

I began to explain to her what this latest project was: Moving the Goalposts, commonly known as MTG, had been up and running for close to five years. Lots of girls were playing and organising their own football activities. But people were getting itchy that MTG wasn't doing enough. Teachers, local government officials, girls and people in NGOs (non-government organisations) and CBOs based in Kilifi were saying, come on, girls have so many issues in their lives; you can do more than this. When MTG started, back in 2001, it had always been an aim to get girls playing football and then add on other relevant development programmes. The time had come to do this.

In 2004, as an initial response to these suggestions, we decided to focus on health and in particular, reproductive health, and HIV and AIDS. We started by training ten young women football players who were members of MTG and no longer in school. Some had finished secondary school but others had dropped out before completing because they lacked school fees.[3] They attended a one-week intensive training course on reproductive health, HIV and AIDS, VCT (voluntary counselling and testing) and participatory peer education. They became the organisation's first peer educators who visited football teams and provided girls with information, support and safe spaces to ask questions about their reproductive and sexual health, and HIV and AIDS.

Launching this health education programme opened up a can of worms. Hundreds of questions flowed out in a torrent from the girls the peer educators were visiting. Questions about adolescence, menstruation, sex, pregnancy, HIV and AIDS, rumours they'd heard, beliefs they held, which sometimes stumped the peer educators, who were desperate to answer all the queries. Girls were hungry for information and I wondered whether we were really giving them the information they thought they needed. We, as an organisation, needed to know more about what girls wanted, what their concerns were.

Mrs Karissa and I discussed the letter I'd written to her, which had requested permission to visit and speak to the girls who play football. I wanted to interview a small number of girl footballers in Kilifi: more than five but fewer than 15, from different parts of the district. I wanted to talk to them over a two-year period—just chat with them about life as a teenage girl in rural Kilifi. She looked out of the window and saw that the footballers were congregating quietly, waiting for her to finish with me. She told me, 'Feel free, talk to the girls and let's continue to work together, for the betterment of girls in Kilifi.' With that we shook hands and I headed out to meet with the girls.

The girls who played football in Mrs Karissa's school knew I was coming. It wasn't, in fact, the school team I was coming to see. It was their MTG league team, which also included girls and women who weren't in school. I walked out into the bright sunlight and found a gaggle of girls, some in school uniform, and others straight from home with babies strapped on their backs, ready for this football meeting. 'Shikamoo', the standard greeting from young people to elders, said one. 'Marahaba', the standard response to 'shikamoo', I replied, shaking her hand, and then came another 'shikamoo', and another, until the whole group had greeted me individually. I asked them where they thought we should go to sit and we settled on the far corner of the football pitch, away from the school buildings and away from the road.

❖　❖　❖

In FIFA's (Federation Internationale de Football Association) Laws of the Game the size of a football pitch is clearly stipulated. The length must be between 90 and 120 metres and the width 45 to 90 metres. In Kilifi, no such dimensions are observed. If there's an open space, you play football on it. There's no mention in the Laws of the Game that the field should be flat; it's assumed it would be. But in Kilifi the only given on a football field is a slope of some sort: from one end to the other, one side to the other or just in patches, small hummocks, trenches, bumps and troughs. And then there's the grass, non-existent in the dry season, long and scratchy after the rains, and there could be thorns, bushes and every so often a tree to navigate. People know their football pitches, they know how to play them, how to dance around holes or dodge past bushes. Football is, quite literally, a different ball game. The pitch where I've played most of my football in Kilifi is really just a beach: a few tufts of grass here, deep energy-sapping sand there and a downward slope from one goal to the other that the local men's and girls' team almost always win on. It takes home advantage to a new level.

The pitch at Juliet's school was one of the better ones I'd seen. It had goalposts at both ends of the pitch, wooden goalposts, with a rope crossbar, but at this time of year there wasn't a blade of grass on the pitch. We walked across it, kicking up dust as we went, to a far corner to sit under some patchy shade provided by an acacia. There were around 15 of us. We all sat down and I explained what I'd come to discuss with them. Juliet sat in that group as quietly as any of the others, politely listening to my every word. There was no indication that she would become the girl who talked so openly to me about her life, bursting with questions the moment I turned the tape recorder on, wanting to talk to me about her dilemmas, the decisions she had to make, the choices and how she was navigating her way through her teenage years. In a group setting she was being the norm, not wanting to stand out, being the quiet, passive rural girl, revealing nothing of her inner thoughts or feelings.

In the discussion I told the girls why I had come to visit their team. I had a criterion for the girls who wanted to volunteer to take part. It was not very complex. They needed to be:

○ A footballer
○ 14–16 years old
○ Willing to talk to me and share their experiences

I told them that the interviews would be confidential and that I would never use their real names, or the names of any of the places they mentioned, in any write-up of our discussions.

I had a form for girls who wanted to volunteer to fill in. As I was handing the forms out the girls were rustling in their black plastic school bags, searching for their pens, which they shared among friends as they thoughtfully began to write about themselves. They wrote their name, age, football team, religion, details about whom they live with, if they were in school, which class they were in, and a short explanation of why they wanted to volunteer for this project. Not all the girls wanted to take part. One, whom I played alongside in our league team, told me, 'There's no way I can talk to you, or tell you about my life, I'm far too shy!' Some were more willing to get involved and had analysed what it would mean to them; others followed the crowd and, wanting to remain a part of this small, exclusive group with a visitor in the school compound for a little longer, filled in the form.

Juliet said she saw it as an opportunity to find out more about life and to help her think through some of the issues she had to deal with daily. She said she volunteered because 'I want to know my rights and to discuss my worries, to try to reduce them'. Mariam, whom we'll meet later, saw it as a mutually beneficial experience: 'Because I will talk to you about myself. It will help you and you will help me.' Salma, whom I'd always known as a keen volunteer for anything, said it would be a chance to use her well-honed narrative skills: 'I like to tell stories about our village, how it is and what people do.' (See appendix 1 for the selection process.)

I sat for over an hour as the girls filled in their forms. It was quiet, that rural quiet where the only thing you can feel is the wind whistling in your ears. It's possible to hear the sound of a vehicle many minutes before it passes, a dull moan from the distance; if you're waiting for transport, you start willing it to be a public vehicle, a public vehicle with a spare seat, or at least some standing space, to take you back home. But it could equally be a pick-up or a motor bike ridden by someone from Plan International or a field worker from KEMRI (Kenya Medical Research Institute). When it gets closer, sounds bigger, a lorry, maybe, bringing supplies or carrying electricity poles for the new rural electrification programme. I could never tell until it swept into view.

I've spent more hours than I probably should have done in such situations, watching rural life pass by and waiting for a route home to my family. Watching groups of young men sitting on makeshift wooden benches and stools, idle, out of work, smoking banghi (marijuana), listening to their radio hanging from the branch of a tree. They don't talk much, the odd comment here, a small transaction there, but mainly they just sit—another day passing in their lives. Girls pass, carrying baskets of maize on their head, off to the posho mill, a diesel-fuelled mill where maize is ground to make maize meal, or with water buckets, down to the tap to collect water. An old man leaning on a stick across the road from where I'm sitting is chatting with friends. He points the stick at me, says something, they laugh and then they go on their way, slowly, back to their homes. I had drifted off as the girls silently wrote and the other school pupils began to leave at the end of the day, snakes of children pouring out of classrooms, running, laughing and chatting, many holding plastic containers in which they had remnants of their beans and maize lunch to take home to their younger siblings. This was one of over a third of the primary schools in the district that ran a school feeding programme, making sure all school-going children had at least one meal a day. The ingredients were provided by a collaborative programme between the Ministry of Education and the World Food Programme. All other costs—the cooks, firewood, water, storage, and so on—were covered by the parents with each school management committee deciding the exact amount to be charged.

❖ ❖ ❖

There was no way I was going to be allowed to leave the school compound without watching the girls play football. They had already decided the format: school team versus out-of-school team. On one side all the girls were in their school uniforms, orange shirts and long royal blue skirts, and on the other there was a mix of flowing *lesos*, colourful cloths used for many things like wrapping around clothes and carrying babies, over biker shorts, trousers, skirts, and even full-length dresses better suited for church than a dusty football pitch. Babies were taken off backs and handed to younger siblings or friends, flip-flops were removed and each barefooted team gathered together, arms linked over shoulders to form a tight circle, heads down as one player recited a prayer at breakneck speed, a pre-match ritual I'd become fully accustomed to. The football was brought from the head teacher's office and the referee, a schoolboy, borrowed a pen lid from one of the girls for a whistle. The school team's number 9 carefully placed the ball at the centre, stepped on it with her shoeless foot and the referee blew the whistle for kick off. It was fantastically frenetic as the ball bounced high and unpredictably off the rock hard ground; it was chased, booted and sometimes, rarely, controlled. The match was chaotic. There were six, maybe seven, girls who looked as if they knew what they were doing. They tried to take the lead, organise, show their skills—a header here, a turn there, a shot on goal—but their efforts were hampered by the sheer exuberance, laughter and shrieks of the others, desperate to touch the ball, just once, to be a part of the game. Through my rose-tinted, biased, football-loving glasses, the girls appeared to be having a whole heap of fun, running, jumping and being free to take part in a team sport in a public place.

It took me back to a match I'd played back in England for Norwich City, because of the stark and absurd differences of the experiences. It's often not the football itself that becomes the memory but what happens around it, the place, the cultural context, the people, the stories. That day in Kilifi and the one in Norwich were tenuously linked by the game of football and the fact that women and girls were playing the game, but after that the similarities dissolve. For hot, dry and dusty in Kilifi read cold (freezing), wet (raining) and very muddy in Norwich. That day back in 1998, one side of the pitch was a complete mud bath, thick, black mud that the ball would get stuck in until someone hoofed it out so that we could continue playing 'football'. We struggled through 90 minutes to a goalless draw and came off the pitch soaking wet and caked in mud. We'd discussed the match all the way home and retold certain instances again and again to our friends, our families—exaggerating a little more each time, tweaking it to fit the audience, reacting to the reactions we got to make each retelling the 'truth' of that cold, wet, memorable winter's day in Norwich. Here in Kilifi I knew that the girls, too, would talk about this match again and again, and the more I sat and talked to the girls during the project I realised how much football, with its potential to both enrich and complicate lives, had become a part of theirs.

Juliet sang beautifully when retelling the story of the day they reached the MTG primary school finals in the middle of 2007. I could imagine the girls in the matatu, singing at the top of their voices, arms out of the windows slapping the sides of the vehicle with the palms of their hands to the beat of their song, letting everyone they passed know that today was their day, their big day to go and play football in Kilifi. She takes up the story:

'I woke up in the morning at the usual time, around 5 o'clock, the time I get up to make sure I get to school on time. We have to be at school by a quarter to seven. I got up, I had a bath and then I got my clothes for school and I put them on and I came to school. In the morning there isn't work to do at home. If there's food to cook then I'll cook it for us to eat but if there isn't we just come to school. I didn't have breakfast that morning; there wasn't any food at home. I didn't even drink water. When I got to school everyone was arriving from their homes. Our teacher told us to go to our classes because we had to wait for the vehicle to come and collect us, to take us to Kilifi. He said he'd call us when the matatu arrived. It was around 9 o'clock when the vehicle came and it brought the MTG T-shirts, the blue ones with 'Tunaweza', 'We can do it!', the Moving the Goalposts slogan, on the back. So everybody was given their own T-shirt and they put it on and we all got into the vehicle, ready to go to Kilifi. We sang on the way, songs to make us happy, some that we sing at weddings, and some that we sing for football. Like, there's the one that goes:

Oh, leo ni leo,	Oh, today is today
Oh, leo ni leo,	Oh, today is today
Teremka bonde kwa bonde	Go down into the valleys
Na mlima mpaka Kilifi	And up the hills until we get to Kilifi

'On the way we stopped for tea. Our teacher took us for tea in a *hoteli,* [a small joint or café for tea and hot snacks]. When we got to Kilifi the team we were to play in the quarter finals was already there, waiting for us. They were practising on the pitch. We knew what we needed to do, everyone knew their position, and we said we'd play the same as we play when we practise every day. The teacher told us we should all have the heart and believe that we can win. We put on our football shirts and went into the pitch to play. In the first half we scored, but the goal was offside. Then in the second half they scored the only goal and we were knocked out. But we played again, against another team, but we even lost to them. We felt so bad. There were two girls in our team who cried because we had lost.

'So we were upset but we were also enjoying ourselves because we had gone to join with other players from across the district. We were the ones who were there, we were the only team from our division. So we had left many girls behind from other schools; we had beaten them all on the way to the finals.

'We stayed to watch the other teams playing and then we were given our certificates and a football and we had the T-shirts we'd been given earlier. We sang on the way home and when people stopped and asked us, "How did you do in Kilifi?" we told them we'd won, but really we'd lost. It was about 5 o'clock when I got home. At that time my mum wasn't home so when I got back I had to do the housework. There was water, so I didn't need to go and collect it, but I cooked some supper, I washed the children, then we had supper and we went to sleep. I was feeling very tired.'

❖ ❖ ❖

Those who don't play [football] are lazy like potatoes!

Kadzo

The tournament finals Juliet described were on Friday, July 6th 2007, at the Karisa Maitha ground in the centre of Kilifi. Fifty-nine teams had participated in the tournament; the finals brought together the last eight teams still in the competition. I hadn't had much to do with organising the tournament; it'd been arranged by a committee of girl volunteers, all peer educators or referees or players or coaches and all girls who were no longer in school, taking responsibility and gaining skills to organise, lead and manage activities.

I'd been told that Juliet's school was one of the teams that had reached the quarterfinals and I was looking forward to seeing her here. It was a cool, overcast July day, my favourite time of the year, just after the long rains when the temperatures reach as low as 18 °C—positively freezing by Kilifi standards. While many people are wrapped up in jumpers and complaining about the cold, I enjoy a short respite from the punishing heat and humidity of Kilifi living.

I arrived at the main ground in Kilifi town at around 2 o'clock, in time for the final. There'd been no need for me to be there at 7 am, marking the pitch, fixing the goal nets, putting up the dais, welcoming the teams, sorting out the fixtures, prizes, entertainments, guests, getting stressed about whether everything was organised. It was a far cry from the early days of MTG. Just four teams played in our first tournament, which I'd organised with the helping hands of a few teachers, team coaches and my husband. We'd bought used oil from a nearby garage to use to mark the pitch the day before. We'd managed to plot the touchline and were halfway through one penalty box when the oil ran out. I'd made a mercy dash to a hardware shop to buy a 20-kg sack of lime chalk, strapped it on to the back of my bicycle and headed back to the field to finish our pitch. I'd worried all night that it would rain and wash away all of our hard work. I'd wanted to put up the goal nets the night before so that we'd only have to deal with the finishing touches in the morning but I'd been advised not to; it was too risky, they were too tempting for someone to steal. About 20 people came to watch that day back in early 2001 and now seven years later I could see well over 500 people standing around the pitch, watching girls playing in the finals of the annual MTG primary school tournament. I'd reported on the women's premier league in England for *The Times* newspaper in the mid-1990s and had never seen 500 people watching the best women's football in those days. Here in rural Kenya men (mainly men), women, boys and girls were on the touchline, cheering the girls on, enjoying the entertainment on show.

I'd walked to the pitch from our office, which consists of five rooms in a shared building. The project couldn't afford an office until 2002 when I'd started with one tiny room measuring 2 by 3 metres. That office, which I worked out of for over two years, now acts as the store, bursting with football kits, balls, nets and all sorts of other accumulated possessions that belong to the organisation. Slowly the organisation had grown, adding another room, then another, as activities expanded and the number of staff went up. My journey that day started with a short stroll past the Hudaa mosque, which is across the dirt road from the entrance to our building. It was a Friday and schoolboys and men were flooding out from their lunchtime prayers. It brought back memories of the days when I wouldn't go for lunch on a Friday. I'd stay in the office, sitting at my desk, to hear the preaching of the imam, blasting through the sound system. I could hear his every word, crystal clear, from where I sat, and I used his sermon as a lesson, a Kiswahili lesson. If I picked up ten words in the early days I was delighted and I'd write down others that I'd heard but didn't know, to find out what they meant. Slowly I could understand more, pick up more, write down less and get involved in the odd heated, moral discussion with my colleagues, sparked by some of his hotter sermons.

So, past the mosque towards the bus station in the centre of Kilifi town, another sound that infiltrated our office, the vehicles leaving to Mombasa, Kaloleni, Bamba, Vitengeni, coaxing passengers in with loud blasts of their horns. I headed right towards the creek, a stunning expanse of the Indian Ocean, which guided me up to the football ground. A narrow road, the newly painted county council offices and the more dilapidated police station separating us from the creek, the District Education Office where I'd had many meetings, up ahead, and the football field to my left.

As I arrived at the ground Juliet's team was the first I came to. They were sitting in a group under the shade of a huge mango tree. Some wore the bright blue MTG T-shirts they'd been given for reaching the finals, others had on their worn yellow football uniform, and some were sharing a packet of glucose. Theirs was a team that had registered to be a member of MTG early on in 2001 and had played in every primary school tournament since. Juliet, with whom I'd spent many hours chatting, was there as their captain, leading her peers and consoling the younger players who'd cried when they lost. We greeted one another and I greeted the rest of the team. A couple half-heartedly said 'shikamoo'; the rest looked up at me shyly and looked down again. Juliet told me they'd lost but she didn't say much more. They were tired and not in the mood to chat.

Having played in many teams that had lost football matches I knew the feeling; there's not much to say when you lose. Juliet and I stood next to each other for a while, surveying the scene in silence, and I then headed towards the dais to meet some of the guests, people from local NGOs, from the government, teachers and members of the general public who had come to watch. There was also a buzz of bright blue shirts, the MTG girls volunteering, organising matches, referees, refreshments, first aid, transport, acting as masters of ceremony, showing the people of Kilifi that they can organise events, take responsibility, deal with issues and put on a great show.

On my way there was a group of bare-chested young men in their late teens and early twenties, hanging around, laughing and joking, getting ready to entertain the crowd. I found out later that this group of young acrobats were heading to the beach to practise in the morning when they had seen the girls playing football. They knew a girls' football tournament would attract a big crowd, and so they took the initiative to seek out the organisers and asked them if they could perform. They said they'd do it for free. They didn't expect any payment, they just wanted to do their acrobatics in a public place. As I got to the dais, Lidya, MTG's head of peer education and MC for the day, was calling all players and spectators round, 'come, come, come to watch the acrobats, come to see our brothers in action'.

The music boomed out and they started their show on the hot sand, an energetic medley of powerful acrobatics, with backflips galore and balancing acts requiring steel nerves and strength. I was mesmerised. I'd seen many acrobat shows in Kilifi, a standard entertainment alongside traditional dancing for tourists in coastal Kenya, but this group was the best I'd seen.

I was feeling the euphoria of the vigour, the energy, the talent of those boys and enjoying the way they were enjoying themselves, loving the way people were loving it, being entertained, having fun during this big day for girls' football in Kilifi. But later, when the euphoria dissipates and reflection sets in, I start to think about the future of young people like these boys and girls: the acrobats were talented young men, disciplined. They worked hard to perfect their show, but what hopes did they really have? They were spending their days practising acrobatics. What for? This day they were given lunch by MTG, but was a free lunch all they would ever get? What productive activities are there for young people in Kilifi, the majority of whom don't make it to secondary school? The answers running through my mind made me feel that there wasn't very much: building sites, transport, selling peanuts, milk, bananas to passengers at the bus stage, all casual work with no security. And for girls, even less opportunity: domestic work, tailoring, bar work, catering. Again, all ad hoc, low paid and insecure.

❖ ❖ ❖

I first came to Kilifi in September 2000, arriving as a white woman from a middle-class European family.[4] Mbilinyi observes that 'our identities are not given or reducible to our origins, skin colour, or material locations. Identities or positions are the product of struggle and they represent an achieved, not an ascribed trait.'[5] Identities are not static; they change over time. I remain with my background and the traits I've mentioned, but today layers have been added, which have built on and shaped who I am.

In Kilifi I have always lived with the man I'm now married to. My identity has been shaped by his identity, as has his by mine. I'm a white middle-class woman married to a black middle-class man, living in a country that is predominantly black. He is Kenyan but not indigenous to the coast and, despite having lived in Kilifi for close to 20 years, would still be considered an 'outsider' of sorts. So we are both outsiders, but also somehow seen as 'insiders' compared to 'real outsiders', such as tourists or researchers straight from Europe. I've gained some semblance of insider status through my work, through living where we live and through learning Kiswahili. It's impossible to live somewhere, in a village, and be completely oblivious to what goes on around you. You talk at the shop, you sit with the neighbours, you eat out, everywhere you go you learn, you build on what you are. I've also become a mother since coming to Kenya. Our daughters were born in 2004 and 2006, and this, too, shapes my identity and changes how people see me. I have a job that combines my passions for football, justice and gender equity, and that allows me to describe myself as a feminist footballer—becoming more of a feminist and less of a footballer with age.

Most of my friends in Kilifi, similar to when I was living in the UK, are middle class. By that I mean that they are all educated, have a profession and are employed. Many of them work in the Kilifi branch of the medical research institute KEMRI, which with over 500 employees is the biggest employer in the town. I live in what could be described as a lower middle-class location. It is a big village, a fishing village, with a complete mix of people. Swahili Muslims, indigenous Mijikenda, the group of nine tribes found at the coast in Kenya, people from other parts of Kenya, a number of Germans, British people and other Europeans, who came as tourists and decided to settle. Most people have built their own houses, or rent a property, and many work in Kilifi town, in small businesses, in research, in development or for the government. Others in the village work as fishermen, in the tourist industry, in small shops and food outlets, and as domestic workers.

I'm in agreement with Temple and Edwards when they write that 'there are dangers in assuming "insider" or "outsider" status'.[6] There is so much fluidity, the boundaries of who we are shift and sway; status is influenced by class, race, gender and it's affected by the status of the person you're interacting with. Your status is not just about how you see yourself but also about how others see you. I haven't lived in the United Kingdom for seven years, yet it was home for the first 28 years of my life. Having been away from 'home' for that long, to what extent do I now understand the shifting culture there, the changing language, dialogue, jokes, concerns that I used to take as given? Am I now an outsider in both of the countries in which I have lived? On an emotional level I feel comfortable in both, I have family in both places and I call both places home. But the reality of what and where my home is remains complex.

But this fluid identity of mine, that insider, outsider that I am, has afforded me an opportunity to learn and to write about rural girls' teenage lives and live the roller coaster of my and their lives over the last two years. But it has taken me a long time to get here, reach a position to be able to take it on, with confidence that the journey we were taking would have some relevance beyond our own small lives.

❖   ❖   ❖

I'd be lying if I said the first six months in Kilifi were easy. They were, in fact, incredibly hard. Before coming to Kenya I'd decided that in the first year I had two main priorities: 1) learn Kiswahili, 2) get MTG established. It seemed so simple. I hadn't allowed any space for my emotional upheaval, my culture shock. I hadn't even contemplated it. I mean, I'd spent a year working in Zimbabwe, I'd been to Kilifi four times before—I knew Africa, I knew what I was getting into. I was coming to live with Collins, the man I loved; surely I knew what was in store. My naivety knew no bounds.

Once I was immersed into Kilifi life I realised it was all going to be a bit more tricky, frustrating and troubling than I'd imagined. All my assumptions about how things should be done needed to be turned upside down, onto their heads, and then they might have some relevance. I was lucky to have Collins's tireless support: this wise, quiet, strong man who managed to calmly advise me, a determined, confident English woman who had bags of enthusiasm but no clue about how things worked in Kenya. I did, slowly, learn to listen, to take advice that often seemed painful and critical but that ultimately was in my best interests. I didn't always heed his advice and got even more frustrated when things didn't quite go according to plan and Collins was, yet again, right.

I'd never been much of a linguist at school, struggling through French and Italian GCSE (General Certificate of Secondary Education), and now I needed to learn a language with structures that made no sense to me at all. I had a book, I tried to teach myself but I was going nowhere. I was saved by Reuben, a charismatic Kiswahili teacher from Mombasa, who was used to teaching hapless adults who'd come to work in Kenya. We quickly built up a rapport and used football as our focus for learning. At that time I was coaching football with girls in four schools in Kilifi town. I would go once a week to each school. The girls were young and mostly spoke one of the Mijikenda dialects as their first language, but all were completely fluent in the national language, Kiswahili. All learning in schools is supposed to be in English, but I soon realised that they could not understand a word of my English. I needed to know commands, 'come here, stand here, STOP! come back, line up there, kick, head, dribble, touch, turn', and Reuben assured me that it wouldn't take long to grasp the language if I started with the girls on the football field. And I did start to pick it up, slowly, building up confidence, hitting milestones: the first time I introduced myself to a district meeting in Kiswahili, holding a full football training session without a word of English, writing a letter to parents in Kiswahili, and talking, talking, talking to girls. One time at practice, when I thought I was getting quite good, I asked a group of 11–14-year-olds to test me, to say words in Kiswahili and see if I could get them, to see if I knew them. For a split second I felt quite confident. Reuben was a good teacher. I thought I had a wide vocabulary now, and I'd been told by quite a few people that I had a good, convincing accent. We'd had a great practice, everyone was in high spirits and they looked excited by my challenge. 'Come on, then,' I said, 'give me a word.'

'*Vipuli*,' a girl shouted. 'Vipuli?' I said. 'Eheh,' they replied slowly, in unison, eyes wide and expectant.

Oh no, I had absolutely no idea. Vipuli, what was it? I knew *vi* meant plural but *puli*? Puli? What on earth was it? I was crushed but they were busy anticipating my response. Humiliated, I told them, '*Ah, sijui, umenishinda tayari*'—'I don't know, you've won, you've beaten me'. These, they shouted, jumping around, laughing, pulling their ear lobes, clapping each other's hands because they'd beaten me. One girl, seeing the puzzled look on my face, said quietly touching her ear, 'those beautiful things you put here, earrings'. I was furious, they were being ridiculous, couldn't they have made it a bit easier for me, started with something I could get like 'ball' or 'bread' or 'milk' or … Earrings, I thought, how obscure. Surely there were thousands of words I still needed to learn before I got to earrings?

But now I was learning, getting back in on teenage life, realising that as much as I needed to know the words for development and evaluation I also needed to seriously get to work on the things that really matter to teenage girls and the vocabulary that accompanies them. It was quite a while after that when I really started to speak and understand Kiswahili, to be able to use it without thinking. The language opened the floodgates for me, opened up the world I had come to work in, the world of young women and girls in Kilifi.

So there I was, in 2005, in what seemed a unique position. I was a journalist, a development practitioner, an outsider-insider, working, having fun and playing football with hundreds of teenage girls in Kilifi: an excluded group whose voices are rarely heard beyond their small social circles. We talk, we plan together, we carry out activities, we like each other, they trust me. They have many issues that are discussed above them, at national level, by adults, by experts. There's free primary and secondary education, but girls still drop out early. What can be done? Menstruation can mark the end of a girl's schooling, what can be done? Girls aged 15–24 years in Kenya are more than twice as likely to be infected with HIV than boys in the same age group, what can be done? I wanted to talk to the girls in more detail, hear what they had to say about these issues, about their own lives, hear about their struggles, their triumphs, their hopes and their fears and get their voices out there, to people who make decisions that affect the lives of teenage girls.

For me, this became a process of uncovering knowledge, peeling back the layers of the social realities, the complexities of growing up as a teenage girl in Kilifi. Through a series of interviews with nine girls over two years, a world unravelled in front of me, a real world. Silverman in his work on qualitative research methods points out, 'interview data display cultural realities that are neither biased nor accurate, but simply "real"'[7] ... displays of perspectives and moral forms'.[8] Many times, when I talked to the girls, I felt I wasn't necessarily getting the truth and it bothered me. But as I went on, the half truths, the falsehoods were all part of the story, further exposing complicated social pressures and moral dilemmas, which, when pieced together, formed a story of rural girls' teenage lives. Barbara Hardy perfectly captured what I felt I was hearing from the girls when she says, 'Before we sleep each night we tell over to ourselves what we may have told to others, the story of the past day. We mingle truths and falsehoods, not always quite knowing where one blends with the other.'[9]

Janet was the most prolific in this: she would tell me a story twice, three times, in the same discussion, changing it slightly each time, from being about her, to being about someone else, back to her, and distant again, confusing me, giving me no time to get to the bottom of what had happened. When I stopped worrying about hearing what had happened and searched more for the meaning, the messages, the context, I relaxed and let her ramble on, tell her story exactly the way she wanted to. And from that I gained knowledge about Janet, about her contradictions, about her life. She was one of the nine girls I talked to, all footballers and all in school in Kilifi District when we started in 2005. This book is their story as much as it is mine, how we've all changed over the two years, but it is also about what I've learnt, how I added to my partial knowledge and continue to do so. It's about what the girls told me, what they said about their own lives, the lives of their friends and families, their own situations, experiences, and a glimpse into how they see the world.

One thing I learnt early on while living in Kilifi is that you don't find things out unless you ask. People do not offer information unless they are probed. I would never have heard these stories if I hadn't consciously made an effort to go out and find them. What that means though, is that my values, the way I see the world, my cultural background and my experience of living in Kilifi as an outsider-insider shape this work. I made the decisions about what we would discuss when we met. I was the one asking questions, probing for what I wanted to know. This was particularly true in the earlier interviews, when we knew each other less well. But still, as we moved along, I controlled the interview. That's the norm for a journalist, for a researcher, who then absorbs and tries to make sense of what she's observed and what she's been told.

This book is a collection of stories and my understanding of them, my personal journey with the girls. But these are not stories of nameless people, they are the stories of nine girls with whom I became close, whose schools, homes, friends and relatives I got to know. Girls who got into my life, under my skin, into my dreams, and who taught me about life, their lives, how they viewed the world and their passage through it. Their stories can't possibly represent the experiences had by all girls in Kilifi, but they can give us insight into the environment in which they chart their way through their teenage years.

Who the girls are, November 2005

Name	Age	Lives with ...	Religion	School
Asya	16	Grandparents; mother passed away, never knew father	Muslim	Standard 6
Carol	15	Father; mother passed away	Christian	Standard 7
Janet	15	Father; divorced from mother	Christian	Form 1, Secondary
Juliet	15	Mother; father passed away	Christian	Standard 6
Kadzo	14	Mother and father	Christian	Standard 5
Kanze	15	Mother; father passed away	Christian	Standard 7
Mariam	14	Sister; mother lives in Garsen, father passed away	Muslim	Standard 6
Mercy	16	Mother and father	Christian	Standard 7
Salma	14	Mother; father passed away	Muslim	Standard 7

One of my favourite things to do while watching football matches in Kilifi is to walk around the pitch, watching from different angles, chatting with spectators and hearing what people have to say about the match. During that final on July 6th, I got talking to a teacher who'd accompanied one of the teams. A short, stocky man I'd never met before, he had nothing but praise for Moving the Goalposts: 'Oh madam, football helps our girls so much, we need to expand the programme ...'

I was used to hearing such sycophancy, which was often followed by a request for football boots, education scholarships, or anything else that was needed at that given time.

But this teacher didn't move on to requests, he stuck right there with the subject in question and he went on: 'In schools like ours the girls have very little and they know very little. It puts them at a disadvantage, even they think they're not worth as much as boys. But this football has exposed them, it's made them realise that they can achieve, it's made them see further, to look beyond the homes from which they come. It's a very important programme in our school.'

He wanted to help the girls, he was open with me about their issues and he wasn't worried that what he said might shock me or offend my sensibilities. He talked about the hard choices a girl might have to make because of poverty, about pregnancies, abortions, their inability to continue with their education beyond primary school. And he didn't judge the girls who had dropped out of school or got pregnant. He was seeing their experiences within the wider social context.

Not all adults, though, were so supportive to girls playing football and many girls faced an ongoing struggle with their parents and teachers to allow them to play. During some work I was doing at a football training camp in 2007 I asked a group of eight young girls to discuss and come up with a list of the five main challenges and problems they faced around football. It was a lively discussion and they eventually came up with these five:

- If you fail your exams at school the teachers say it's because of football
- We are not allowed to go to the field by our parents because we have to go and look for money
- I don't like the backbiting that happens at the field
- When you're in your period you are scared of going to play
- We don't have shorts to wear

These difficult problems weren't easy to deal with or easy to solve. Pressure at school to perform in class, pressure at home to contribute to the family income, teenage issues—periods and gossiping—and poverty. But these problems came from girls who'd been selected to attend a football training camp, girls who were committed players and coaches. They seemed prepared to face these problems because they wanted to play football.

Why, then, do girls play football in Kilifi? The reasons that I've been given over the last few years have not been very different from anyone else who might play team sports: to keep fit, to be strong, to have fun and to make friends.[10] But domestic chores and schoolwork can jeopardize their participation, parents might not see any immediate benefits, and while being a player, belonging to a team and belonging to an organisation has the potential to enrich a girl's life, showing commitment to that team can become a struggle when the forces of other demands are in full swing.

Janet claimed to have very understanding parents who supported her decision to play football. The help of a teacher who motivated the girls also contributed to her early, positive experiences with football: 'We started playing football in Standard 4 with Mercy Karisa, who was in Standard 6. She taught us football using tough styles. She taught us slowly until we knew it, so the teacher said he would buy us a ball. When I joined Form 1 [secondary school] I used to go to the field until 6 pm. My mum would ask me why I was late home. I explained to her we were playing football and she would say it's OK if you were playing football. My dad knows that we are footballers, he was a footballer, and he knows the importance of playing football so when we ask him for permission to go and play football he says "you go and play".'

As time went on Janet found it more and more difficult to keep playing football as she tried, at all costs, to stay in secondary school. She shuttled from her dad's place to her mum's, then to a sister's and finally a brother's in a desperate bid to find the financial support to pay her fees so she could finish school. During her struggle, playing football was not a priority.

Salma, meanwhile, was one of the most committed players I knew. She was very clear about why she was playing football. She told me, 'I really like football. My mum says it's my talent and if I'm chosen I should play to use my talent because it might help me in the future. When you are playing, people get to know you, you can be sponsored to go to secondary. It happened to another girl at Mitsedzini Primary. Football has helped me, I am active and I have many friends from other places.'

Having a mum who supported her to play and having a passion for the sport didn't make Salma immune from some of the more negative attitudes held by people about girls playing football. She told me a tale during one of our conversations about what boys thought and did about girls playing football. She started like this: 'With the boys, some respect players but some want to make fun of us. If they see you making many mistakes like falling down or missing the ball while playing, any time they meet you on the way, they laugh at you or make fun of you.'

So for Salma, girls were now putting themselves into the public arena, into a place where people could watch them, decide whether to respect them or to make jokes about girls. I felt sorry for her when she told me this and I asked her if it made her feel like she wanted to stop playing football. She thought about this question for a long while and then, taking a deep breath, she said to me, 'You know, there are boys who call me names when I pass. They call me, I don't know, I can't say … they call me Mama MTG!' I laughed, we both laughed. OK, it might not have been the most flattering name for a 15-year-old girl, but I thought it was great that she was getting recognition for her leadership in MTG. She wasn't of the same opinion: 'But I don't like that name because I'm not the only one playing for MTG. They call me this because they see me telling players in the field to stand up and practise because I'm the coach. When I get to the field and I find players sitting, doing nothing, I tell them to stand up quickly. They obey me and do as I say so they gave me that name because they see the way I'm respected by the players.'

She hadn't answered my question about whether she ever felt like she should stop playing football but she'd given me a glimpse into her footballing life. She'd told me about the name reluctantly. She didn't like the fact that the name put her above the rest, which she claimed she was not aspiring to be. She wanted to remain a part of the crowd, but this juxtaposed with her actions as an ever-willing volunteer, taking on responsibility, being a leader. The status this gave her didn't sit comfortably on her shoulders because of the pressures of being a teenager, being a part of the gang and not wanting to be above her peers.

Mariam, a wonderfully skilful footballer, came from the 'keep them busy, keep them out of trouble' school of thought when talking about why she played football. 'At the beginning I didn't know that girls in Kenya play football. I thought it would be good to play because most girls just sit idle. They don't concentrate on anything and they can just be caught up by people and get pregnant when they're still young. My mum thinks it's good that I play football because I haven't started this behaviour of going here and there with anyone. My brother says I must continue playing, continue with my class work, and he will help with my school fees for secondary. Then he said if his work goes well he will buy me a ball and football boots.'

The youngest of the nine girls, she had just turned 14 when we started talking, but by then she'd been playing for a couple of years and it seemed like football had got into her blood. 'If we leave the field we talk a lot about the football league, our league for the under 12s. Everybody wants their team to win. Last year the under-12 league team I am coaching came third but this year we want to win. I have the same players in the team but now I have some new, very young players. I have made another team so now I have two teams. I am also in Coach the Coach, MTG's football coaching course. Now we are working with the new coaches who are joining. Some are older than I am and others are younger, but we are the ones who are coaching, and I can do it. Being a coach helps because the team I play for has really improved because we have been taught to be coaches and we have become good players too. If you have learnt to be a coach and you can do it well, you can get your own team and coach it until it is famous and you become famous too.'

Someone who is famous in MTG and a little further afield is Mbeyu Akida, a quite phenomenal football player. She is, without doubt, the best player in MTG. She lives with her mum, her dad and her three brothers. I had arranged to visit her mother at her workplace at the agricultural college in Kilifi. I didn't know exactly what her job was as I walked into the room, an isolated space with a desk and little else. During our conversation we were disturbed a number of times by people bringing in fresh milk and payments, which she would deal with politely, quickly and efficiently before getting back to the story about her only daughter.

Mama Mbeyu: My daughter's a footballer

Mbeyu started playing when she was nine years old, with her brothers. She's the only girl. I didn't have anyone to look after her when I was at work. I would leave the house in the morning and come back in the evening. Mbeyu didn't like just staying at home and this environment we were living in was bad. People drinking mnazi, or palm wine, drunkards, banghi, the issue of prostitutes—it was all going on here. So the time for her to be going to play, it made me feel relieved, like there was someone taking care of her.

When they first had a team at school, people were telling the coach Mbeyu should play, but she was only nine and he thought she was too small. In the end they convinced him to let her play. She was in Standard 3 when she first started playing in the school team. After some time she told me, 'I have been chosen by MTG', so she was also playing with them. They said she was a good player. I felt happy. I didn't mind that she was playing football. Her brothers were with her, taking care of her.

Now she plays with boys down at the field at Mgandini every day. They don't mess about with her. She doesn't go with another AOB, they know what her objective is. They give her respect. She goes with her brothers too to watch football in the video den. She goes to watch the best players, to pick up tactics. Like in the evenings she'll cook early, leave it in the pot and go to watch football.

But I have one problem in my house with Mbeyu and this issue of football. If she comes from the football field and they have won, we'll hear the whole story, how she scored, we'll all laugh, the whole house will know. Even if she's been injured but they won, she'll do all she can to be up and about. But if they have lost, ha, Mbeyu — she'll be ill and the whole house will be ill! She'll say her stomach hurts. You'll feel so bad, even though you were not there at the football field. If she's lost, there's no laughter in the house.

❖   ❖   ❖

Having lost in the quarterfinals on that cool July day, Juliet's team had had to make do with watching the rest of the primary school tournament from the touchline. As the whistle had blown at the end of the final the supporters of the winning team had rushed onto the pitch, cartwheeling and screaming, hugging any player they could find. The players had scattered in different directions with arms aloft, running as fast as they could, everywhere, anywhere, in sheer jubilation. They then came back together, regrouped to sing their victory song as they made their way towards the dais to be awarded their prize. I reflected on how universal our celebrations of victory can be.

I left the football field after the chief guest, the area manager from Plan International Kilifi, a dynamic woman from Coast Province, had given a speech about the importance of staying in school. She was a good friend of the organisation. She had a captive audience—eight girls' football teams and plenty of others who'd come to watch. She explained how she had walked over five kilometres, barefooted, to primary school and had struggled to achieve what she had now achieved. She was from a background similar to that of most of these girls and her words rang true—an incentive for girls to try to stay in school. She also encouraged them to keep playing football, that football provided an opportunity to get recognition and support, and that there were benefits beyond the prizes they were receiving that day.

At such events there's little chance to go into the complexities of what football really means to girls, or what football and an organisation like MTG can achieve for girls in a place like Kilifi. For every supportive parent there's a family that won't allow their daughter to play. Many promising players get blown off course by family events outside their footballing lives: the impact of poverty, the need to look for money, to contribute to the family income, a family member passing away, a lost job, an unintended pregnancy—all can spell an end to their participation in football, and for many, their attendance at school.

It is in this context that MTG operates, dealing with complicated lives with pressures, morals and concerns that determine whether they play football, and keep playing football. However, for girls in Kilifi District football is now becoming a norm. Speak to almost any primary schoolteacher and they will tell you girls play football in their school. Whether girls who play football in Kilifi are self-selecting and by extension more confident, from better-off, more supportive families is a moot point that requires further investigation. My observations indicate that this is not necessarily the case. Football might provide a chance for girls who, because they come from the most disadvantaged backgrounds, have missed out on other opportunities in education and training. Whether they can remain active and keep playing, when family pressures to contribute productively can be so strong, is where their participation can become problematic. But at this point, I'm not going to look much further beyond the fact that girls are playing football and that this project has opened up a teenage world to a larger audience. What potential sports has for solidarity and empowerment among girls and its ultimate impact on individual and collective lives becomes another fascinating study altogether.

2

On home ground:
Families and domesticity

Kanze lived with her mother and had eight brothers and sisters. Some of her siblings had completed school and others were still in school. Her father, who had had two wives, passed away in 2001. He was sick but Kanze didn't know what the illness was. Her mother was the second wife; the first wife had five children, all of whom were married. Two of Kanze's sisters were married and had moved to their husbands' homes but one had returned after a disagreement at her husband's place. After Kanze's father passed away the relatives quarrelled. Her family was told to move and go live somewhere else. The disagreement was between her family and the family of her dad's first wife. Her brother came and helped resolve the problem and they were told they should remain in that home, which is where they were still living. They had three houses of mud and *makuti*, a thatch roof made of dried palmtree leaves. Kanze had to walk for half an hour to the tap to fetch water. They had nine goats and five chickens. Kanze did the normal domestic chores at home, like collecting firewood, cooking, washing clothes and looking after her younger siblings. She also baked half cakes (small round cakes cooked over a fire), sold for one shilling), just under two cents, to sell at school during break time so that they could get money to buy food. She would take the money back to her mother, who would then send Kanze out to buy things. Her mum sold mnazi, the local brew, going to collect it from where it was brewed and selling it at her home.

When it rains in Kilifi, it pours. But the long rains in 2006 were particularly heavy. During those rains two of the houses in Kanze's home were destroyed by the pounding rainfall and all the family was forced to stay in one house. One brother whose house fell down left the home altogether to go to Malindi to stay with another relative.

Kanze finished primary school at the end of 2006 and left the rural home to go stay with her brother in town and attend a tailoring college. Her brother was paying her fees and her upkeep in his house. She was planning to finish her training and buy a sewing machine so she could return to her rural home and set up her own business.

Kanze's home life gives a snapshot of the kind of situation a girl in Kilifi might find herself growing up in. It involves heavy domestic duties, helping to bring income into the family, parents surviving through tilling the land, selling local brew or other produce and relying on older siblings who may have found employment away from the rural home in a town such as Kilifi, Mombasa or Malindi.

While I'm saying that Kanze's life is representative of rural Kilifi girls I've also seen a complex world where circumstances within the home of each girl were contrasting and unique: Mariam living with her sister, away from her mum; Mercy with both parents, who eventually split up; Janet moving from one parent to the other and back again, away from her home in her quest for an education; Carol and Asya both having had to cope with the loss of their mother; Kadzo looking after her elderly parents; Salma's close relationship with her mum; and Juliet heading the household while her mum worked in town. There was no typical family set-up but there were universal experiences: domestic work, work in the *shamba,* a plot of land for cultivation, and assisting to bring income into the family, all jobs that girls were expected to do.

I'd come into this project with my own romanticised assumptions about families in Kilifi. They were big, extended and secure with structure and intergenerational communication and support that, despite the impact of poverty, provided a solid bedrock from which girls could grow. What I found, though, against a fading backdrop of traditional rural family life, was a picture of fragmentation, of families crumbling under the strain of poverty and illness. It was a community in flux: an older generation of grandparents and many parents who had not been to school; a younger cohort, most of whom had some education, who were working, or unemployed and looking for work, or no longer looking; and an even younger group of mostly school-going siblings, which included the girls here.

I knew Kilifi was poor, I'd read about it and I had written about it in the many funding proposals I had written for MTG. I cannot remember how many times I had written 'Kilifi is one of the least-developed districts in Kenya; 66% of the population lives in poverty and around 8% is infected with HIV and AIDS. Poor women in Kilifi District have the lowest rates of both literacy (26.8%) and school enrolment (54.4%) in Kenya.'[11] So there you go—Kilifi District equals poverty, HIV and AIDS, illiteracy and inequality. The reality, of course, is much more interesting and much more complicated.

❖ ❖ ❖

Understanding the complex family structures of the Mijikenda was a tall task for my brain, which had been conditioned to see 'family' as a small, simple, nuclear set-up. In the UK brothers and sisters were brothers and sisters and cousins were cousins; the distinction was very clear. They were not the same, and nor were your relationships with them. Here in Kilifi cousins are brothers and sisters, there's no separation; the children of the siblings of your dad, and of your mum, are your siblings too. Hence the family can look pretty big and confusing to an outsider.

And then the language used for family members was a minefield. One minute I would think a girl was talking about her aunt, her mother's sister, and then I'd come to realise that, in fact, the whole story had been about her dad's second wife. I still have to think hard when they say *mamangu mdogo*. The literal meaning of 'my young mother' is used for two quite different relatives: the younger sister of her mother *or* another wife of her father, *if* her mother is the first wife. Whenever I heard such words I had to raise my attention, focus hard on the rest of the sentence, to try to get the context. I drew a chart for myself of the Kiswahili-English-Kigiriama[12] translations. Kiswahili is not the mother tongue for most of the girls, so 'mamangu mdogo' is imported to describe a relation. If we delve into the Kigiriama there's less confusion because the words resonate more with the traditional culture and structures. For example when looking at aunts on your mother's side and the wives of your father the distinction is clear in Kigiriama. Aunt is *mzhere,* your mother's older sister, or *mhoho,* your mother's younger sister. The wife is *misomo;* mzhere is only used to clarify that the wife is the older wife.

Kiswahili	English	Kigiriama
baba	father	baba
mama	mother	mama
babu	grandfather	tsawe
nyanya	grandmother	hawe
shangazi	aunt (father's sister)	tsangazimi
mamangu mkubwa	aunt (mother's older sister) or your father's wife who was married by your father before he married your mother	mzhere
	father's other wife (married before or after he married your mother)	misomo
mamangu mdogo	aunt (mother's younger sister) or your father's wife whom he married after your mother	mhoho (aunt only, not used for father's wife)
babangu mkubwa	uncle (father's elder brother)	bamzhere
babangu mdogo	uncle (father's younger brother)	bamhoho
mjomba	uncle (mother's brother)	ahu
ndugu	cousin or sibling	ndugu
kaka	cousin or sibling brother	ndugu wa kilume
dada	cousin or sibling sister	ndugu wa kiche
wifi	sister-in-law	hawe
shemegi	brother-in-law	mlamu

In families where the parents were married and dowry paid, the children would live in the home of the father; that was where they belonged. Girls would talk about their sisters-in-law who would also live in the home, having moved to the home of their husband. Interestingly the word for grandmother and sister-in-law in Kigiriama is the same, *hawe*. Both play important roles in the lives of young girls, sharing domestic duties, teaching the girls about adult life and providing social support. However, in some cases the sister-in-law might be a burden to the girl, insisting that she help look after her children as well as doing other work expected of her. An uncle on the mother's side, *mjomba*, remained important in the lives of girls once they had left their family home. If for example a woman was having problems in her marriage, and her father wasn't around, it would be the uncles, not her mother, who would step in to mediate with the other family, to act on behalf of her family to help resolve the issue.

Something that I should have known, but didn't, was that death knocked on the door of most families of teenage girls. It wasn't just the death of grandparents and elderly relatives, but a parent or a sibling, which disrupted the delicate balance of their family.

Of the nine girls, six had lost a parent and three had seen a sibling pass away. Kanze, Salma, Juliet and Mariam had all lost their fathers, while Asya had never known hers. Her mother and Carol's mother had died. Kadzo had lost a younger sister, Salma a brother and Juliet's teenage brother died, suddenly, out of the blue, at the beginning of 2008.

The absence of Asya and Carol's mothers seemed to me to make them more rudderless, less secure than the rest. Asya talked of how her uncle, who was now caring for her needs and those of her siblings, treated her in a way that, if her mum had been around, he wouldn't get away with. She told me, 'Now, if I do something wrong my uncle shouts at me and uses abusive language. If my mum were here he wouldn't be able to do it.' Her mother had provided protection for her and that protection was no longer there.

My own father had died when I was 12. This made me and my siblings the odd ones out, suffering something than none of our friends had experienced or were likely to experience soon. Divorce was a much more common phenomenon among my friends' parents. My dad had been ill for a long time. We would visit him in hospital but I had no idea he was dying. One freezing cold, dark evening as my mum and I walked back to our car across the icy car park at the Hope Nursing Home in Cambridge she broke the news to me. He had cancer. My memory of my response is so clear, yet so hazy, an important moment in my life, remembered for what it was or what I've made it over time. I asked her, 'Have you told Henri (my sister, who was two years younger than me)?' 'No, not yet,' was the reply. 'Well, you'd better not tell her, mum,' I said, 'because Henri's only ever heard of people who've died of cancer.' Was it really what I had said, or was it, in hindsight, what I wish I had said? How do we really remember our own histories, significant moments in our lives? I asked my mum over the phone recently if she could remember what I'd said when she told me that dad was dying. She couldn't. But she started telling me about how she, 25 years later, can so clearly see and feel my brother's achingly painful and silent response on hearing the same news.

We all have our own memories, containing some truth and some imagination, distorted by time, blending what we remember and what we want to remember, to explain our moments within our lives that can't be consigned to the past and forgotten, that remain painful, defining and significant.

I've thought about this moment and my memory of it many times in the years since he passed away and more so during the past two years, because I truly believed at that point that my dad was immortal. Of course there was no way he was going to die—he was *my* dad. What illness he had didn't matter to me. He was alive. It has come back to me when I've talked with the girls about their parents passing away. I've always asked them, was he or she ill? Had they been ill for a long time? Do you know what the illness was? Me as an adult, or me as a journalist wanting to know everything, wanting to know exactly what it was, to get some explanation, so that I could feel OK, settled that they knew and I knew, which would somehow make us more comfortable with the loss.

But it just wasn't like that. Only one of the girls, Carol, said she knew what her mum had died of. In our second interview she told me she'd died of TB. It wasn't until the sixth time we met that she said that her dad had told her that her mum had died of AIDS.

But for the rest, all of their parents had been ill but none knew what illness had caused the death. I wanted to know and I struggled, probing, to get the information from the girls. I wanted clarity about what illnesses had hit their families. But they wouldn't say, they genuinely didn't know, no one had told them and they weren't about to ask. Or, if they did know, they didn't want to tell me. Their responses brought about a reflection I'd never had before on my own life and my own experience of the death of my dad. In trying to understand what the girls were saying I dug deep into what I had felt, feelings that were buried deep under overlying layers of my life.

My dad had cancer, so what? At that time, when I was 12 years old, I didn't think he would die, full stop. That he was alive mattered and knowing he had cancer meant nothing. He came out of hospital to spend Christmas with us, and died on January 15th 1983. Coping with that, the loss of a loved one, the loss of a parent, someone who supported the family, is what concerns us when we are young, not what made it happen. How we come to terms with it, how we deal with the sadness, when they're with you in your dreams at night, laughing with you, playing with you, just as they always had done, and the jolt when you wake up, the realisation of the truth—how we cope with that and how we move on is what concerns us. That's what I was hearing from the girls, what their silence was saying to me. We don't care what illness it was, my dad/mum/brother/sister is no longer around and it's hurting. It's difficult. It can be a long, lonely road and was one that too many of the girls were travelling down.

Kadzo was one of the few girls with both parents, and by the end of 2007, she was the only one who still lived with them both. Her problem was that they were both quite elderly and intermittently suffered from bouts of illness, which obviously affected the whole family. Their ill health, coupled with the demands of her in-laws—her brothers' wives all lived with them—conspired to make Kadzo's life a lot busier than she might have liked. Her family wanted to support her to play football, but sometimes what they wanted and what was possible just didn't go together. 'I started playing a long time ago because my mum and my dad told me to play,' she said in our first interview. 'My dad says football is good, don't be lazy, be one who is fast. All my brothers play and they say I should play because I have strong legs. Also if you play football you can get many presents and you might be lucky enough to get your school fees paid by a good spectator who will have seen how well you play.' It wasn't long after this that she told me, 'I've had to stop playing football because my mother was sick and there was no one to take care of her. My sister-in-law was at home but she had just given birth to twins and she couldn't look after my mum. As soon as school finishes I rush home. Now I just don't have enough time for practice. I already feel heavy and I can't run that much and I'm only 15. I want to play because if I don't play when I wake up in the morning I feel tired. Football makes me active and quick but right now I feel lazy.'

Kadzo said her mum didn't want her daughters to be burdened with domestic chores but the reality for Kadzo was that, as the oldest girl, she had a lot to do. She talked about going to collect water from the well very early in the morning, before others were awake. While her mum worried about Kadzo, her sister-in-law had no such concerns. Kadzo didn't have much time for her sister-in-law but she had no choice but to help out. The sister-in-law would order her about before she went to school: 'In the morning I don't even think about eating. I've collected water, washed the children, washed their clothes because you can't allow them to be dirty, I'm so tired I don't get any time. It is like "do this, do that". She delays me for school with all her demands.'

The domestic burden girls in Kilifi face remains alien to me; by the age of 12 you're probably collecting firewood and water, washing up dishes, helping with the cooking, looking after younger siblings, going to work on the shamba and you might also be sent out to sell grass brooms, peanuts, maize, and so on, to contribute to the family income—lots and lots of hard, often very physical work.

Just the other day, early on a Sunday morning, as we were finishing our breakfast in the cool, bright morning sun, there was a knock at the gate. The dog started barking and I heard the shrieks of a gaggle of young girls from the other side of the gate. It was six girls from MTG with their yellow cylindrical 20-litre jerrycans, coming to our door to see if we had water. I knew it must be serious because the girls never came here to ask for water. There'd been no water in Kilifi for close to a week and people were getting desperate, walking further and further to find water. They used our tap to fill their jerrycans and helped each other to put these incredibly heavy vessels on their heads. It made me feel weak. I may have lived in Kilifi for seven years but I struggle to pick up 20 litres, let alone manage to lift it onto my head. If I ever did get the water up, I doubt I'd get further than a few metres. These girls are strong.

Before they set off on the 'short' two-kilometre walk, across the bridge over Kilifi Creek back to their homes, one of them asked me if they could come back again to get more water and then quietly said, 'How much do we pay for each can?' I sent them on their way, chuckling at their good fortune that they hadn't had to part with three shillings (five cents). So they came to our house twice that morning, two kilometres each way, that's eight kilometres before you've even started thinking about breakfast, washing clothes, homework and anything else you might do on a Sunday. When I was that age I would be lying in bed on a Sunday morning, listening to music, reading magazines and then later, I might, if I was asked because I certainly wouldn't volunteer, help my mum make the Sunday lunch.

Our domestic situations as teenagers, theirs dominated by domestic chores and work in the shamba, mine lacking in any domestic responsibilities, were so different. I found it difficult to imagine what it must be like to have to do so much physical work, to sleep on a bed shared with siblings, or on the floor, to worry about whether there was going to be food on the table, going hungry so others could eat, knowing that as soon as you get home from school your work starts and it's only if you work very hard and quickly that you'll get time to do any homework. Through my eyes, it's a stressful existence; for them it's just normal.

Underneath this, though, I also saw some very strong and supportive relationships—Salma and her mum, Janet and her dad, Mercy and Kanze and their brothers, and Asya and her sister, who in the face of isolation after the loss of their mother bonded to become a united force in dealing with their issues.

❖ ❖ ❖

My mum says that my talent lies in football and if I'm chosen I should play to use my talent because it might help me in the future. Salma

Carol was one girl whose family story spilled out like beans from a sack every time I went to see her. It wasn't a particularly happy tale but I feel obliged to tell it because she so openly told it to me.

One of the first things Carol told me was that, when her mother died, her father told her that she should go and find her real father because he was not her dad. We were sitting in a big, high-roofed room at her school, which was used as a nursery school in the mornings. I looked over at the colourful but worn alphabet on the wall and the torn pieces of paper blowing about on the mud floor, imagining how it must have looked this morning, jammed full of noisy young children, laughing, jumping and singing without a care in the world. The room felt cold and empty. I really didn't know what to say. It completely knocked me off balance. But she just continued, telling me that one of her sisters had told her to stop going to school and go and look for a job. But Carol had decided that her education was more important. 'I told her that I will learn,' she said. 'I will remain here and live with these problems but I'll complete school. I have a friend who says if I have any problems, like if I don't have money, she can help me if she has money at that time.' Her resilience, a supportive friend, made the situation bearable.

Later that day, when I was back in the office, her words kept ringing in my head: 'He told me to go and look for my real dad.' She was 13 years old, her mother had just died, and she was being told she didn't belong in the place she'd called home all her life. I couldn't keep it to myself and told Collins what she had said later in the evening. A man of few words he just said, 'That's terrible,' with such a pained expression on his face that I knew I wasn't being ridiculous to be so disturbed by what I had heard.

Whenever I went to talk to Carol we would meet at her school. To begin with, I couldn't read her face. In the company of teachers, she would greet me with a completely blank expression, but as soon as we started talking she'd open up and talk frankly. She wanted to tell me things, she wanted me to know about her life and she wanted me to know what she thought.

One time during the holidays, Carol and I met at a nearby trading centre and went to her home to chat. There were a few chickens scampering around the compound and a couple of dogs. Carol took me into the small entrance to her brother's house, a mud-walled room with no roof where we sat on two rickety chairs and began to talk. Her sister-in-law and a neighbour were sitting and chatting just a few steps from where we were and went quiet as our conversation started. I felt uncomfortable. I didn't think we could chat openly, laugh about the things we normally laughed about and talk in the way I was used to talking with her. I asked her if she was OK to talk here and she said yes but I told her I felt too inhibited. She laughed at me for being shy but agreed we could walk up to the school to continue. As we left the compound we found her brother slashing the grass. He had a big cut on his face, which she said he'd got when he fell off a bicycle coming back from a wedding.

Carol had lived here since she was born, but her father had told her she didn't belong. It was against this backdrop that she talked to me about her family life and her own struggles to take control of the situation. According to Carol her father's contribution to the welfare of the family wasn't adequate: 'Sometimes he taps palm wine or he goes to cut trees to sell the wood. When he gets money from selling the wood, he buys banghi. He sells some of it and smokes some. He gives us money for food but if he doesn't get money we go to bed on empty stomachs. We normally eat the ugali (the staple food cooked from maize flour and water) with *omena*, the small fish. He only provides money for the flour. You don't know how to get money for other food. Sometimes I make brooms or fetch water to sell to others or dig other people's shambas to get money to buy the things I need. When I get the money, I buy soap and paraffin so I can study at night. When I finish school I am going to leave this place because if I need money just for soap for washing I have to look for the money myself.'

Both her sisters were married and had moved to their husbands' homes nearby. They'd both come back home, gone back to the husbands and returned home again during the two years in which we met. One had disagreed with her mother-in-law, the other with her husband and this instability was a feature of Carol's home life. Twice she told me of incidents when her brother, whose house she lived in, had been violent towards her. The first time she said, 'When my sister heard him shouting she told him, "If you drink alcohol and you come here to beat your family it's not good." He got very angry. He wanted to beat her as well. It was everyone for herself. I spent the night in the forest near home; I was alone but there was moonlight. I don't know where my sister went. When I woke up the following day I went home, took a bath and then I went to school.'

The second incident, sparked by Carol going against what her brother had told her, left her with injuries that were bad enough for her to miss school. She'd made an effort to get to school that day because she knew I was coming to visit. I could see a wound under her eye and she explained what had happened: 'My brother told me not to pick the tangerines without his permission. But I did, I picked a few. And when I got home he hit me on the face and the back until I couldn't see properly. I was beaten so badly I couldn't go to school. I went to see a doctor because I had a headache and he gave me some medicines. My brother told me I couldn't sleep in his house so I went to my uncle's place. I can't tell any teacher about it because I don't know where to start or where to end.'

I had often thought about the options Carol had. One time early on in our meetings, she had told me she would finish primary school, go to secondary school and then college, and make sure she had a job before she got married. I wondered whether this was a mantra from school that she'd repeated to herself enough times until she believed it, or whether she thought that it was what I, as an adult, wanted to hear. She seemed too sharp and aware of the situation in which she was living to really believe it would happen. In our later conversations she talked much more about wanting to make sure she finished primary school and get away from where she was living. These were her priorities but it looked to me that her options were limited.

She had an aunt who lived nearby, her mother's sister. Carol thought of moving to live with her aunt, but it would have meant changing schools and she knew that to be accepted into a new school she would have to repeat a year, to go back into Standard 7. She was already in Standard 8 and, it seemed, she didn't want to stay in school for longer than was entirely necessary. She said she'd stay with her dad, deal with the problems and finish Standard 8.

This was Carol's situation in November 2006: she was about to finish primary school; she came from a poor and broken family and had no obvious relative who could take her to secondary school or college or help her find work. What happens to a girl in Kilifi in this predicament? What path is she likely to take? Carol and I met up in June 2007. She had failed her Kenya Certificate of Primary Education (KCPE) exams the previous November, and she explained to me how life had been since finishing school:

'I was at home. I was told that my aunt was calling me to go there. When I went to see her she told me that she knew of someone who wanted a worker. I went home and I told my dad, but he said he wouldn't give me permission to go there. He said he needed me to stay at home and cultivate.

'I wanted to go back to school.[13] I went with my sister to Matuga Primary to ask for a place in Standard 7 and they agreed. When I went home and explained to my father he told me he wouldn't give me permission to go back to school. He said my work was at home now and going to the fields to farm. I went to Mombasa to stay for a week with my sister and then we returned home.'

Her father had refused to allow her to follow two of the possible options she had. He wanted her to remain at home. I couldn't understand it. He'd told her she didn't belong there and now here he was, insisting she stay put and work on the shamba. It then became clear what he'd been holding out for:

'When we returned home, I saw John and he told me that he wanted to marry me. I'd seen him passing our place a few times. I didn't know him and I didn't know his intentions, so he went to his home then came back with his uncle. This uncle of his came and told me that there is someone who wants to talk to you and then I went to where he was. He told me that he really wants to marry me. I told him I will go home then I will come back to tell him the answer. I told my sister and she said that it's my decision to go or to remain at home. She told me, "You know your problems at home." I was forced to tell my grandmother and she said that if you, yourself, have decided to go, you go. This was in March, so I went and told John. Then he came on a Wednesday and I took my clothes and went to his home. I said I better go because at home if you want money to buy soap you have to fetch water or you have to work in the fields.'

So she left, she got out of her home. Her father would get something in return, the dowry, and that was enough for him to let her go.

When we met in June she was wearing a new light blue dress with intricate ribbon binding, her hair was neatly braided, and she told me she was already pregnant. She hadn't had her period since April and she'd been feeling sick. I asked her how married life was:

'Whenever I tell John what I want he gets it for me. Like money. If I see something that is good for me or something I desire, when I tell him he gives me the money. Like with clothes, he buys clothes for me. He even bought the dress I'm wearing today. He's paid the dowry. He was told to pay 25,000 shillings (US$375) but he managed to pay 6,000 (US$90) and he was told to pay the rest in December.

'I do the daily chores at the home, like washing utensils, fetching water and cooking. I'm helped by another woman but they are a big family. I cook lunch for some of the children in the family when they come home from school. In the evening I work, I fetch water, I boil it for John, he bathes, then at night we sleep. Well, sometimes we sleep, sometimes we make love. It's better now because when I was at home I had to work for what I wanted, but here I don't. I get what I want. I can't say if I am happy or not [about the pregnancy] because I haven't ever had a baby so I don't know what that life is like. I don't know it, so I can't say if I am happy or not.'

Having talked to Carol for so long I ended up with a similar feeling of ambivalence that she displayed about her life. Sometimes she looked like she was so in control, staying in school to complete, suffering to get what she wanted, choosing to go to her husband's place. At the moment her husband was providing for her needs. Carol was happy that for the first time in her life she was asking for things and getting them without having to work for them.

But in my mind, she was working, cooking for all her husband's younger siblings, making sure her husband was comfortable and very soon, she was going to be looking after her own child and catering for its needs. Her life looked tough to me. Having grown up in the comfort of a middle-class English home, I got a good education and I've almost always had a job. Carol's grown up in rural Kilifi, scraped through primary school and is now, aged 17, married and expecting her first baby. But this is where she's always been. I've seen other lives and I'm making my comparisons based on my own views of what makes a comfortable life.

But for both of us, all of us, our lives are about our social lives, our relationships, friendships, homes, parties, celebrations, weddings, funerals, music, and beyond that we diversify into our work and other interests. The context may be different but we all talk, discuss issues, tell jokes, gossip and entertain each other, wherever we are.

Carol's life looks hard and confined to me and the thought of moving into the home of your husband, whom you hardly knew, would have been a frightening one for me. But she didn't seem fazed. She took it in her stride and was now developing new relationships, laughing with other women and girls as they prepared food, collected water and did their daily chores. Learning and gossiping about other people, going to celebrations with different people are what any of us do when we move to a new place in our lives.

I want to finish this chapter with Salma, who lived in a more urban or semi-urban setting—a very different home, where she and her mother have a strong and supportive relationship. Salma is a Swahili Muslim and she describes her domestic situation as one dominated by women—her grandmother, mother and aunties, her sister and Salma's nieces. Official figures show that one in every six households in Kilifi is headed by women.[14] Through Salma's eyes her household would be female headed. The women are the ones that she sees as important, but there are men present: her uncles, who live in their compound, would be considered by others to head the home. Salma only talks about the men in passing and in fact never mentioned them in our discussions until the third time we met and I was asking her for some clarification on her family set-up:

'We have four houses,' she told me. 'In our house I live with my mother, then there's another house for my aunt, who stays with her husband and her kids, then up a bit there is a house for my other aunt, who lives with her family, two of her children, a daughter and a son. The son is married and the daughter, Mwanaidd, has two children. The other house is my grandmother's. She comes to our house during the daytime and spends time there, then at night she goes to her house to sleep. My grandmother's is a mud house and my first aunt's is made of coral blocks then thatched with makuti. The second aunt's house is built with blocks and roofed with iron sheets. It has a cement floor. We have tapped water, and our house and that of my first aunt have electricity. My first aunt has 15 goats and my second keeps chicken. We use firewood and charcoal for cooking.'

I knew Salma well before she volunteered for this project. I'd always been impressed by how hard working and organised she was. She wasn't, in my opinion, one of the most talented football players but she had a determination that I just couldn't fault. I soon realised that this will to succeed had been drilled into her from a young age, that her mum had shown her that hard work and good planning were the key to development: 'I was born at my grandmother's place and then my mother got money to buy a plot. She was working, *vibarua* [casual work], with my first aunt. She still does that, cooking food for the workers on construction sites. When construction starts on a certain plot she gets called by the workers. She takes food daily and then they pay her on Saturdays. She wakes up very early, at 4 am, cooks, carries the food to sell and then returns at 2 pm from Monday to Saturday. When she was paid, she saved the money until it was enough to buy a plot. She bought a plot and started to build a mud house. She continued to work and put her money into micro-banking. She got money from the organisation and she bought blocks for building and she continued like that up until now. Now she has bought cement and sand and wants to finish off building more rooms. She wants to do this so that even if she doesn't get work she is getting money from renting out the rooms.'

Salma had lost her dad when she was very young, around two or three years old. He had been her mum's second husband after she had divorced her first husband. Salma had an older sister (same mother, different father) but the second-born, a brother, had died when he was a baby. She was, by all intents and purposes, a single child, surrounded by her female relatives. Living in a homestead dominated by women wasn't unheard of, particularly among the Swahili, where there's more leeway for divorce and remarriage for women. Salma's mum was now on her own, and according to Salma, not looking for another husband. Despite living in what might be considered a not very typical Kilifi homestead, with just one sibling and seemingly matriarchal, Salma still conformed to the role of a teenage girl burdened with domestic chores. 'I help my mum wash utensils, sweep, I wash my sister's kids at 6 in the evening, I prepare tea for them and I then give them their tea. When they have gone to sleep, I eat and then I continue with my studies. Sometimes I look after the goats, taking them for grazing and bringing them back at 7 pm. I don't do it every day because there are some boys who help to look after the goats. I have to do the work at home, if I relax the work will pile up. I am forced to do it quickly so when evening comes, I am very tired. In the holidays I helped my mum to take food to the construction site. We take tea and food, like *sima* [maize meal staple, another name for ugali], *chapati* [round, flat, unleavened bread), beans, cabbage and meat, down to the site. When they finish we record the amount, we wash dishes and then return home. When I finish washing the dishes, my work is over. Sometimes I go to the field to see if people are practising. If they are I join them or if there is a match, like now the boys' tournament has started, I sit and watch the match.'

3

Pepeta, pepeta![15]
Juggling football, free time and religion

You know those bicycles, those boda boda [bicycles with a seat for carrying passengers, serving as taxis] that you see at the corner? There was this man, he was drunk, and he got on one of the bicycles when the owner wasn't looking and he went as fast as he could across the bridge, to town. When he reached the bus stage he knocked someone down and he was taken to the police. The owner of the boda boda bicycle was looking for him everywhere and he was told that the man was at the police station. So he went to the police station. When he got there he told them the boda boda bicycle belonged to him and he wanted them to release the man. Then the drunkard, when he was freed, instead of going home, started singing to the police, 'Bah bah bah banjuka tu'.[16] People were laughing and asking is he mad or what? He kept singing for the police until he was about to be beaten and that's when he ran away saying, 'I thought you were going to lock me up but now you've let me go free. Bah bah bah banjuka tu!'   Kadzo

We were all together and the girls were laughing and giggling at every small development, waiting for the punch line, of Kadzo's theatrical story that she recounted with relish. It was one of those stories, funny at the time, funny in the first retelling but probably for most people, somewhat lost in the translation!

We'd met up as a group in December 2007 at a small hotel with a conference room, situated on the cliff overlooking the mouth of Kilifi Creek with a panoramic view of the Indian Ocean. In

MTG, we normally held our meetings and trainings in places in the centre of Kilifi town, at Pekele or Titanic, or we'd squeeze into someone's office at Jakob's building where we had our five-room headquarters. But I'd chosen this place, Chambai, because it was away from the town, a short *tuk tuk* (three-wheeled vehicle used as a taxi) ride from the bus stage, a private place for this group, to keep their identities away from the MTG bunch. They all came from different parts of the district and this was only the second time that the girls had spent any time together as a group. We'd come together a few months before for a party to meet with their family and friends. They were starting to get to know each other, linked by this project, but no-one outside of this group knew who all the nine girls were.

We had a lively discussion, dominated by Kadzo and Janet's story-telling and Asya's jokes. It was hard for the quieter Mercy and Kanze to get a word in edgeways. Carol was eight months pregnant and wasn't in much of a mood to talk to anyone. Salma, Juliet and Mariam were not able to attend the meeting; Salma was away playing football for her school, Juliet was playing for her division in an MTG Super Team tournament[17] and Mariam had travelled to her family in Garsen.

I wanted to use this opportunity of us being together to hear some of the stories they like to tell, things they like to do and what really makes them laugh. I thought a group discussion might bring out much more of these stories because they could play off each other and enjoy each other's tales. That was as much of an agenda as I had and we chatted, laughed and covered an array of subjects from dreams to drunkenness, discos to funerals, girls loving girls to me being a grandmother in just three-quarters of an hour.

Janet had just gone home from secondary school and retold a story she'd been told the night before by her sisters. It made us all laugh too because we'd all met her dad, a larger than life character, and we could envisage him stumbling out of his house in the dark: 'Last night I was laughing so much when I got home, I thought my sides were going to split. They told me that my sister had been sleeping, she was dreaming and she was shouting in her sleep. She was shouting, "That one is an insect, that one is an insect, it's got four legs." She shouted so loud that my dad came running out from his house, he came and he asked, what's going on? When they were telling me this story I laughed and laughed until I was in pain.'

Asya then started talking about how she couldn't sleep the night before because she was excited about coming to this meeting and Kadzo tried to outdo her with a story of how she overslept this morning and the resultant comedy of her running around the house trying to get ready, not finding her clothes, banging her head, being chased by her neighbour's son, who wanted to come with her, and eventually did.

It took me back to a very different time: the time when I first started interviewing the girls. One area of their lives I wanted to find out more about was what they do in their free time. Asya's first answer was, 'I go to work at the shamba.' I wondered if she'd understood me properly, and I tried to explain that work wasn't free time, work was work. Free time was when you didn't have any work to do, domestic, shamba or schoolwork. She told me, 'OK, play football. We have a small field at home and we play with *matufe*—balls made of papers and plastic bags. I practise with my sisters every day. Other times I sit with my friends and we tell stories, like stories about school. In the holidays we were at home looking after goats, we didn't go on any outings. I read on my own. If I stop reading I go to wash the dishes.' Asya was trying to tell me about her free time but was getting caught up with her duties, looking after the goats, washing the dishes—these were the things she did in her 'spare' time. Others said they read, studied, talked to friends, had their hair plaited or braided. If they were lucky, in the holidays they'd go and visit relatives who lived away from the rural home.

Salma and Juliet both spent time playing football and got the chance in the holidays to go to visit relatives. Salma loved football: 'In my free time I go to the field. Even if I am on my own I will go to the field to play football. If girls see me there at the field it makes them happy so they come to play as well. When we closed school we went to Mombasa. We visited Likoni and then we went to the beach. My second aunt has a house in Likoni. We stayed there for three weeks. Then the fourth week of the vacation we returned here. We went to the beach and watched boat races. I was with my three cousins and my sister's kids.'

Juliet was a player in the MTG league: 'For now we are going to the field for the MTG league. My sister also plays, in the under 12s. I also visit my friends for a chat or discussion when I'm free. We talk about things that have happened at home. During my school holiday I went to visit my sister in Mtwapa, the one who is married in Mtwapa. I went on December 22nd and I stayed there until January 3rd, when I came back home. Each day we prepared for Christmas. One night there were prayers at the church through the night but we didn't go because we had work to do at home. We cooked *pilau* [spicy rice and meat dish], *mahamri* [sweet doughnuts], *chapati*. I was supposed to get my hair braided but it was late and I didn't get taken to the salon in time, so a girl at home braided my hair in a Rasta style. When she finished we just sat. Lots of people were already walking around but we stayed at home—that's me and another girl who lives with my sister. We sat around at home, chatting and talking about everything that was going on, Christmas and about the people who were walking past. We were looking at what they were all wearing and we were sitting and laughing, me, my sister and some other girls.'

I'll admit that I've never been to a real, traditional rural disco. I use traditional in the loosest sense of the word because in these discos it's not drums, mnazi and everyone dancing to traditional Mijikenda music. It's a more modern event that has become a part of rural culture during the holidays, at Christmas, Easter and on other public holidays. The requirements for a rural disco in Kilifi include a big clear space, a temporary fence of wooden poles and sacks tied up to become the walls, a mega sound system, which normally arrives in a pick-up truck, a DJ, plenty of drinks and plenty of people. The disco starts any time in the afternoon and goes on all night.

Asya's impression of an old man going to a disco had us all in stitches: 'Come, Sarah, come to a disco during Christmas, come and see something. Every person, even the elders, even if they have a walking stick they'll be there. An old man will come and he'll say, "Where's the DJ?"'

At that point the other girls were all saying 'Where's the DJ?', 'Where's the DJ?', doing their best impersonations of an old man speaking in Kigiriama, wanting to be a part of the disco.

Asya continued, 'Yeah, even if he has … if he's carried his walking stick, walking, he says "Where's the DJ? I want the DJ, how much does it cost to come in?" Then that old man, he stands there in the disco and then he starts to dance, he dances like a child and he's an old man. Then he sits down somewhere and says, "Go, go and get a soda for me," and he sends a child to get a soda and he enjoys himself a little bit and then goes on his way home.'

The girls told me people dance, people fight, people drink, people get seduced. Just like a disco in any other part of the world, I thought, or certainly the same as any other disco I've ever been too. Having seen girls in Kilifi exhibit excruciatingly painful shyness I wondered aloud how shy girls were in such places. I was immediately informed that there was no shyness in discos these days and Janet told me in no uncertain terms, 'You have come from your home and you want to get into the disco, your shyness should be far away. If you get tired, OK, take your shyness back at the door, go with it to your home, but if you are going into the disco, remove it. You keep it aside.' I really enjoyed imagining that; it's as if you peel off your veneer of shyness when you go to a disco, leave it at the door, like you would leave your coat in the cloakroom at the door, collect your ticket so you don't forget it, and pick it up on the way out.

What the girls said they did in their free time
Play football, chat with friends, read books, visit relatives and friends, have their hair braided or plaited, go to church, go to the beach, go to discos, play 'appo', go to weddings, drink soda, do

homework, help look after relatives' children, go to visit relatives in town, such as Mombasa, Malindi, Mtwapa.

❖　❖　❖

Religion took up a lot of their free time. When I came to the coast in Kenya I was hit by the strong presence of religion in people's lives. Christianity, Islam and traditional beliefs lived side by side, rubbing against each other in schools, workplaces and the lives of everyone.

Idd ul Fitr was the biggest Muslim celebration in the year in Kilifi. Kadzo explained to me what hers had been like:

'The day before Idd people were texting each other, telling them, tomorrow is Idd, tomorrow is Idd. Other people were texting words from the Koran so that they knew tomorrow is truly Idd. Some others were not so sure. In the evening, they stood on the balcony of our neighbour's house. They looked to see if the moon could actually be seen, to know whether tomorrow would be Idd or not. I climbed up too with my elder brother and we were looking for the moon.'

This was only Kadzo's second Idd. Her family had recently converted from the Baptist church and this time she had fasted[18] for the whole of Ramadhan and was proud that she had made it; that she was proving to be a good Muslim girl. Kadzo was engrossed in anticipating the sighting of the moon and the celebrations that would follow.

'When we saw it, when we saw the moon,' she continued, 'we got so excited. Our neighbour, the father, started laughing and shouting, and then he started the disco in their house with his big, I don't know what it is, DVD? So he started playing songs really loudly! I mean if a person had been trying to talk downstairs, outside, you couldn't have heard them. I mean there was so much noise, people didn't even know how much noise they were making. We were up on the balcony. We didn't know that people were down there but when we looked we could see many people dancing to the music. So the father was happy and he increased the volume when he saw the people dancing. They danced more, he increased the volume more and then his wife said, I want to pray, but she was told there's no praying, you will pray tomorrow. That's what she was told by her husband.'

So it looked like the neighbour wanted to make sure that the sighting of the moon was met with as much celebration as possible. No praying, just dancing. This was the family that had been instrumental in Kadzo's conversion to Islam. They were a relatively well-off family with a car and a hardware store and a shop on the ground floor of their two-storey home. Kadzo describes the relationship she had built up with the neighbours as something very special. It seemed as if they had taken her into the bosom of their family, involving her in their Idd celebrations, buying her clothes and treating her like their own child. For Idd she would travel with them to another part of the district to enjoy the celebrations there: 'We hadn't eaten food during the day, then he slaughtered a goat, we roasted it at night, we ate the meat until morning. We didn't sleep. Then the meat that remained, he gave it to other people. Now, you know he has a shop, he weighed up ten bags of one kilogram of rice, he again went and bought meat and he divided it up to give to the poor people.

'We went to Shanzu on Friday. That was Idd. Two goats were slaughtered for us and we cooked *biriani* [a spicy rice and meat dish]. Then when we finished eating we put on our new clothes and came back home. I went with our neighbour and her husband and their housemaid. We went in their car. My family stayed at home. It was only me who went to Shanzu. It was my neighbour who said I should go with her to see how their Idd is. My Idd clothes were so nice, they were bought by my neighbour. They were fashionable, the current style. She bought the clothes because I had fasted for the whole month, 30 days, so she bought the clothes for me. She bought me a black skirt, another T-shirt, a white blouse with small sleeves and she bought me some shoes. She is not my parent but she gives me things because she is like an older sister to me. When people ask her she says this one, Kadzo, is my sister.'

This relationship with her neighbours was a good one for Kadzo, a bright girl growing up in a family with very limited resources and parents whose illnesses were a constant source of worry for her. This new family was helping her deal with many of the problems she had talked of before. She was getting clothes bought for her; her neighbour also bought her sanitary pads. Her basic needs, which she'd so often said the family could not cater for, were now being met with her switch to Islam. But it wasn't just one way, I'm sure the family enjoyed Kadzo's company and their son, who was about eight years old, adored Kadzo to the extent that when she came for the meeting in December she brought him with her because he wanted to go wherever she went.

When I was growing up in the UK in the 1970s and 1980s religion, and what we learnt about religion, was simple. I didn't live in a multicultural part of the country and at both primary and secondary school Christianity was the dominant religion. It wasn't just dominant, it was virtually the only religion I grew up knowing. In our religious education classes we were told that other religions existed, such as Islam, Buddhism and Hinduism, but that was about as far as it went. You were a Christian, you might go to church, you might not, but you were still considered to be a Christian. It was a bit more complicated for me in my early teenage years because my mum became a more regular church-goer and insisted that we all attended Sunday school. We battled with each other for what felt like years, me hiding under the blankets on a Sunday morning, pretending to still be asleep, trying to avoid Sunday school.

In the small town of Kilifi different Christian denominations proliferate. There must be around 20 churches, Catholic, Anglican, Methodist and Apostolic, all housed in more traditional concrete churches, and then others, Royal Tabernacle, Full Gospel, Temple of Praise, Miracle, and many more worshipping in places at various stages of development. At the top end are the more established, better-funded churches in huge buildings with high iron sheet roofs, concrete floors, altars, powerful sound systems and no walls, so the breeze passes through and the word of the Lord spreads out.

I've watched the development of a church in our village over the last two years. It started when someone began a fellowship on a grassy knoll behind the bus stage on the main Mombasa–Malindi road, just behind the shaded tree where the Sunday newspapers are sold and maize is roasted for passing travellers. He started with a sound system, powered by electricity from the local hair salon. The electric cable would snake out of the salon, lie across the road and charge up his system. He had a captive audience with people passing to go to other churches, going to buy the newspapers, wandering around on a Sunday morning. Slowly the congregation grew, he bought a few benches, he preached and they sang all morning long, for most of this side of the village to hear. Then a fence went up around the small area to indicate the land was now theirs. Then the church went up—coral block foundation stones, wooden posts and iron sheets for the walls and the roof. Now it looks like a fully established church, still using the electricity from the hairdresser, singing the praises of the Lord every Sunday and with a Sunday school of around 20 children who sit under the tree next to the church for their Sunday morning lessons.

Islam is also omnipresent, particularly along the coastal strip. Our office is situated opposite a mosque and from our home we can hear the call for prayer from the mosques of the village. In our village there are two; in Kilifi town there are at least five and alongside each mosque there's a madrassa, where most Muslim children study after school. Salma and Mariam were Swahilis born into Muslim families. They both talked of going to the madrassa. Mariam said it teaches her 'to a deep level so that I understand a lot. It teaches me discipline, how not to sin and how to live peacefully with my parents.'

❖ ❖ ❖

*God and menstruation: Salma and her teacher dispel a
religious myth:*
*Some people say that if you see the blood it is a sin and when it's
over God has forgiven you. I tell them it's not a sin, it's a normal
thing for a girl to experience when she gets to adolescence.*
*Some people say it because they don't understand. But recently
we were taught science by our teacher, and he taught us about
menstruation. That's when they started to understand. They
asked questions and they were told it is not a sin.*

Underlying the conventional religions that are so visible through
their churches and their mosques, there was an equally powerful
force of traditional religion that girls were born into, live with in
their homes and adhere to in their daily lives. This traditional
religion explains phenomena, events, good and bad fortunes and
heals the sick. It adds to the decision-making melting pot that the
girls exist in. Which religion should they follow? Who or what
is influencing them? Can they mix them up and take what they
want?

Even if you belong to one religion it is impossible not to
be exposed to others. You will have friends, classmates and
neighbours who have different religions and you will learn
from them about their own beliefs. While Salma and Mariam
were exposed to other religions, they were born Muslims and
they remained Muslims. All the other girls, who were from
the Mijikenda community, had more diverse and complex
relationships with religion. All were born into families with a
history of traditional beliefs. This history was being challenged
by both Christianity and Islam, and the girls were often struggling
with the messages they were getting from different quarters. The
tension between home and school, parents and teachers, was a
real one in the field of religion. It looked to me like a constant
balancing act, one that some of them consciously negotiated and
reasoned through, choosing one religion over another, while
others dipped into two if not three religions, extracting the parts
that were most relevant and needed at a particular time.

But all the girls agreed on one thing. If you pray, regardless of the god you pray to, you will be helped and many of your problems, particularly those concerning poor performance in school or illness, will be solved. Kanze once told me, 'It's important to pray because if your performance in school is not good, you can pray and do well. If you want to pass your exams you pray. You might be sick and you don't have money to buy drugs—you can pray and get better.'

So, if you prayed hard enough you would do better in your exams or get better if you were ill. They all believed this. When I probed Kanze a bit further she said that sometimes your prayers are not answered, so you better just pray some more. There were, it seemed, many things that happened in their lives that they couldn't control: the quality of education they got, the amount of work they had at home, the amount of time they had to study. So a level of belief and faith that someone, somewhere, is listening to your prayers, was all part of a coping strategy, helping them through their teenage years.

Asya was a Muslim when I met her, but her uncle was a *mganga,* a traditional healer. She'd also dabbled with Christianity but told me, 'I was a Catholic but I became sick. I am not sure what it was. I had rashes and I was told to go to this place. I went and I got healed, so I changed my religion to Islam. All of my family changed their religion.' Healing and religion were a critical part of Asya's life and, despite being a Muslim, traditional beliefs remained a central part of it. She told me that she didn't eat meat because she had a health problem; there were times when her body would swell and the elders had told her not to eat meat because if she did her body would swell up.

I noticed once that she was wearing a coloured string necklace with a tiny bunch of small twigs tied into it. I knew that it was a traditional charm of some sort and I asked her about the story behind it: 'I had a sore throat. It was so bad I couldn't eat. I was taken to the hospital and I was there for two weeks. The elders gave it to me, the necklace, to protect me and to make me better. There are some people who do not want to see me move on in my life so this protects me from them. You know, I came back home with the radio[19] after the last meeting. People got jealous and said, "Next thing you will be coming back with a TV." That's when I started to get ill.'

I was asking Asya and her sister many questions about traditional healers until her sister, looking a bit annoyed, said to me, 'What, do you mean you don't have traditional healers where you come from?' It's at that point that I was hit again by the gaping difference between us. I stumbled through an explanation: well, no not really. If we were ill when we were young we would go to the local doctor, the medical doctor and in my mind I'm seeing my mum driving us on smooth roads through the country lanes of north Essex to the local doctor's surgery where we would get free medical treatment. I was realising that this huge gap was a two-way street and I wondered whether they sometimes felt tired having to explain things to me—me with my silly, ignorant, biased questions about their culture and their religion. As a group they were very forgiving of me, but there were probably things they made a conscious decision not to even discuss with me because it might just have been too complicated to explain.

It became clear the more I talked to Kadzo that her family had flitted from being Baptists to Muslims while still maintaining strong traditional beliefs. When her elderly aunt, her dad's sister, died, Kadzo explained it like this: 'She was discharged from hospital and then she was admitted again. She died in hospital. Her stomach was burning but the doctors could not detect any illness. They don't know if she was bewitched or what sickness it was.' That she was over 90 years old didn't seem to be reason enough for her demise.

Janet claimed that, as a committed Christian, she didn't have any dilemmas or tensions between traditional beliefs and conventional religion. She had strong ideas that you should stick to one religion, whatever that religion might be, but that you really shouldn't mix them. In articulating her beliefs she demonstrates powerful insight into religion.

'I am not sure whether there are others who balance between the two, so the balancing is what I don't know,' she told me. 'I mean today you will be going to what, to a traditional healer then tomorrow to the church? It's not good: if you go to the church, just go to the church. And if you opt for things to do with traditions then follow those. OK, when you were born, you didn't have religion then and you did not know, and your parents maybe put some things[20] on you. OK, but now, you know, there is, now I am a church youth, and then if I go to a traditional healer, what am I going to take? Even if you have problems, you just tell your friends, ah I have such a problem. OK, you call each other and pray nicely.'

I knew that religion had spread far and wide, but I still couldn't help being surprised when I came across a church or a mosque, perfectly built in a remote part of the district. Janet worshipped at one such church, far from the main road where I had got out of the matatu. We were walking together to her school during the rainy season. I hadn't been able to get out to see her because of the heavy rain, but that day there was a lull in the downpours and I decided to go. I walked to the bus stage in Kilifi and got into the matatu. The vehicles that went out towards Janet's place were ancient. They say that when a matatu retires from the Mombasa–Kilifi route it's taken to the interior roads that go deep into the district to die a dignified death on those dirt roads. They rattle and they creak their way slowly to their destinations, journeys that I used to find exciting, to new places, with new experiences: breakdowns, heated arguments over the fare, stories and the squeezing of more people in a matatu than you could ever imagine. But now I find travelling by matatu a frustrating experience. I still like the stories, but the discomfort, the danger—I'm not sure it's still so exciting and I get annoyed that this is how most people in rural Kenya have to travel: squeeze in, head down and pray.

The matatu was almost full when I got in, the conductor called for more passengers and we were soon on our way.[21] The road had recently been graded so there weren't huge potholes, but I knew that because of the rain it was unlikely to be the easiest of trips.

At one stage the matatu slid along the surface of the road, gliding forward towards our destination. At another point we squelched through the huge gorges of tyre prints where an overloaded lorry must have got stuck before eventually being hauled out. Our wheels sprayed mud high into the air and the matatu's back end swung from side to side as we willed it through. I was lucky to be squashed against the window on the second last row of seats. The vehicle was jammed full. I could see out of the side but I couldn't see much of what was going on ahead. I preferred to travel that way.

When I arrived at the bus stage nearest to Janet's home, she was there waiting for me under a tree. There were puddles everywhere and the air felt fresh. The rains always brought respite for everyone, a sign that another season had started, planting should begin and after months of stifling heat we could now enjoy a more bearable climate, where we didn't feel completely lethargic and incapable of achieving anything.

We'd agreed that from there we'd walk down to the school, greeting her dad on the way. We then bumped into Mama Sarah, a formidable local woman leader in her fifties, who had been a player in the MTG football league the previous year. She started telling me a long story, explaining why she was no longer playing football. It was a tale of disagreements with other players and her own fundamental belief that there weren't enough incentives coming from MTG to get girls playing football. Mama Sarah had wanted to control the football team, believing there were big pickings to be had. Some of the younger players had revolted against her because they thought she was involved in too many things in the village. Whenever an NGO came along or if food relief was brought, Mama Sarah was right there at the forefront, coordinating things, putting herself forward as the voice of the community. When their prize for being runners-up in the football league wasn't as big as Mama Sarah had expected she tried to convince players to stop playing. She succeeded in causing a big split in the team, from which it was still trying to recover.

The Anglican church Janet attended every Sunday was being built. It was going to be big. The main body of the church, including the porch, had been constructed. It was hot and dark inside so we stood in the more breezy doorway as Janet told me what the Sunday service was like:

'I come here with my sisters. The young children have already been here from early in the morning in Sunday school. You find there are flowers all over the floor of the church, because the children have been playing with them. We sweep the floor and others come in, young and old people, for the main service. There's the youth choir, and the mothers dance too. They have their choir and they dance. There's a song for everyone, the praises. When you finish, you pray, then you sit to listen to the word of God. Afterwards you sing again, then there are the announcements, then you give the offerings and then you go out. You greet each other outside, then the youth get together to practise next Sunday's songs.'

It seemed that traditional culture was woven into these adopted religions. Conventional religion, while taking a judgemental stance on some aspects of traditional culture, embraced many others. Staying up all night is an integral part of Mijikenda culture. During burials, remembrance ceremonies, weddings, people will stay up eating, drinking, playing drums and dancing. When Carol attended a funeral she fell victim to her local church's strict rules on what was expected of its congregation. She told me, 'I don't go to church any more. I was a Christian. One Saturday we had a funeral at home so we stayed up throughout the night. When I went to church we were told it's not good for Christians to attend all-night events so I stopped going to church. I just decided not to go any more. People from the church came to ask me why I don't go any more. I just told them I had decided myself not to go.'

Motsemme[22] states that 'religious discourses are always mediated by one's own experiences, which are influenced by gender, race, class, location, family, generation, etc.' Our cultural location shapes how we worship, with whom we worship, where we worship and what we worship. Religion here illustrates the fluidity and flux of rural culture. In Kilifi, as in many other parts of Kenya, the concept of staying up through the night has been taken on by religion. Remember Kadzo on the eve of Idd ul Fitr. In churches all-night prayer meetings have been incorporated into the annual calendar. In all churches, members of the congregation are not supposed to drink alcohol or go to bars, and some of the stauncher believers take a dim view of traditional celebrations and ceremonies. But perhaps church members need something to do, more than just attending the Sunday service. There may not be alcohol at the all night prayer meetings, but there will be praying, fellowship, singing and dancing all night long.

Juliet described herself as a Christian and attended an all-night prayer meeting on Christmas Day in 2007. However, when her 15-year-old brother died, the family turned to their traditional beliefs to explain his sudden death.

'He woke up on Saturday morning, and I was making tea. After I'd made tea, he left and he didn't even take tea. He went out, down to the shamba of our uncle, the younger brother to our dad. When he came back he said he had a stomach ache. My mum told him he should go and buy some drugs. He told her he couldn't go because his stomach was hurting too much. So my mum took the money and went. I wasn't there. I was washing clothes at the tap. When mum came there, to the tap, she told me, "Your brother has a bad stomach ache. I need to go and buy him drugs." So she went and bought them, took them back to him and he took them. Then when it got to around 3 o'clock he said he couldn't eat anything. We cooked him some tea, he drank a tiny bit and then told us, "Stop, I can't drink any more," and he went to sleep. When night came he said he couldn't sleep. He was crying and saying that his stomach was so painful, it was burning, so my mum told him, "In the morning we'll take you to the hospital." When morning came we got a bicycle to come and take him. When he got up, he got to the door of his room and then he couldn't go any further and he fell down, he collapsed and he died right there. So we put him on the bed. Then we had to tell people about it. My dad [brother of her father], and others, we called them using the phone. I'm feeling so bad because it was me and him and then our small brothers and sisters at home, so we used to really help each other at home. Now, if my mum leaves, it will be me on my own looking after the small children.'

This was what Juliet told me as we talked in the library at her school. When we'd finished we walked to the stage where I would take a matatu back to Kilifi. As we walked I asked her, 'So what are people saying, I mean, what are they saying to explain your brother's death?'

She told me, 'My dad's brother and sister are saying that he was bewitched. There was this neighbour of ours, a woman, an old woman—her husband had died a long time ago. They were saying it was her, she had bewitched him. She and her husband were not from here. They had bought land in this area and they had been here for a long time. They were from Vipingo [in another part of Kilifi District]. She knew what people were saying about what she had done and she got scared. Three days later she died. She was taken to Vipingo and buried there.'

I asked her if she also believed he'd been bewitched: 'I have to, otherwise how else could he have died?' I wanted to know why this old woman would have bewitched her brother. She told me, 'I don't know, I just don't know.'

I could understand that her family wanted an explanation. People need explanations: he'd died suddenly, something must have made it happen. This woman was an outsider, she was not from the area and despite having lived there for many years she was still an outsider. I wondered later how much her outsider status had to do with it. I wondered if the old woman had been bewitched in return. Or had she died from fear? Was it a punishment from God? Was it better that she was dead? Did that help in the healing at all?

❖   ❖   ❖

The girls' views and discussions painted a picture of a fluidity of religion where not much was set in stone. You had to navigate through different religions in different settings, making your own decisions on where your beliefs lay. Mercy, the granddaughter of a bishop, Kanze, whose brother was a saved Christian, and Janet all said they held strong Christian beliefs and regularly went to church. Carol had left the church after a clash with rural traditions and Juliet was a churchgoer but also needed her tradition when confronted with death in the family. Salma and Mariam were Muslims from birth, while Asya and Kadzo had dabbled with all three religions to epitomise the complexities of religion as experienced by rural teenage girls.

Religion served a purpose: to explain illness and death, to assist you in schoolwork, to give you something to do on a Sunday, a group to belong to, to give you moral guidance. I got the impression that religion was just something that you did or you had because everyone had to have a religion. But the girls also made conscious decisions: Carol to leave the church altogether, Asya to switch to Islam because it had helped her recover from an illness, Kadzo to stick with Islam because of the support from her Muslim neighbours. I liked the way they used religion for their own benefit and took the parts that they felt worked for them and left other bits behind.

4

Off the pitch:
Education and school life

NARC, the National Rainbow Coalition, swept to power in
Kenya in December 2002, dislodging the Kenya African
National Union (KANU), the party that had ruled the
country since independence. KANU was also the party of Daniel
Arap Moi, who for 24 years was president of Kenya. This was the
third 'multiparty' election in the country. In previous elections the
opposition had been split but this time Mwai Kibaki's Democratic
Party (DP), Raila Odinga's Liberal Democratic Party (LDP) and a
number of other smaller parties had come together to form a force
strong enough to remove KANU. Kibaki had been Moi's vice
president and sat in his cabinets. Odinga had announced *'Kibaki
tosha!'* (literally 'Kibaki is enough', which was meant to urge all
his supporters to get behind Kibaki) at a pre-election rally. At that
point, Moi must have known that KANU's days were numbered.
On December 28th 2002, Kibaki was sworn in as the newly elected
president of Kenya at Uhuru Park in Nairobi in front of thousands
of cheering Kenyans.

One of the very first policies the NARC government announced
was free primary education for all. Throughout the country
children who'd previously been staying at home because their
parents could not afford to send them to school were turning up
to learn. Schools reported classrooms with over 100 pupils, and
one octogenarian taking the 'free education for all' quite literally
became a national icon when he enrolled for Standard 1 in his
local school.

In Kilifi it was no different. Schools burst at the seams with
new pupils and while people working in the education sector
wanted to embrace the new policy it had many teething problems

that still reverberate today. John Katana had been a head teacher at various primary schools in Kilifi for over ten years and had first-hand experience with introducing free primary education. I'd called him to ask if I could come to talk to him about how he'd implemented the new policy in his school in 2003. No problem, he said, and we fixed a time. Minutes later he called me back. What exactly did I want to ask him? He wanted to be prepared. When I turned up at his office later that day he sat behind his gigantic desk with an A4 pad in front of him. He'd written two lists: 1) the positive effects of free education and 2) the negative effects. It was an overwhelmingly comprehensive list, typical of John, making sure that everything was covered, that he wouldn't miss anything out and that he'd provide me with as much information as possible. He started to read them the lists to me, giving me time to write and think about what he was saying:

'First, it helped the parents. They no longer had to pay levies to the school, which meant they could use that money elsewhere. It reduced child labour; some children who hadn't been in school had been sent by their parents to work, selling *barafu* [small ice lollies] and peanuts, because they didn't have anything to do and the family needed the money. But now they were in school. It helped reduce poverty because parents only had to buy uniforms now. Everything else was covered by the government. It meant more girls enrolled in school. Children had better access to learning materials because these were all provided now: text books, exercise books, pens, rulers. Before 2003 the parents had to buy these things and often children just missed out. It helped improve health because children were learning about a balanced diet and were learning to cook in health education; socially, it helped children learn how to interact with others.

'But there were some downsides. Personally, I believe that when it started the government wasn't ready and had not planned it properly. There were a lot of repercussions. We couldn't cope with the influx of pupils. It diluted the quality of education because there were just too many pupils. We lacked physical facilities and resources so what we had were overused; children didn't have desks so they had to sit on the floor. We are still acutely understaffed here. We have over 1,250 pupils and the average class size is 70. In Standards 1 and 2 we have three teachers and 236 pupils, and in Standard 8 there are 65 children. The government rate recommends a maximum of 50 per class.

'There's also more indiscipline with the re-admissions. We absorbed former street children and beach boys and girls, who used to follow tourists on the beach for sex. They've seen a lot more of the world out there and they bring that knowledge into the school, which influences the other pupils. There are huge age discrepancies in classes and some of the older pupils bully the younger ones. They can't relate with them and some of the younger ones are scared of the older ones. I can give you an example. At my previous school a 27-year-old man came back to school and went into Standard 4. He stayed for a term but then left. He said that the others in his class were laughing at him, they were too noisy and he didn't want to stay any longer.'

One major shift for girls through free primary education was that if they became pregnant and gave birth they could return to school and continue with their studies. It wasn't that they couldn't before but in a place like Kilifi the parents would think twice before paying the school levies. According to John parents felt that if they sent their daughter who'd given birth back to school it would be like educating someone else's wife and that would be a waste of money. It's generally expected that a woman will marry and when she does she moves away from her parents to the home of the husband. Even if the girl didn't leave her parents' home when she gave birth to go and live with the father of her child her status in the community changed; she's now a mother, a woman, and regardless of her age, she would be seen as such. John tried to put a positive spin on girls returning to school after they'd had babies, but it wasn't as easy as it might seem: 'On the one hand it's good. She can act as a role model to show girls that you can get pregnant and then go back to school. But it can also encourage those who might not have thought about it to think about having sex and getting pregnant.

She's feeling different now, she's a mother and she might not feel comfortable in school.' And that is the crux of it. Girls do now have the opportunity to go back to school after they've given birth. But the practicalities, how she has changed through giving birth, how society now sees her as a mother, as a woman, makes it complicated and difficult for both the girl and the school.

❖ ❖ ❖

Teachers say football is good. It gives girls confidence and drives away shyness. If you don't perform well in class but you're a good player the teachers understand that at least you are good in the field.

Kanze

I started talking with this group of girls two years after the introduction of free primary education. They were all of school-going age, between 14 and 16 years, and at that time they were all in school. Most girls in Kilifi who had chosen to play football were in school teams because that was where football had first been introduced to them. Some also played football for their league teams on Saturdays but any player in a league team who was not in school was invariably older, in their late teens or early twenties. After two years, five of the nine girls were still in school: two in primary and three in secondary.[23] Two were married, one was attending a tailoring college and the other had just sat her KCPE and was not sure if she would go on to secondary school.

	November 2005	November 2006	November 2007
Asya	Standard 6	Left primary before completing Standard 7	Married, baby daughter aged 10 months
Carol	Standard 7	Sat KCPE	Married, 8 months pregnant
Janet	Form 1, secondary	Form 2, dropped out, lack of school fees	Form 2, repeating in different secondary school
Juliet	Standard 6	Repeating Standard 6	Standard 7, will repeat in 2008
Kadzo	Standard 5	Standard 6	Standard 7
Kanze	Standard 7	Sat KCPE	Tailoring college, Malindi
Mariam	Standard 6	Standard 7	Sat KCPE
Mercy	Standard 7	Sat KCPE	Form 1 secondary, sponsored place
Salma	Standard 7	Sat KCPE	Form 1 secondary, sponsored place

I soon realised that there were only two things in school that the girls consistently worried about: 1) academic performance and 2) school fees for secondary school. Everything else was a by the way. The only extracurricular activity we talked about was football, apart from Kanze, who was an active member of the Scouts. Everything in primary school was about achieving the magic 300 or 350 out of 500 in their KCPE results and going on to secondary school. It was touted as a goal, something they all aspired to, but when they talked about their end-of-year results, 320, by Kadzo, was the highest any of them ever achieved. Most were getting between 250 and 280, just reaching the 50% pass mark. When it came to Standard 8, the last year of primary school, everything intensified in the quest for academic success, including the amount of praying that went on. It was in the series of second interviews that the girls told me they prayed to do well in exams, to do better than last year, for academic success. Prayers were needed: when the girls' aspirations were curtailed by forces beyond their control, such as the amount of work they had to do at home, they used prayers as a source of encouragement, to support their belief that they could fulfil their hopes.

At the beginning of 2008, 1,976 of the 4,051 girls in Kilifi District who had sat KCPE were accepted into secondary school.[24] That is 49%, which means that 51% of those who finished primary school didn't do well enough to be offered a place in a secondary school. This '300–350' that was bandied around didn't look like a realistic ambition, so why was I hearing it so often? Were they being built up in schools to believe they could achieve the unachievable in an attempt to motivate the students? The chances of girls getting the grades to go to one of the coveted secondary schools was relatively low. If they did get the marks they were sent into a spin, trying to find some way to take up their place in secondary school when they knew it hadn't been catered for in the family budget.

It wasn't until early 2008 that 'free' secondary education was brought in. However, this policy was announced during the post-election violence and all schools, including those in Kilifi, were thrown into chaos in trying to implement it. Schools opened late because of the political problems. Information was not getting down to the district about how to implement it. So the promised land of free secondary education became a botched job. In any event, 'free' didn't actually mean free. It meant fees were waived but there were many other costs such as contribution to physical education, administration costs, medical, PTA development and boarding fees for those in boarding school, all to be borne by the parents.

It's unlikely that free secondary education will significantly reduce the worries and fears expressed by the girls about reaching secondary school. I'd talked at length with all of them about their home situations and not one of them had a parent in full-time paid employment. Janet's dad, a retired teacher, got a small monthly pension, but he struggled to support her secondary education. Others had parents who did casual work: Salma's mum as a cook. Mercy's mum had a sewing machine and would get a lot of work when school uniforms were being ordered at the beginning of the year, but nothing steady or guaranteed after that. But when Salma failed to raise the money she needed to go to secondary I could see that the inconsistent income her mother's work brought into the family would not stretch to fees for secondary school. Or secondary school might not have been a priority in the family budget, considering the hole it would burn into it. The only hope, often, for a secondary education, came through an employed older sibling, who more often than not had their own young children to support, or the chance of external assistance.[25]

❖ ❖ ❖

Salma moved from Standard 7 to Standard 8 at the beginning of 2006, but not without anxiety. This worry increased as she prepared for her KCPE exams and wondered whether she would make it to secondary school. She was concerned about whether her mum could afford the school fees, not whether she would pass the exams.

'I did well in Standard 7. I had 275 marks but we were not allowed to go to the next class because some pupils had cheated. They stole answers from another school and used them, so all of us were told to re-sit the exams. In the second week of term we did them again and I passed with 285 marks so I was allowed to continue into Standard 8. This year I am targeting 300 marks or above in KCPE. I am doing tuition with Mr Sadiq. Over 50 of us are doing tuition there with one teacher. We are in different rooms for Standards 5, 6, 7 and 8. It's now time to be very serious so that you can get a good secondary school to go to. There's no time to sit idle and we should always be studying. I want to go to a school near my home. I would like to be able to get a chance to come home. Like now, there is this football tournament, so if I'm selected for the team and there is a tournament, I'll be able to come and participate.'

So that was how Salma felt in her final year in primary. She was working hard and going for tuition. Tuition meant more expenditure for the parents, some of whom just wouldn't be able to afford it. But almost everybody in school is strongly encouraged to go for tuition. And now, with classes jammed full of children, more than before many parents see tuition as a necessary expense. There is, as Salma said, no time to rest, and you can often see school buses from local private schools ferrying children home well after 8 pm.

When I saw Salma after she'd sat her KCPE, she was confident that she had performed well: 'The KCPE exam was not hard. It was a bit easy. I'm expecting to get over 300 so that I get a good school. When I asked my mum about school fees for secondary she didn't say anything. I think she has the money but I don't know. I think she has because she has work, taking the food to the workers at the construction sites. We are just from there now. She told me that when she gets 2,000 or 3,000 shillings, she takes the money to the cooperative. Then on January 1st she will check if the money's enough for my school fees, then I will go to school.'

❖ ❖ ❖

The selection process for secondary school in Kenya is complex. In their final year of primary, all students who have paid to sit their KCPE have to choose schools. They select two national, two provincial and two district schools. National schools are open to pupils from all parts of the country, as the name suggests. These schools get the pick of the bunch, selecting the pupils with top academic qualifications. The selection takes the learning conditions of the district into consideration. For instance, in Kilifi District the 19 girls who were accepted into national secondary schools in 2008 all got over 400 marks but it's likely that those from Nairobi would have needed over 430. Those in even more remote places, such as the districts in North Eastern Province, may have achieved 380–390 marks and still have been given a place in a national school.[26] So in February 2008, 47 students (28 boys and 19 girls) out of 10,530 who sat the KCPE in Kilifi District were selected for place in a national school.[27] It seems that there is no fixed number of pupils from each district selected for secondary school. While there is some weighting applied to counter disparities in learning environment and access to resources, academic achievement remains the guiding factor in the selection.

You can apply for provincial schools only in the province in which you live, so girls in Kilifi District can apply for schools in Coast Province. Provincial schools require higher academic qualifications than district schools and are, more often than not, boarding schools. This bumps up the price because of the boarding fees. In district schools pupils still need to have achieved a certain mark in their KCPE. This is generally lower for girls than boys as they, unsurprisingly, given their domestic burden and the many other factors that undermine their schooling experience, still perform less well. The table that follows specifies those who have been accepted into a secondary school. Figures were not available at the time of the number who actually took up the places, which was likely to be fewer than recorded here because of parents not being able to afford the costs of secondary education, despite fees being waived as of January 2008.

Secondary school intake for Form 1, Kilifi District, 2008

	Boys	Girls	Total
National	28	19	47
Provincial	946	793	1,739
District	838	743	1,581
Private	665	421	1,086
Total absorbed	2,477	1,976	4,453
Total registered for KCPE	6,479	4,051	10,530

Unfortunately it didn't quite turn out how Salma had expected. She didn't get close to the 300 she was predicting. Her teachers had described her to me as an average student. She said she'd been consistently achieving around 280 marks in her mock exams through Standard 7 and Standard 8. Those marks would have easily got her a place in a district school. I'd assumed that Salma would mirror her form on the football pitch—limited ability but outstanding effort that shaped her from an average talent to an effective first team player—in the exam room. But, it seemed, that wasn't going to be the case.

'First we were told to collect the results slip. When we arrived at the school, we found the headmaster there. He gave us the results and ... I had failed. I scored 236.' I remember my reaction to her news, a kind of squeaky hurrumph. I couldn't mask my surprise, which was tinged with disappointment. Her mother, knowing Salma better than I did, was sympathetic and pragmatic. I speculated later whether her mum had actually breathed a sigh of relief, knowing that Salma had such high hopes of going to secondary school while she, as her only parent, would not be able to afford the school fees.

'I took the results home,' she continued. 'My mother told me "you did not fail as such if the last student scored 96. You've really tried." I asked my mum about going to secondary school, so she said she had money but it wasn't enough and she wasn't going to get any other money in time for me to join. I asked her, what will I do? And she told me to be patient. That's when Anze from MTG came to the football field where we were playing. She asked me if I would be joining any school. I told her that I didn't know because I hadn't been told so. That's when Anze told me that at MTG there was a plan of taking some girls who are good footballers to Masinga Secondary.'

This was an opening for Salma. Her commitment to MTG might show some dividends. If ever there was an MTG activity, Salma would be there—a committee meeting, a league match, a tournament, a coaching course, Salma was present, learning, contributing, giving ideas, volunteering, coaching her team, advising her teammates and playing a game that she said she loved.

'I thought about what Anze had said,' she continued. 'And I told her, "If they will accept me then when my mum gets the money, we will pay it back." But Anze said, "Since you are in MTG, and a player, they will take you, it's no problem. You just need to buy uniforms and the things you need to go to school." She told me to collect the results slip and photocopy it, get my leaving certificate, photocopy it, and take it all to the office so that it can be taken to Masinga.'

This school, Masinga, had some sponsored places for good footballers. In Kenya the publicity secondary schools get from reaching the national finals of school ball game competitions is huge. Pictures and stories of the finals sit alongside the ubiquitous English Premier League news in the national newspapers. Success here elevates your school into the national limelight. The teachers knew that MTG was producing lots of good young footballers. That is how the relationship between the school and the organisation started. Salma was one of five girls from MTG to go to Masinga in 2007. Despite failing her KCPE, Salma was accepted into the school because she was a good footballer.

There's much that conspires against girls getting an education in Kilifi, as both John Katana and Mr Wanje from the District Education Office told me. 'Boys do better than girls, not because they are brighter but because more boys sit the exams than girls,' John told me. I couldn't quite work out why that would be reason on its own until I discussed it further with Mr Wanje. 'Girls feel outnumbered,' he said. 'It can affect their performance. It's as if they feel they don't belong there, surrounded by all the boys.' But it wasn't just that; other issues are at play. John continued, 'Girls look shy and sometimes the boys in class bully them. Sometimes the girls themselves think they are too big, too old, to be here in school. Some are worried that they will spoil their clothes because of their periods. Girls are given a lot of work to do at home so that when they come to school they are exhausted.' Mr Wanje agreed with John that another big problem for girls in school is menstruation: 'Girls' performance in school is affected by the issue of sanitation. Girls lack what they need and the toilets are not adequate. Some toilets don't even have doors, so girls don't feel like going to school; they feel embarrassed.'

There are so many pressures on girls: there's no food on the table at home. Your mother is ill, so can you really still go to school? And then how are you performing in school? What standard of teaching are you getting in a class of 60 or 70 when the exams are around the corner? And then, you, yourself—you've just started your periods, they're irregular, you can't afford sanitary pads, there's only one girls' toilet at school—wouldn't it be better to just stay at home? Getting an education in Kilifi is a battle.

In Salma, there's a promising tale. She'd gone through all the struggles to finish primary school and now through hard work, perseverance, a bit of good luck and no doubt a few prayers she'd reached the holy grail of secondary school. It's not an easy path. When I went to see her at her new school, she told me things were a bit tough in class, that she wasn't performing well academically. On the football field, though, she was practising every day and was now a key member of the squad. And she was very popular. She'd been voted class leader, a stamp of approval from her peers, confirming that she was happy, confident and settled in her new school.

❖ ❖ ❖

Juliet's story about her family's efforts to keep her siblings in school, and her role within it, starts with a frank yet ambivalent assessment of her life: 'My life is not too bad and not too good,' she said.

'Sometimes there's no money at home to pay for exam fees for me and my brothers and sisters. So I have to struggle to go and look for work, like cultivating other people's fields. My exam fees are 155 shillings (US$2.30) a term. Two of my siblings need 95 ($1.40) each and the other two 65 ($1) each. I can get maybe 30 shillings for doing work in one day, maybe my mum pays for one of us, or maybe two and then I look for money for the others. So my life is not too bad and not too good. But my mum helps, she buys me underwear. And this year I have a school uniform that isn't ripped.'

As I sat in the matatu going back to Kilifi this bit of her story got stuck in my head. She's grateful that her uniform isn't ripped this year, she's happy she has underwear and she'll work with her mum to ensure the children continue in school. Her family couldn't afford this unless she worked in the fields. That to me is a serious struggle. To Juliet it's a reality, 'not too bad and not too good'. She carried this heavy load with a sense of responsibility towards her younger brothers and sisters. It's her duty to help them.

My parents had provided everything for me. If I did do any work to earn some money, that money was mine. Full stop. No sharing with anyone, no responsibility to anyone else. Juliet was growing up in such a different setting to mine to the extent that it might be hard to imagine that we had any connection. But we had and we both looked forward to seeing each other. I liked talking with her, hearing her stories. She was always bursting with questions, which were invariably about decisions she needed to make in her sexual relationships. When I saw her at the tournament in Kilifi in the middle of 2007 she asked me when I was next coming to see her and with a giggle she said, 'You must come soon, I've got so much to tell you.'

I didn't fill a gap in all the girls' lives but Juliet saw me as someone who could advise her, someone who wouldn't judge her decisions, someone to whom she could open up and know that the discussions would be just between the two of us.

We always met at her school, a place I enjoyed visiting because I'd got to know the staff. The games teacher had attended a coaching training course I'd run in the early days of the MTG project. He wanted to become a better coach so that he could help the girls' team in his school improve and become successful. And they did. I remember the first time they reached the quarter finals of the MTG primary school tournament in 2002. It's likely that some of the girls in the team had never been to Kilifi town before and that they headed back to their homes with tall tales of the teams they'd played against from other parts of the district, from places they might never have heard of. These stories, once told and repeated, had acted as an incentive to the teams around. The teacher in this school had built on that initial success. But their superiority in the area was short lived as other schools, piqued by these stories and wanting to be the next team to get to travel, upped their efforts. Local competition became much stronger. It wasn't until 2007 that his team qualified for the finals again—the day Juliet describes at the beginning of the book.

When I'd go to visit Juliet we would head to the dusty library to chat. Her academic performance wasn't great. She certainly wasn't one of the pupils helping to improve the school statistics. She'd repeated Standard 6, gone into Standard 7 and when we met in December 2007 she told me she'd failed and was being forced to repeat Standard 7. I wasn't entirely surprised by this fact. Her father, who had had two wives, had passed away five years ago and her mother had moved to Mtwapa, a town in Kilifi District, to set up a small business selling charcoal. Her two older sisters were married and had moved away, and her elder brother had recently moved to Kilifi town with his wife. That meant Juliet was acting as the head of the household at home, looking after her six younger siblings—three girls and three boys. Her father's first wife—her 'stepmother'—also lived there but it was Juliet's responsibility to look after the family. At the beginning of 2006 she told me, 'I did the exams but I didn't do well. I failed. The pass mark was 250 but I only scored 235 so I had no choice but to repeat Standard 6. I felt terrible because I wasted one full year. I felt so bad. I'd like to complete school then join college but if I can't then I will have to look for a job so I can help my mother. I did OK in maths, Kiswahili and science but I failed GHC (geography, history and civics: now known as SSR, social studies and religion) and English. I think I failed because at school we have to use English for communication but we are so proud of Kiswahili—and I think that is why I failed.'

I had asked myself about this many times: How can children in Kilifi learn and understand subjects when they are taught in a language most of the girls I came across, and with whom I still work, couldn't really speak? I'd even found communicating in English a problem with teachers early on, especially with my strange English accent. One example was the word 'football'. I used to swallow the 't' when I said football as most English people do. Here that just doesn't work, you have to pronounce all the consonants, so I now say 'footy-ball' and we all know what we're talking about. I realised very quickly that working in Coast Province if you can't speak Kiswahili, you're not going to get very far. But then, equally, if you don't speak English in Kenya you are also not going to get far. I struggled to learn Kiswahili but at least everyone around me was speaking it, which made it much easier than it must be for girls to learn English. When I went to the shop I could try out my Kiswahili, but what about a rural girl in Kilifi, trying out her English? Where could she do it? For most, school would be the *only* place where she would hear or speak it. In most homes they communicate in their mother tongue; at the shops, with your friends it would be your mother tongue or Kiswahili. So where, in your day-to-day life do you speak English? Even in Kilifi town, there'd be no need to speak English. Maybe if you went to Mombasa, you would hear it a bit more, and then travelling to other urban centres—Nairobi, Nakuru, etc. But surely, that has a serious detrimental effect on your schooling experience?

Kilifi's KCPE results for 2007 illustrate the impact of the issue of language on educational attainment. The top subject for the district was Kiswahili with a mean score of 57.28, higher than SSR (53.40), science (52.62) and maths (51.28). The bottom subject was English with a mean score of 48.12, which is a fail. Should that not be telling us something about how children are learning? At the coast, and in many other areas of Kenya, Kiswahili is the main language of communication. Teachers speak English in the classroom and occasionally use it outside, mainly in official meetings. How impossible it must be to teach in a language you yourself don't feel comfortable using. And with free primary education bringing with it larger classes, heavy workloads for teachers, very limited infrastructure (classrooms, toilets, desks), what of the quality of education?

According to Juliet three things contributed to her lack of success in exams: having to use English, not getting enough time to study and getting distracted by thoughts about having sex. She couldn't do much about the first one, that was a national policy, but she said the support of teachers, God and a little self-discipline could combine to reduce the effect of the other two: 'I don't really get time to rest or study because I don't finish my home chores until 10 pm and I'm expected in school at 6.45 am. But the teachers are really trying hard and encouraging me. I try to get my work done early at home so I have time to read later in the evening. I want to read a lot, put in a lot of effort and try to stop this issue of thinking about sex. I'll pray to God to help me. It's a problem because if you are trying to read and you start thinking about your boyfriend you get distracted.'

Juliet was soft spoken but loved to talk. She spoke poetic Kiswahili, using the language to tell her stories with intricate detail. Her good performance in Kiswahili at school had elicited a rumour among a group of girls that she was sleeping with the teacher. One holiday she told me: 'Some girls in the school are saying that I'm having sex with one of the teachers. They told another girl and that girl came to tell me. I followed those girls who were spreading the rumour and I asked them, where have you seen me and the teacher together? And they denied ever saying it. When school reopens I want to take these girls to the teacher and ask them to tell him where they had seen the two of us together. They say he gives me good marks because we're together. I feel very bad about it. If my mum hears about it there will be a big problem.

'But Sarah, you know, girls do sleep with teachers. You remember Halima? She was a footballer and she got pregnant. Everyone says it was a teacher but he is still teaching at the school. But I wouldn't be able to do it with a teacher because they're like a parent and I respect them too much. I don't know why these girls are saying it. The teacher is a Christian, he's married and lives with his wife and two children. I spoke to my friends about this issue and they advised me to talk to the teacher about it. I'll do it next term.'

I wondered about this story. She wouldn't have told me about it if the rumour hadn't been spread, but with only Juliet's side of the story it was difficult to know what had set the rumour off. She'd been told by another girl that the rumour was being spread by a group of girls. When she confronted the girls, they denied it. Over the years in Kilifi I had heard many anecdotal stories of teachers sleeping with girls, sometimes with the parents' consent because the teacher, with his income, might provide the family with a few provisions. Juliet herself understood how the rumour could have started because, after all, Halima had slept with a teacher right there in her school. While Halima had dropped out of school the teacher continued to teach. What I find interesting here is Juliet's reaction to the rumour. Her first move was to confront the girls, the second to ask for her friends' advice, and in the telling of the story she wanted to make it very clear to me that it had not happened. How could it? He's like a parent to her? He's married, he's a Christian, surely that's enough to prove it could never have happened? Her final move would be to follow the story through, to talk to the teacher about it and prove it wasn't true.

The last time I visited Juliet at her school we waited under the shade of an *mkilifi* tree [neem] for a matatu to take me back to Kilifi. I asked her how she was feeling about going into Standard 8. She told me, 'I'm repeating Standard 7 this year. I got 272 and the cut off was 280 to go up. I was told I need to repeat. I'm wondering, why, why do they keep holding me back?'

I asked both Mr Wanje and John Katana about repeating years at school. They both told me that the school administration cannot decide alone. The teachers can recommend to the parents and the child. Then it is up to the parents to decide if their child repeats the year or goes up. In Juliet's case she was repeating Standard 7 when she had already spent two years in Standard 6. Her mum was not around, so maybe another relative had been consulted. The school must have known about her family situation, that they were poor and Juliet was the head of the home. They knew it was incredibly unlikely she would go to secondary school or find a paid job, so what would she do if she finished primary? I wondered if the school was somehow trying to protect her, to keep her in school, to keep her from heading into marriage and life as a mother for a couple more years.

Juliet had developed her own theory. She'd tried to transfer to another school but her current school had refused to let her go. She thought they wanted to keep her there because she was a good footballer and they needed her in the team. I just didn't like the thought of repeating years at school. I have always thought it would be soul destroying, being kept back while your friends move on. I was even more concerned that Juliet might think that her success in football was holding her back. I hoped it was my theory, rather than hers, that was right or that her 'failure' in class was the sole reason for her repeating. It would be difficult to know, and we both clutched to our own reasons to explain something that needed to be explained.

There's no doubt that girls are marginalised in school in a district like Kilifi. Mondoh and Mujidi[28] observe that there are many reasons for this in Kenya: the deferred entry of girls into school system, frequent absenteeism, poor performance, lower aspirations, and higher level of wastage when girls drop out of school early.

Some of these reasons ring true in Kilifi. Girls generally perform less well than boys in school. Girls have more domestic responsibilities and pressure to contribute to the family income. They are the ones who stay at home to look after a sick relative or younger siblings. Girls tend to get a lot less time to study at home than boys. Both girls and boys drop out early, but an early pregnancy will almost certainly end a girl's education. A major issue for girls in Kilifi is the toilet facilities in schools. Toilets, which have been highlighted as a concern for many years in Kenya, remain a huge problem, despite the national recognition that it must be addressed.

Families, too, are critical. There were two very good footballers in MTG who, we recently found out, were regularly playing truant. Not because their families didn't value education or because they were being sent here and there, doing jobs for the family, but just because the girls didn't feel like going to school. They had other fish to fry, and there was no one around to keep track of them. It's often not customary beliefs about education that lead to girls dropping out but more the result of crumbling family fabric in the face of poverty and AIDS. In these two cases, neither girl had much social support. One was an orphan living with her aunt, who was extremely ill, bed ridden with AIDS. The other, aged just

15, was living with friends and the only adult in that home was also ill and admitted at the local hospital. No one was making sure they went to school.

John makes an interesting point, though, about truancy. He says it affects boys more than girls and that family, if it is there, is in a good position to ensure that girls go to school: 'I think boys are more likely to miss days off school. They are more likely to play truant, especially those who are not doing well in class. They leave home in the morning but they don't come to school. They hide in the bushes. Boys can just decide that they want to leave school and their parents don't seem able to control them but with girls the parents have more control. They generally drop out of school if they get pregnant or married. When they do drop out they tend to just stop coming to school—they disappear without telling us. It is then the responsibility of the teachers to follow their absence up but, you know, cultures are different. If a teacher goes to a girl's home asking questions about the girl, people will ask, "What is his intention?" It is difficult to follow up.' In John's view it's unacceptable for a male teacher to go to the home of a girl student, even if he is going to see why the girl was no longer in school. I also wondered if teachers really had the time to follow up lost students, with huge classes to teach and tall piles of marking to be done.

Janet was the only one of the nine girls who was in secondary school when we started talking. The first time we met she was in Form 1 in a day school and we decided to go and sit under a tree in the school compound to chat. The tree was on the edge of their football field. The school classrooms and administration block gave us some shelter from the Kilifi wind, which was blowing up the sand and dust across the field. It was a pretty bleak spot. The school compound was on something of a ridge giving an expansive view, of undulating, sparsely populated, forested folds to the west and an area stretching far to the north, with homes, shambas and more sporadic bushes and trees. It was November. It was hot and there hadn't been much rain. When we started talking about her family, she told me her dad had four wives. Well, he had had four wives, but he'd split up with each of them and they had all returned to their homes.

I was to meet him, twice at their home and once when he came to a get together we'd arranged in Kilifi, when all nine girls were invited to bring a couple of relatives or friends along to a meeting and lunch. As the elder statesman of the group, and a retired head teacher, he ruled the roost that day, bubbling with good ideas, general support and good humour about MTG. His quick, witty comments had us laughing throughout the meeting. It was obvious that he and Janet had a close relationship. She laughed at his jokes in a 'that's my dad' kind of way, with and at him, along with the crowd. But Janet was the only girl who'd come to the meeting with a parent. All the rest had come with sisters, brothers or friends.

I never quite found out exactly how many children he had but Janet was the first-born of her mother's children and she had three sisters and two brothers. Her mother had since remarried nearby and Janet became embroiled in a tug of war between her parents, which stemmed from the struggle to find her school fees, spilled over into a complex family dispute and consequently completely disrupted her education.

When I visited her that day in November I was lucky to find her in school: 'I was sent out of school because of not paying the fees. I stayed at home for two weeks, missing classes. Then what I do, when I think the teachers have forgotten, I go back to school and they think maybe I have paid but I haven't.'

At that time Janet was living with her dad but by the time I went to visit her again she'd moved to her mum's place: 'My dad said he couldn't afford my school fees any more so I was forced to join my mother. She is a farmer, she has livestock so when she has no money, she sells livestock to pay for my school fees. She has cows and goats; she has five cows and many goats, about 15 or more, and she has around ten chicken. My dad doesn't have livestock. He has two chickens and two ducks. My mum lives with my stepfather. After my father chased her away she married another husband. My stepfather and my mum are paying for my school fees. It's not how it was last year when I stayed with my dad. I used to stay at home most of the time. He used to give me 1,000–2,000 shillings (US$15–30) and then I'd go back to school. After two weeks I'd be sent back home. But now I was given 5,000 (US$75) by my mum and stepdad, so I think I won't be sent home because I only have a balance of 3,340 (US$50). This term it is 8,340 (US$124). This Friday those who have a huge balance to pay will be sent home.'[29]

Janet told me that if she wanted to stay in school she had to stay with her mum. She couldn't benefit from staying with her dad because there was no way her mum and stepfather would contribute to her school fees unless she was living under their roof. So for the first two terms of Form 2, from January to around September 2006, Janet was living with her mum and stepfather and going to school regularly because the fees were being paid.

I went to visit her at school in October 2006. I never felt particularly welcome at her school, probably because my first point of contact was the secretary outside the head teacher's office. To say she was dour would be an understatement; she was downright hostile. This day she told me to wait on a bench outside for the head teacher. Twenty minutes later the district audit officer, whom I knew well, came out of the head teacher's office, saw me waiting and came up to greet me. As we talked he told me I'd be in for a long wait if I wanted to see the head teacher; they were doing an audit and the head wouldn't be dealing with anything else all day. He suggested I see the deputy, which, it seemed, the secretary had had no intention of suggesting. The deputy told me that Janet had been sent home for non-payment of school fees. I asked him if he knew where she lived and he directed me to a shop that her uncle owned and ran. He said I'd be shown to her home from there. I knew the place and I knew it was the area of her father's home, not her mother's. As far as I had known, she was staying with her mum and paying her fees regularly. It looked as if there'd been some significant change, and not for the better, in Janet's life, again.

I started to walk to their place, out of the school compound and along the dark murram road. It was a long walk for me, about four kilometres, without a hat or sun cream, in the burning sun. There was a cool breeze, though, and walking time was thinking time, or just time to enjoy, relax and unwind, greeting the odd person, feeling the calm of how rural life looks from the outside.

I found her uncle sitting outside his shop. It was painted blue and white and black, advertising Crown pens—a new biro that had recently hit Kilifi and was being advertised all over the place. It seemed like shops and houses, in need of a lick of paint, had turned into Crown adverts overnight. He was resting on a cool concrete bench built as part of the entrance to the shop, a place to sit, drink a soda and share stories. He told me I'd find Janet's home just behind his place. I hadn't walked far when I saw her sitting on a wooden stool in a small, sparsely stocked *kibanda* [a stall for selling things such a vegetables, peanuts, snacks], a covered wood and makuti stall for selling things such as vegetables, peanuts and snacks, selling sweet cakes and nuts to people strolling past. If she was surprised to see me, which I thought she should be, she hid it well. She told me she'd been at home for a few weeks now. We went to greet her dad, who was sitting at the side of the house. He was old, with a full head of white hair, wearing an *mshihiri*, a piece of cloth wrap men wear in and around the home as a long skirt, and a collared shirt. He had on leather sandals. His feet were big, and worn, and swollen. He stood up and walked towards us, slowly with a stick. 'Shikamoo', I said. 'Marahaba' he replied and we started to chat. I told him I'd come to see Janet, that we'd been meeting regularly for about a year now. He told me he'd also been a footballer in his day and he thought MTG was good and that it was nice to see that girls were playing football these days. Janet and I went back to the kibanda and agreed we'd meet later in the week to talk more. I wanted her to be ready to talk. I'd be coming to visit Kanze in two days anyway so we agreed to do the interview at Kanze's school, which was not far from Janet's home.

When we met up later in the week she explained to me that there'd been a disagreement between her parents. In Mijikenda culture the children belong to their father: 'There was a struggle between my stepfather and my biological father. The issue became so serious that my stepfather decided to stop paying fees and told my father to take over, but he refused to pay. The case went to the chief [a local administrative officer, employed by the government] who made the decision that my stepfather should pay.'

That meant that her dad had lost 'ownership' of his daughter and that even when she completed school she would remain with her stepfather. Her father didn't stand for this and demanded that she return to his home. 'I was forced to obey my father's demand and come back but I asked him whether he would be paying for my school fees. He said he would but he rarely gets enough money. My stepdad and mum have stopped paying, saying they will only pay for someone who stays with them.'

The issues here are complex. Children are your investment for the future. They're expected to look after their parents when they're old. When the man pays dowry for his wife she is expected to provide him with children, who will belong to him. If Janet wanted to stay with her dad she wouldn't get an education, but he was refusing to allow her to go to her mother and stepfather, who could afford her school fees. Their investment in her education would give them a claim to Janet's future earnings. It may have been more complicated than her father just being stubborn. She was his first daughter by her mother and perhaps he just couldn't bear to lose her even if it meant she would forfeit her education. He was lucky, though, that Janet had decided that it just wasn't possible for her to miss out on finishing school.

So that was how things were for Janet in October 2006. I invited her to come to our offices in December but she never turned up. I found out through a teammate that she'd moved, she'd gone to stay with a sister in another part of the district, to go to school. I travelled out to see her dad and he told me it was true. He gave me the mobile number of his first daughter from his first wife, Rose, the woman who was now taking care of Janet.

For Janet, dropping out of school was not an option. While staying idle at home she'd considered going to college, which would have been post-primary school vocational training such as tailoring, but she'd reasoned that it wasn't something she could face doing. She'd been in secondary school for two years and going to college would be humiliating. 'I had thought of dropping out of school to join a college, but then when I look at those ones from the college, how they are, I pity them. I can't leave school and join them. I thought if I join the college the students at the college will laugh at me, they will say you were in Form 2 and yet you are here with us now. Secondary school and college are very different. The ones who have finished secondary are more experienced, the college students are not. After finishing Standard 8 [the end of primary school] you will join college, train and then find a job but still you won't be like the one who reached Form 4 [end of secondary].'

So while sitting at home she hatched a plan to tell her eldest sister, Rose, who was a primary schoolteacher in another part of the district. 'I didn't know what she would say but she agreed to help me. She would be paying little by little so long as I complete school. She said, "Move to my place, then when schools open in January I will take you to school." And I said OK. I went to join her in November. Now she's planning how to finance my education and the education of her second born.'

But things didn't turn out quite as planned. When I called Rose to say I'd like to come and visit Janet in July she told me Janet was no longer living with her and she wanted to come to explain to me what had happened. It was a long story, started by Janet claiming that Rose was mistreating her. Rose wondered whether Janet felt constrained, staying with her, because she kept Janet and her own daughter on a tight rein. They had to come straight back home from school and were only allowed out of the compound to go to church on Sundays. Janet had a school fees debt of 12,000 shillings (US$180). Rose had told the school that she was no longer responsible for Janet's fees. The supportive relationship from one sister to another had broken down completely.

When I caught up with Janet at school the next term she was looking remarkably healthy, her face was getting quite round, her eyes were as sparkling as ever, and in her husky voice she told me her side of the story:

'I came to stay with Rose, I stayed with her the first month. The second month, then, she started mistreating me. On Saturdays she would tell me to go with her to the shamba to farm but her child [a daughter in the same class as Janet] was allowed to stay at home to study. I realised that she would make me fail my exams so I went and told my teacher, Madam Mwaro. Madam Mwaro told me to persevere because it was Rose who had helped me to stay in school. She told me, "Persevere until school closes in April, then go and report the matter to your parents." So I said fine. When we closed school, I told Rose to give me bus fare but she said she had no money. I went and told my brother that I wanted bus fare to go to home so he gave me 250 bob [shillings]. At home I told my parents about the problems and they advised me not to return to Rose's place but to go and stay with my brother. So in April I went back and I told her that I was going to stay at my brother's so she told me to go. She said who will pay your school fees? I told her I would tell my father to pay in instalments even if it's 200 or 300 shillings.

'Rose had said that she would help me but when we did the exams her child failed and I passed. I mean, I wasn't studying; all the time I was busy doing housework and farm work. At night her child had time to study but I didn't. I didn't have time to eat, to bathe, I was always doing something. So I had many problems. So when I complained she asked me what I would do about it. So what was I supposed to do? When the exam results came her child had an E and I had D+. So she asked her child, "Were you taught by different teachers, because you scored an E and she scored a D+?" That's when the quarrel started. She started mistreating me more. This made me uncomfortable so I left and came here. At my brother's I don't work in the evening after school. I only fetch water. At 7 pm I'm told to study. I have enough time to study here. He encourages me to play football. When it's time to go to the field, he reminds me, he says, "Your team-mates are there at the field. What are you waiting for?"'

Janet was determined to finish her secondary education. She understood how restricted her options would be if she didn't finished school. She reckoned that a secondary school education would also give her status both in and outside her family. Only Rose and one brother had finished school and she wanted to be the third in the family to do so.

But she also liked her freedom and she wasn't a pushover. I could see it in her dad, and I could see it in her. I also think she didn't mind bending the truth when she got carried away with some of her stories. Many times when we talked about boys, love and sex, she would tell long stories of the exploits of her friends, of her own close encounters. She was quite a contradiction, dedicated to her education, but only on her terms. It wasn't important enough for her to stay suffering at Rose's place, but she made sure she had another option. One time when we were sitting under a giant mango tree at the side of the football field at her new school I asked her if someone was to give her anything, what would she ask for. She told me, 'It's my education. You know, in the near future, even qualifying for sweeping the roads will need a KCSE [Form 4] certificate.'

4½

'The future of football is feminine':[30] Mbeyu Akida

When the FIFA president, Sepp Blatter, announced that the future of football was feminine it's unlikely he was thinking of someone like Mbeyu Akida. Mbeyu, who lives a couple of kilometres from Kilifi town, is MTG's best-known player. She would have been four years old when Blatter made his pronouncement to launch an 'era of development' for women's football. While the game still lags way behind men's football in sponsorship and TV coverage, anyone who saw anything of the Women's World Cup in China in 2007 would have seen football of the highest standard: for the most part a much more cerebral approach to the game with enough professionalism, excitement and flair to impress the men I watched it with, many of whom were seeing international women's football for the first time.

❖ ❖ ❖

Mbeyu was just nine years old when MTG started in 2001 but she was already making waves in her school team. When the teacher eventually agreed to let her play she showed him that her selection hadn't come a moment too soon. It was MTG's second ever tournament and the finals were being played in front of a larger crowd than usual—two women footballers from the UK, some guests from the British Council in Nairobi, which was the first donor to the project, the Kilifi District sports officer and a spattering of teachers, people from local NGOs and passersby.

At that time Mbeyu was tiny but she was fast and tricky and could control a ball in a way that none of the other girls could.

She was outshining everyone. At one point in the final she turned a defender with utterly deft skill, leaving her for dead, right in front of the dais where all the guests were sitting. We were all left speechless at the confidence of this pint-sized player. That day she won the prize for the best player—a football strip, shorts and a shirt, in which she was swamped then, but now six years on, although a bit worn, is only just starting to get a bit small for her.

Since then Mbeyu has won best player or top scorer in virtually every competition she has played in and last year was featured in one of the national newspapers in a two-page spread.

It would be very easy for a player with such immense talent to let the accolades go to her head but the 16-year-old Mbeyu remains one of the most level-headed girls I've come across in Kilifi. She's lucky to live with both her mum and dad, who are very supportive of her playing football, and four brothers, who keep her feet firmly on the ground. She is focused. Football is central to her life and because of that she's become involved in other aspects of MTG—peer education, coach training, girl-child rights seminars and strategic planning. She's building her own skills at a very young age.

When we met at my office she was just back from tuition at her secondary school, her short hair as neat as ever, and looking cool in jeans and a vest T-shirt. As we chatted she told me, 'I play football to avoid being idle, to keep myself busy. I have a great interest in football and I have realised that it is where my talent lies. That's why I like it more than other games. I knew my talent was in football after MTG was introduced. MTG taught us more about football and gave us more skills. I have really benefited from playing football. It has helped me avoid being idle. If I look at the girls in our community many of them are idle, so they end up going to video dens, which are full of boys. Instead of going to video dens I go to play football. The problems at the video den depend on the environment and the time. You will get boys and men there and they get tempted to seduce the girls and then the girls end up getting pregnant.'

❖ ❖ ❖

On the pitch, Mbeyu is the same as any young player. Sometimes she has great games where everything she does works and sometimes she doesn't, choking on big occasions, missing every chance that comes her way—a typical, talented, inconsistent, young player. But her commitment is impressive: 'I go running in the morning at about 4 am with my brother. We go to the beach, we run from home to the beach. It keeps me fit. I also train with boys around my home. If I have a match, about one week before, I think about how I will play and win. So when the match comes round I'm already prepared. When I enter the field I'm OK, but when we play against a tough team I feel nervous. After the game starts, the nervousness subsides because I will have seen how they are playing and maybe we realise we can defeat them.'

And off the pitch Mbeyu is no different from most other girls in Kilifi. She told me, 'At home, every day, I do the domestic work, like cooking, washing and going to the shamba. But when it reaches the time to practise I go to the field since my parents understand that I have to practise. When I come back from the field I finish the work. For those girls whose parents are not so understanding, they should prepare a schedule to help them do the work at home and also get time to play football. I'm lucky. My parents support me and when I don't go for practice they always ask why I didn't go.'

The highlight of Mbeyu's football career so far came when she represented the youth of Kenya at the All Africa Games in Algiers, Algeria, in 2007. She was one of just two young Kenyans chosen to attend the Youth Summit at the games. MTG received an email from the Coast Province Director of Sports to say Mbeyu had been selected to go and she needed to be on a bus to Nairobi the very next day. Mbeyu was sitting her KCPE exams later that year and would miss three weeks of school by going to Algiers. But her parents wanted her to go. She didn't have a passport and that evening she frantically got everything ready: birth certificate, letters from both parents, and travelled to Nairobi the next morning. Within a few days she had a passport and was on the plane to Algiers with the Kenyan team.

Mbeyu tells the story: 'I was told that the person who organised the Uwezo wa Kipekee tournament [a Coast Province under-17s tournament for boys and girls played in early 2007] saw how I played and decided to give me the chance to represent Kenya at a conference in Algeria. It was very sudden but I had to agree to go. I was very happy. I stayed at the camp in Nairobi as I waited for my passport to be ready. When I went to Algeria I saw boys and girls of my age playing different types of games. At that camp in Algeria I was the only girl playing football. We were taught that players should not use drugs, how to avoid problems between players, how to communicate with other people, and the problems that players get and how we can avoid them. We had lessons every day. After the lessons we were given certificates to show what we had learnt.

'We were taken to see different places like to see Algiers Stone and we were told about the people who lived there. We went to watch the different sports that were being played [at the All Africa Games]. We were taken to museums and told about how people lived in Algiers in the past.

'The people with me were coming from different African countries. People were talking in French and in English. I enjoyed staying there but the weather was not nice. The sun was very hot. You could wake up at 4 am and find that the sun had already risen and you think it's morning but people are still asleep. When I came back my friends were happy because I explained to them how Algeria was. I had many stories.'

When Mbeyu returned from her three weeks in Algeria she had to buckle down to her schoolwork because her KCPE exams were just a few months away. When her results came out in early 2008 she'd performed well, getting over 300 marks. She secured a place at a provincial secondary school, an all girls' boarding school in

Kaloleni. Rather than slowly easing herself into secondary school life as a new girl she got straight into sports and was immediately chosen as captain of the football team. She led the team, scoring the only goal in the final, as they won the MTG secondary school tournament in March, the first time that school had ever got to the finals of the competition. When I asked her what her ambition was in life, she had only one: 'My aim is to be an international player. I want it to be my profession.'

5

Let me play!
Menstruation and peer
education

I play during my monthly period. Nobody can know, because
I put cotton wool then two pairs of underwear and then biker
shorts. Then I play without any worries. Some girls don't want
to play during their period but they don't say why.   Juliet

When the idea for this work was first put forward, MTG
was in a better position, financially, than it had been
since its inception. It was 2005 and we had just secured
a three-year grant from the Ford Foundation that crucially,
covered core costs, including salaries. I'd been with MTG in Kilifi
for four years. During that time girls had been taking on roles as
coaches, referees and peer educators. There'd been one other staff
member who'd joined in 2003 and many volunteers, but I was still
synonymous with MTG. It wasn't quite Sarah = MTG and MTG
= Sarah ... but it wasn't far off. The new grant from Ford gave the
organisation a chance to grow. I'd take a step sideways, to work
on developing participatory monitoring and evaluation and to do
this work, while still being involved in fund raising.

We advertised, and got, a new programme director, a
woman with over 15 years of experience working in community
development in Coast Province. One of the girls was heading the
peer education section full time, one was in charge of football and
we had another as an office assistant. All of the girls had started
as volunteers for the organisation and were now employed in
their first-ever job. We'd grown from two staff members to five. I
was looking forward to having a less central role and it felt good

that the organisation was more secure and expanding; it was affirmation that it was having a strong positive effect. What had started as a relatively radical programme was gaining legitimacy, both locally and, through the support of funders such as Ford, further afield.

❖ ❖ ❖

I've talked to many people about MTG and I've been asked thousands of times about how the project started. Football for girls? In Kilifi? You're joking? Why? That doesn't happen here. Why not netball? And sometimes a glazed expression that says to me, 'Not another *mzungu* [white person] with an irrelevant idea thinking you're going to help Africa.' Only when people dig a little deeper, or better still, come and see the girls in the project in action, do they get a real feel of what MTG is. Now in 2008 MTG is much less about me than it was in 2005. The programme director, Margaret Belewa, has stamped her authority on it and the expansion continues. We're recruiting four new staff members as I write and I write in my own small office, undisturbed by the daily goings-on of the projects. I come up for breath by attending the weekly staff meetings and advising on monitoring and evaluation but otherwise things just go on, and continue getting bigger and better. It's not that I'm quite yet completely irrelevant but we all know that MTG can now survive without me—something we've worked hard to achieve in the last three years.

So how did I get to Kilifi? What was my motivation, what made me make the choices I made, what were my risks and my journey through the last seven years? When people ask me about how MTG started my story goes something like this: I came to Kilifi to visit a very good friend with whom I had studied at university. She knew I was a football coach and had heard of a girls' football team that played close to Kilifi. So I went and practised with them a couple of times. It was my first experience of a Kilifi football pitch and the studs on my boots clacked against the hard dry earth and sank into the soft patches of sand. Their coach had brought out all the cups they'd won and arranged them on a school desk at the side of the pitch—huge gold and silver trophies, proof to the visiting white person that this was a serious team, worthy of support. I was suitably impressed.

These girls could play football, and they did so without boots. So while I sounded like a herd of zebras they glided across the pitch like gazelles but with a tenacity we severely lacked in the team I played for back in the UK. They were tough, but some of them also had some very exciting skills that they wanted to make sure I saw. It was late in the afternoon but we were playing in 30-degree heat, and stifling humidity. As the sun disappeared behind the mammoth green mango tree highlighting its tempting, drooping fruits, the coach eventually called us together for a cool down. We sat in a circle in the middle of the pitch and started to discuss what it was like to play football in Kilifi and in the UK. It wasn't easy. At that time my Kiswahili was non-existent and their English wasn't much better. But what I did get, mainly from their coach, a young guy from the village, was that they needed more equipment, balls, football uniforms and boots. But he also told me that they couldn't play many matches because, being in rural Kilifi, they were far away from other good teams and they couldn't afford the transport to go to play them. That sowed the initial seed of an idea in my head. If they had more teams to play with nearby, they would have to spend less on transport, they would be able to play more matches, enjoy playing more often and become an even better team.

After discussing this with a few other people, other ideas came up: link football with health, education, income generation, community development, etc. People asked me, have you heard of the Mathare Youth Sports Association? It's a big sports and development organisation in the slum of Mathare in Nairobi—a model to aspire to. This initial meeting with the team in Kilifi was the catalyst for 18 months of planning, after which MTG started as a pilot project with a seed grant from the British Council.

During the same two weeks that I hung out and practised with the girls playing football in Kilifi I met my husband. I've always been cynical about 'holiday romances' but here I was in the midst of one propelling me towards a completely different life. So I left Kenya that April in 1999 with a hare-brained scheme to return to be with him and start a girls' football project.

Fast forward through two return visits to Kilifi, which included long meetings discussing the project with the District Education Office, the Ministry of Youth, Sports and Gender, the Kenya Football Federation, teachers and coaches; setting up Moving the Goalposts as an organisation; spending hours writing funding proposals; trying desperately to get anyone to support this untried project—and I was eventually on my way back.

For me, it hadn't been a hard decision, but my mum was bewildered about what I was up to. I was a 28-year-old woman working in a steady and interesting job for the BBC as a sports journalist, writing on women's football for a national newspaper, coaching young kids, mainly girls, to play football and playing football for Norwich City Women's team every Sunday.

I was working for BBC Radio Norfolk. I enjoyed it but I needed to make a move, a move up the career ladder. That was when the doubts started setting in. I'd been in the media long enough to know it was a very competitive business. The sports media, too, was a particularly testosterone-driven environment. I was getting tired of the comments and the quips about being the only woman in the press box. People with whom I worked had been telling me I could make it to national radio. Work hard, get a sports producer job, a couple more years of experience, and you'll make it. You've got the voice. But I'd worked on the early shift, starting work at 5 am for over three years. Kudos for being on the breakfast show, but I would have preferred to have been in bed. I was realising that I just didn't care enough about whether David Beckham had broken his toe, and more importantly, whether I was the one who broke the news of the broken toe to the world. It didn't mean enough to me. I couldn't spend the rest of my life, or the next few years at least, in the cutthroat world of journalism chasing stories that I didn't give a hoot about. I'd get found out.

At the same time I'd passed my football coaching certificate and was getting very involved in Norwich City Football in

Community, coaching girls and boys after school and in the school holidays and coaching in the girls development programme. So how on earth does all this tally with a move to Kenya? I'd spent a year in Zimbabwe in the early 1990s and had carried out my university dissertation there. I'd travelled in eastern and southern Africa and always used my leave from work to visit friends on the continent. It seemed to me that this plan was bringing together many pieces of my life, my passions: football, girls, development, Africa. I was ready to take the risk of going on a new journey.

I'm now married to my holiday romance man, Collins, whom I met in Kilifi nearly 10 years ago. We've got two young daughters and I'm still working with Moving the Goalposts. I used to play for Coast Riders in Mnarani, the village where we live, before I had my children. After having my first child I returned to play for the same team, now known as Moons FC. I can't ever claim to have been the world's fastest player but I remember so vividly one half-time talk from our captain when I was still easing myself back into football after maternity leave. I used to play in midfield but was now playing at the back and had been beaten down the wing by a sprightly young 14-year-old with beautiful close control. There wasn't a great deal I could have done but our captain, Lilian, buoyed with confidence, told us, 'Now, look. Everyone knows Sarah's very slow. You must get back and help her there.' It was crushing—no sugar coating, just the cold facts. You're too slow, you're the weak link! This was something I'd noticed over the years in Kilifi; people will say it as it is. You need to be tough, there's no time to feel bad about it. Don't be sensitive, just get on with it. I wondered whether she would have said it a few years before, not because I was any faster then but in deference to me as an elder. I mean, it was a good analysis of the game. She had seen I was struggling when faced by a nimble young winger. She wanted to do something about it. Even though I was her elder she would tell it straight. That was what MTG was all about: building confidence, inspiring leaders for the future. And being the captain, and coach, of a team was the start of that process for Lilian. She might still have been a bit rough around the edges and needing slightly more developed diplomacy skills, but the analytical skills she was showing, the leadership skills to direct her players, the confidence to take control of a group of her peers were all a step forward.

MTG is primarily a football programme; we always say that football is the core activity. But we always had the aim, from Day One, of incorporating other development activities into the programme. Yes, we could see football as a means to an end: developing teamwork, confidence, a collective and empowering energy, giving girls opportunities on and off the pitch to organise their own activities. But it also provided an entry point—an entry point for related programmes in a rural district where girls were a marginalised group, an often invisible group, when it came to youth development projects. The first one that we developed was around reproductive health and HIV. We started with a small grant from the National AIDS Control Council (NACC) to do a situation analysis and a participatory planning process to learn from others working in reproductive health and HIV and AIDS and come up with an appropriate plan. The first activities we implemented came about from linking with KEMRI VCT (Voluntary Counselling and Testing) in 2004, with a programme that reached out to our secondary school players. KEMRI VCT is funded by the International AIDS Vaccine Initiative. Its aim in the project with us was to get more people to go for VCT. Later, with funding from the Ford Foundation, we could reach out to more girls, especially those in primary school and to others who were no longer in school.

The first topics covered in MTG's peer education were puberty and menstruation. The peer educators would come back to the office with their session plans jammed full of questions the girls had asked. They tried to answer them, there and then, but if they weren't sure of the information they would bring the questions to the next peer educators meeting. The peer educators would discuss the questions so that they could go back and provide the right information during their next session with the girls.

Lidya Kasiwa is now the organisation's health education

coordinator. Lidya lost both her parents while she was still in school but struggled through with support from other family members until she finished secondary. She played football at school and on leaving she started volunteering with MTG. Since joining MTG she's been to Nigeria for training, to Namibia to make a presentation on MTG and to Scotland to run three workshops on setting up a girls' football and development programme. On the football field she plays left back and is one of the most feared defenders in the league.

Being a peer educator in MTG: Lidya Kasiwa

The first time we went to do peer education with a primary school football team we had to talk to the head teacher first. MTG had sent a letter to the head about what we were coming to do, the topics we would cover. So when we got to the school the first thing we did was go to the staff room. I was with another peer educator, Eunice. Before we went into the staff room, we were nervous; it was full of teachers. I told Eunice, 'You go in first and talk,' and she said, 'No, you do it.' So we were there, arguing, and we said, 'OK, we'll go in together,' but I still wanted to walk behind her. We walked in and we greeted each of the teachers in turn. Then we started to explain what we had come to do. Eunice spoke first. She said we were from MTG and we had come to do peer education with the girls' football team. We told them MTG had sent a letter to the head teacher. They directed us to the head teacher's office. He told us it was no problem, it was good we had come and he got the teacher in charge of girls' football to organise the girls in a classroom.

When we got to the classroom there were so many girls, close to a hundred. We had told the head teacher we could only do peer education with 30 girls but when we got there, the class was packed. There were even other students looking through the windows, standing at the door, trying to hear what we said. What could we do? The head told us we had to be with all the girls because they needed the information, it would be very important to them. It's difficult for me, as a young woman, to tell the head teacher, no, we must only have 30. So we struggled to control the girls but luckily most of them were very interested and they asked so many questions. And some of the questions were really hard. There were times we didn't know the answers because we didn't have enough information ourselves so we had to use different methods to get round this. Like I could say, 'OK, that's a good question and we'll cover it in another session that is coming up next week or the week after.' The more we did peer education, the better we got. We had to make sure that we made jokes with the girls, laughed with them, so they felt free with us. After some time I stopped feeling nervous with the girls and now I'm more confident but still teachers might give you a challenge, test you to see if you really know what you are talking about.

I like peer education because by talking to girls you find out that they are also going through what you went through, so you can help them. You can learn from other peer educators and from other girls. You are always learning. It also means I am always getting updated with new information. And through being a peer educator with MTG I was chosen to go to Nigeria to visit the Girl Power Initiative for a three-week training course. It was the first time I had been outside Kenya. We went with others from Kakamega in Kenya and from Pemba in Tanzania. I liked the way they organised their peer education in Nigeria because they get the girls when they are still young and they make sure that they really understood everything before they can graduate. The city we went to in Nigeria, Calabar, was very clean. I liked that, not like Kenya. Ah, but the roads, they were so busy with motorbikes everywhere, driving very fast. I was scared to cross. On the first day our Nigerian friends had to help all of us from East Africa to cross the road!

❖   ❖   ❖

During sessions held on menstruation, peer educators were asked over 100 questions. Here is a selection:

- Why do some girls have heavy periods and some light?
- Why do some girls get periods twice a month?
- What are the signs you are about to get your period?
- Is it possible not to get my period for one or two months?
- What can a girl do if she is 15 and she hasn't started menstruating?
- Why do girls get their periods on a day when they don't expect it?
- Why should a girl get monthly periods while a boy doesn't?
- Why is it that some periods smell?
- Why do some girls eat a lot when menstruating?
- Why do some girls like drinking milk when menstruating?
- What causes a girl's nipples to ache when they are about to get their periods?
- What causes abdominal pains during monthly periods?
- If one gets her period today, misses the following day and gets it the day after, does she have a disease?
- Why do I get pimples on my face when I'm about to receive my period?
- How are sanitary pads used?
- If you are pregnant do you get your periods?
- What should I do if I get my period while I'm at school?
- Are there side effects when one takes drugs while in periods?
- Why is it that when you are menstruating you often get angry?
- If a girl is menstruating and she meets with her boyfriend, how can she make him understand her situation?
- What happens if one sleeps with a man while menstruating?
- If one had sex when young, is there a possibility of her not getting her monthly periods when she grows up?
- Why do some doctors tell some girls that they must have sex to reduce stomach aches during periods?
- Is it possible to tell your father when you are in periods?

○ If somebody is too shy to tell her mother that she has started getting her periods, what can she do?

❖ ❖ ❖

I remember very well the first time I got my period. I was 13 years old and in my second year at secondary school. We'd had lessons about it from the science teacher in the last year of primary school. It was very much biology, facts about adolescence, how your body changes, how boys' bodies change, but most of what I learnt about menstruation came from my best friend. She'd started her period when she was 10. She was very open about it and had told us all about what it felt like to have your periods. She showed us the sanitary pads she used. She had an elastic belt that went around her waist and she then clipped either end of the sanitary pad to it. It looked big, mechanical and, quite frankly, frightening. Everything she told us was based on her own, very personal experiences. She suffered from terrible period pains, she would be bedridden for at least two days a month, her periods lasted for seven days and she had a very heavy flow. She'd scared me senseless and made me never ever want to get these period things.

I was often called a tomboy because I was always playing football. If no one else would play with me I would kick the ball against the brick wall of an old store in our tiny backyard. I would make up games—two touch, one touch—spending hours challenging myself to pass the ball through smaller spaces, kick it harder, lob it higher, more keepy-uppies. I spent most of my time outside, riding bicycles with my brother and sisters, making camps and dens, climbing trees, having fun and playing more football.

I got my period during the school holidays, one of those times when I was out in the fresh air, running through cornfields, hiding from friends, enjoying myself. I'd quickly come into the house to go to the loo and that's when I saw a kind of brown stain, the blood of my first period. I cried and cried and cried. I sat on the floor of my parents' bathroom, with my back against the bathtub, looking at the swirling patterns of the colourful wallpaper, sobbing and thinking that now my life is over. The fun would stop. I thought about the number of times in my life I would have to suffer this. I tried to calculate it. How many days per period? 3, 4, 5? 6 or 7? 12 times a year multiplied by how many years? It would be well over 2,000 days of my life spent menstruating. That upset me even more. I certainly didn't feel ready to celebrate becoming a woman; I wanted to remain a girl. My mum was there for me. She tried to console me, support me, talk to me, she made sure that I had sanitary pads and showed me how to use them.

There were many similarities between my faded memories of my first period and the more recent experiences of the girls in Kilifi: the roles of our mothers. They were the ones we turned to; the confusion, wanting to know more and wondering what the future held. But one big difference was knowing what menstruation was. Mariam was the *only* girl who knew, prior to the onset of menses, what periods were, and she knew only because she had been taught by the MTG peer educators. The others said that they knew nothing about periods before they started menstruating. This mirrored what I had heard from other conversations with girls in MTG; most told me they hadn't known what menstruation was before their own experience of it. I remember one girl in a planning meeting saying, 'Girls could think they'll just bleed to death if they don't know what's going on.'

❖ ❖ ❖

Kanze describes her experience: 'I felt like there was some water coming out, and then I thought. ... No, I didn't think ... I just went on. I was at home, it was during the holiday. I went on and when evening came I found out that I had stained my underwear. I didn't know what it was. I told my mother and she told me this was a sign of becoming a woman. She also told me that I should be careful now. I asked her what I should be careful about. She replied that I should not have boyfriends and that if I sleep with boys I can get pregnant.'

It was interesting that Kanze focused on what her mother had said to her about boys. Did she already have boyfriends with whom she was sleeping? She never talked to me explicitly about having sex with boys, but she had many stories of others, her sisters, her friends, her neighbours, doing it. She had one very religious brother; she'd flirted with Christianity and was well aware of the abstinence messages it preached. When her mum had told her she must now not sleep with boys she went to her friends to get more advice: 'I talked with other friends who told me that now that I have come to this stage of adolescence, I should know how to say no to boys. I asked them what I should do if a boy approaches me. They replied, "You will tell them that if you love me then wait for me until I complete school. I go to secondary school, afterwards I go to the university and when I am through and you still love me, then you can marry me."'

I wondered how I would have felt if I'd been given that advice. Surely, that would be a pretty hard thing to manage. I asked her, 'Is it really possible?' Her response was an ambivalent one I had heard so many times from girls and others in Kilifi: '*Nitajaribu*', 'I'll try', which means nothing and everything. In this instance I took it to mean, yes, I'll try, but I know as well as you do that it's highly unlikely, but it's what *I'm supposed to do* and what I tell adults I will do. And that's the dilemma that girls grow up in. They have messages coming to them from all directions: their school teachers, their churches or mosques, family members. And they know that decisions they make around sex can also affect their education. What happens if I get pregnant? Is that the end of my education? With the messages raining down on them to abstain from sex while still in school, that their time has not yet arrived, that they will ruin their education if they start having sex, they rarely get the chance to ask, what do *I* want? What if I *do* want to make love? What are my options? Are they really as limited as they seem?

❖   ❖   ❖

Kadzo's mum helped her out when she first got her period but there was little she could do about Kadzo's severe stomach pains. Kadzo talked about missing days off school because of her periods, a situation that didn't go down well with her teachers: 'If you are having your period and you get stomach aches to the extent where you don't know what to do, you tell your mum and she wonders what she can do. You feel like your waist will detach making you unable to do anything. So you just cry. You can miss about three days of school because of the stomach aches and when you get back to school, you are questioned by the teachers. When you tell them, they complain of you giving them the same reason of stomach aches every month.

'The first day I got my period I was in school and I asked for permission from my teacher to go back home. On reaching home, I told my mother and she asked me to sit down. I sat and the pains got worse. I fell asleep and I stained my clothes. I asked my mum what it was because I didn't know and she answered that it was my monthly periods. She said, "Take that money," and I went to the shop to buy sanitary pads, which she showed me how to use. I stayed at home ... the first day, second day, third day, then the fourth day I placed the pad but the bleeding stopped. I asked my mum and she said that if it has stopped then that is the end of the period this month until next month. I then asked her if it would come every month and she answered yes.

'The next month there was no money for pads so I used pieces of leso. My mum showed me how to use them. We cut several pieces. She told me to wash them after using them. We call them "special pieces" and I would take them during my periods and put them away after.' After Kadzo's family converted to Islam she put her special pieces away for good: 'Our neighbour, who is a Muslim, buys me sanitary pads. She says she will help me because a young Muslim woman should not use rags. So she buys me pads every month.'

Mariam was the youngest of all the girls. She was just 14 when we started talking and was the only one who hadn't started her periods. She had found out about menstruation from the

MTG peer educators and was waiting for it to happen: 'I have developed breasts but I'm wondering. Others like Sarah have already received theirs but I haven't. It's better to get it earlier than later, isn't it?'

She'd heard some things that had made her worry about what she perceived as a delay in getting her period: 'I had asked my mum why I hadn't got my periods. She said maybe I have a tough womb.'

I didn't know what she meant by this so I asked a number of the girls I work with what a 'tough womb' is. They told me the implication in this statement is that a tough womb is not necessarily a good thing. It meant you could have problems later on in getting pregnant. Mariam had also heard from someone that 'if you reach 16 and you haven't received your period, you are sick'. So when she did receive her period she did so with a huge amount of relief that she was now, more than ever, one of the crowd.

'We had gone to play football in Kwale. I was sitting in the vehicle and when I alighted, another girl told me that my skirt was dirty. A girl helped me with sanitary pads. I was happy because now I was like all my friends.'

The complexities of how to absorb the blood was a whole new, ingenious world, unknown to those of us who can afford sanitary pads. I had a good idea from my own friends that tampons were not widely used by women in Kenya. Most who could afford them bought sanitary pads, not tampons. I also knew that sanitary pads were likely to be beyond the budgets of many teenage girls. But I had very little idea of what they used instead. It was only when the peer education started up and we began to have more discussions about such issues that I found out more. The conversations with these girls painted a more detailed picture of the dilemmas faced, strategies used and resilience demonstrated by the girls when they were menstruating.

The struggle to find money to buy pads was a monthly one of asking relatives or doing small jobs such as selling half cakes or digging shambas. Those who couldn't find money used cloth; others who got small amounts of money used cotton wool while some managed to afford sanitary pads (a packet of 10 costs between 45 and 80 shillings, US$0.67–1.25). Most did not rely on one person to buy sanitary pads. One month a sister might buy them, the next her mother, a brother, and so on, depending on who had spare shillings that month. Communication regarding periods was kept mainly among the female members of the family.

Another major issue for girls was the toilet facilities in schools. Much has been written about the inadequacy of these facilities and the detrimental effect it has on girls' attendance at schools. I fully concur. In Kilifi schools, toilets are often poor, run down and insufficient and do nothing to help girls feel comfortable in the school environment when they are menstruating. And when I say 'toilets' I'm not talking about the sit-down, flush toilets that many people might be used to but of pit latrines, a hole in the ground, surrounded by concrete walls and a concrete floor, usually a dark place where you wouldn't want to stay for longer than necessary.

Head teacher John Katana's story of building new toilets in his school highlights some of the issues: 'When free primary education came in, all schools were given 50,000 shillings (US$746) to put towards toilets. I was in a different school then. We built the toilets there: one block with four separate toilets. When I came here to this school, I found five toilets: three for boys and two for girls. The teachers have one toilet, shared by the men and the women. The new toilets hadn't been completed and with only 35,000 shillings left there was not enough to finish the job. I looked for help and got 35,000 from a tourist I knew, who happened to be visiting at that time. We completed the block and now we have two more toilets for girls and two more for boys.' So now they had nine toilets for over 1,200 students. But look back to what they had before: three for boys and two for girls.

I had assumed that the investment of 50,000 shillings from the Ministry of Education towards improving toilet facilities was a direct response to evidence that girls were missing days off school every month during their periods and that poor toilet facilities were a major contributory factor. But now, still, in this school, the boys had more toilets than girls. There were only four loos for over 600 girls. Whichever way I looked at it, it made no sense, and the building of a new toilet block had done little to reduce the problems the girls faced in preserving their dignity while menstruating and trying to attend school.

❖ ❖ ❖

When I went to visit Kanze at her home one holiday I saw for myself the *boma* [the enclosed place for bathing, normally fenced with makuti or sacks], where she would bathe, but only from a distance. We had agreed that we would meet at the bus stage closest to her home. We were to meet at 11 o'clock. I got out of the matatu at the stage, which amounted to an open area of dark brown dust surrounded by trees. There was one small makeshift bench of two V-shaped branches dug into the ground with a plank of wood between them. I couldn't see Kanze anywhere but there were two boys, about her age, sitting on the bench. I started towards them and as I got closer there was no mistaking who one of them was. It had to be her brother. He had the same tall body, long limbs and pointed face. We greeted each other and I said I was looking for Kanze. He told me she'd sent him here because she was busy collecting water. We set off towards their home. It was the time of year when the maize was ripening in the fields. As we walked along the small paths the bright green leaves of the maize brushed our bodies. It felt good to me and I thought it must be an even better feeling for people around here, knowing that this year the harvest is going to be OK, this year they would be able to roast maize over the fire, enjoy it at its freshest, share it with their neighbours, and still have enough to dry, grind and store to carry them through to the next harvest.

We kept walking and came to a homestead, where two men, one old and one much younger, were sharing a smoke, sitting on two small wooden chairs under a central tree providing shade. We greeted each other and Kanze's brother then led me to sit outside his small mud room. He brought a chair out for me and placed it under the dappled shade of a sparse tree. He told me Kanze would be coming and disappeared into his room.

It gave me time to survey the scene, which reflected much of what Kanze had told me about her life. It was bare; there were few people, not much livestock, just a few chickens. Kanze didn't talk much about her home life. I knew her father had passed away, and I knew she had an elder brother that most of the family looked up to and respected. It was this brother who had come to resolve the issue when her mother, as the second wife, had been told to move out of the homestead when her dad had died. This brother was to later play an even more important role in Kanze's life, in helping her when she finished primary school. As I pondered Kanze's life she appeared from behind her brother's room, carrying a yellow jerrycan of water on her head. She put it down, wiped her face with her leso and greeted me. One sleeve of her T-shirt was wet where the water must have drip-drip-dripped as she walked the half an hour walk back to her home. She still looked cool, unruffled and told me she'd been expecting me. It was here that she told me more about her strategies when she's menstruating: 'I use cotton wool. I ask my mother for the money to buy it. Sometimes I buy it myself. I get the money from selling half cakes at school.' She talked about how to keep hygienic: 'I bathe a lot when I'm menstruating. I try to bathe every time I change the cotton but this is difficult when I am at school. At school I just change it in the toilet. But it's important to wash because the blood has an odour. If you are around others, it can disturb them.'

When we finished talking I told her I needed to use the toilet. She looked worried. I just needed to pee but I hadn't told her that and I don't think she felt she could ask me *exactly* what I needed. I asked if they had a boma, or whether I should just go on my way to the bus stage. She said yes, that going in the bush would be better. We passed the boma, a rickety affair, four wooden posts with sacks roughly sewn together to make the walls. I was used to going to the loo and washing in total privacy and this boma looked a bit open to me. Not quite as open as going in the bush but Kanze and her brother politely walked on as I did what I needed to do.

My colleagues in the office have really laughed at me about this, and other questions I've asked them about ablutions in the rural areas. I asked Margaret, the programme director, why she thought Kanze wouldn't let me pee in the boma:

'You didn't tell her what you wanted to do,' she laughed. 'She probably thought your need was bigger than it was and you can't do that in a boma. The boma is for washing and weeing. Normally there are two stones in there that you stand on so your feet don't get dirty from the earth. If you need to do a poo, that's done out in the bush.'

'And what about the boma? I mean, it's not very private is it? I'm not sure I'd bathe there, with everyone able to see me. Or am I just being prudish?' I asked Margaret.

'Well,' she said, 'nowadays, because there are more people around, you would normally bathe at night, when people can't see you. A long time ago you would just go the river to wash or just collect your water and bathe in the bush or behind your house at night.'

❖ ❖ ❖

Juliet also lived in a homestead without a pit latrine, and told me in detail how she managed her periods: 'Sometimes I use cotton wool and sometimes I use cloth. If I change the cloth at school I throw the old cloth down the pit latrine. If I am at home I wash it with soap when I am in the boma having a bath.[31] I put it on a string to dry in the boma and put a costume [underwear] on top of it. It dries in the sun. I cover it because of the shame; I don't want people to see it. It's not good, because it a woman's secret. I change the cloth in the morning, lunch time and when I get home. We do not have a pit latrine at home so if I use cotton I just throw it in the bush. I bathe many times when I'm menstruating.'

Why is it that women have to suffer so much while menstruating? As if dealing with the pain and managing the flow is not enough, we've been socialised in our patriarchal societies to feel shame and embarrassment about it too. It's absurd that we worry that people know, that we keep it as a 'woman's secret'.

When my mum remarried I used to leave my packets of tampons on top of the loo, not hidden, as a teenage act of defiance, trying to embarrass my stepdad, who didn't have any daughters of his own and had now thrown himself into a household with four girls. I don't think he was remotely fazed but it was a small source of power for an angry teenage girl, using my own understanding of the secrecy and shame of menstruation to try to assert some control.

My most memorable menstruation moment from my adolescent years involved another girl. I'll call her Samantha. She was in our class but she wasn't in my group of friends. She was a loner. It was after lunch that one of our friends noticed Samantha had stained her skirt, badly. But not one of us would go and tell her. We discussed it, 'What shall we do? I can't go and say anything, it's too embarrassing.' 'Well, I'm not going. Why don't you mention it to Jane, her friend, so she can tell her?' 'No I can't.' Well, who would, then? The answer was no one. We knew that poor Samantha would leave school in the afternoon, walk to the train station and take her train home. Not content with not helping her we then went on to refer to this incident if we were ever worried that we might have 'leaked'. Instead of asking friends directly, have I leaked or stained my clothes we'd say, 'Have I done a Samantha?' So that was the group I hung out with. We were the cool crowd in a not particularly cool school. To me, now, it just seems that we weren't very nice to girls who didn't quite fit in our group. But weren't we just being teenagers?

I've seen girls in MTG behave in this way—and worse—towards each other. Normally it's a rumour about something a girl has done or hasn't done, said or hasn't said. A favourite introduction and icebreaker in MTG meetings is for everyone to say one thing they like and one they dislike. The dislike mentioned most often is *kusengenya* or *kusengenywa* [to gossip or to be gossiped about], yet at the tea break you'll see them at it, indulging in their local pastime, like any other teenage girl the world over.

However, when it comes to offering social support to each other, Kilifi girls are leaps and bounds ahead of the girls I grew up with. Girls help each other just because they do, because that's how they behave towards their friends or their peers. For instance, Carol's friend Gladys told her what she should do: buy cotton or sanitary pads if she had money, use cloth if she didn't. She even helped Carol buy sanitary pads when she had money. Salma was once caught unawares at the football field. Whereas my group of friends giggled, gossiped and did nothing about the predicament Samantha found herself in, Salma had someone to turn to. 'There was one time when I had to tell Fatuma my problem when we were at the field. I had received my period while we were playing football. We went to her home where she helped me with a *kanga* [a colourful length of cloth] to cover where I had spoiled my clothes. When I reached home I changed in to my own clothes and I returned her kanga to her.' Mercy too was regularly helped by her friends: 'I tell my friends my flow is heavy and they tell me it's just normal. I'm scared of staining my clothes so sometimes I borrow a sweater and tie it around my skirt at the back. My periods bother me. I feel so bad but I force myself to go to school when I have my period. My friend helps by bringing drugs for me or cotton wool so that I don't have to use cloth.'

The only times I wouldn't play sport because I was menstruating were if my period pains were too bad. On day one and sometimes day two I could be in agony with crunching stomach cramps. Every third or fourth period I would get it really bad and vomit. But I don't remember ever not playing because of shame, or embarrassment, or worry that people might find out I was menstruating. That's likely to be because I used sanitary pads or tampons. I had to take precautions, make sure I'd changed before going to play sports but I wasn't worried that they would fall out, or they would leak, or that somehow people would know I was menstruating. But if girls playing sports in Kilifi don't feel safe and comfortable that there's no way people will *know* that they are menstruating they will often sit out a practice or a match. It's just too high a risk to take. As Kadzo said, 'I don't play during my monthly periods. I am afraid, if I jump ... if I use a piece of cloth it will fall. It is better I use sanitary pads. If you use a piece of cloth you can't play, but if you use sanitary pads you can play.'

During competitions, Mercy was a player her team could ill afford to lose. The solidarity her friends and teammates showed in making sure she played was impressive. 'I won't play football when I have my period because my blood flow is a lot and I use a piece of cloth, which I'm afraid might fall as I play. Sometimes my friends help me. If there is a match my friends give me sanitary pads. That means I can play.'

Juliet had developed a fail safe way of making sure she still plays. I loved the way she said it, so matter of fact, so practical, but it must have been hot: 'I play during my monthly period. Nobody can know, because I put cotton wool, then two pairs of underwear and then biker shorts. Then I play without any worries. Some girls don't want to play during their period but they don't say why.'

MTG is currently involved in an East African initiative to produce affordable sanitary pads. It has linked with The Kids League, an NGO in Kampala, Uganda, and Marsabit Girls High School, the only secondary school for girls in the remote Kenyan town.

The three groups came together with Professor Musaazi from Makerere University in December 2007 to discuss the way forward. Professor Musaazi has developed sanitary pads made from papyrus grass and wastepaper. Each organisation is carrying out a feasibility study, and if we find the innovation is satisfactory it will be implemented as a social enterprise, employing local young women in all three locations. We're also planning to include information on reproductive health, hygiene, HIV and AIDS, sports, and so on, in the packets of sanitary pads. We're hoping that this local solution to a local problem is workable and affordable and will ensure that girls can feel comfortable about staying in school and playing sports when they're menstruating.

❖   ❖   ❖

A brief history of MTG's peer education

Year	Training	Topics	Girls reached
2003		Situation analysis and participatory development of an action plan	
2004	10 girls in peer education	Menstruation, adolescence, HIV and AIDS, VCT, prevention of mother-to-child transmission, family planning, sexually transmitted infections, communication	Football players in 5 secondary schools
2005	24 girls in peer education, 16 in child rights	Menstruation, adolescence, HIV and AIDS, decision making, problem posing re: rape, incest, domestic violence	Football players in 24 primary schools
2006	33 girls in peer education	Menstruation, adolescence, HIV and AIDS, decision making, problem posing re: rape, incest, domestic violence	22 schools, 930 girls (players and non-players)
2007	44 girls in peer education, 12 trained as counsellors	First 6 sessions: knowing MTG, self-esteem, decision making, adolescence, menstruation, HIV and AIDS	2 schools, 420 girls (players and non-players)

Donors: NACC, KEMRI VCT, Ford Foundation, Safaricom Foundation, APHIA II Coast

6

Play by the rules:
Teenage girls' sexuality

You start making love secretly. Your mum is not aware. Then,
unluckily, you get pregnant and you have nobody to come to your
defence. The boy denies doing it with you ...   *Mariam*

The sexual stories of the girls were a complex mix of restraint,
pressure, sexual activity and desire, combining girls'
emotions and fears in a torrent of narratives. Plummer in
his book *Telling Sexual Stories* makes a point that resonates here
when he states that 'instead of taking these stories as givens—as
providing rays of real truth on sexual lives—*sexual stories can be*
seen as issues to be investigated in their own right. They become topics
to investigate, not merely resources to draw upon'.[32] That is what
this chapter and the next are all about: hearing the voices of rural
girls, hearing how they talk, their muddled stories containing
truths and falsehoods, and the pressures and realities of rural
teenage life.

From the beginning I had had the journalistic desire to search
out their stories but at the same time I knew the girls had probably
never spoken to anyone before about their own sexual experiences
and thoughts. Not in detail and not with an openness I was
hoping to expose. In Kilifi discussing such private matters wasn't
common—you kept your own tales to yourself, they weren't
anyone else's business.

I'd hoped, though, that this oddly unique set-up that we
had would unearth some of their thoughts, their experiences,
their desires. I wasn't from their community so they could have
little fear that I would discuss what they said with their friends,
families and teachers. I wouldn't judge their stories through the

same cultural lens. I had no social vested interest in knowing what they said. I wasn't constrained by their cultural boundaries, only by my own, and they were fully aware of this. Every time I went to visit the girls I reiterated that their stories were between me and them and that their names, and the places they came from, would not be mentioned in the final write-up. They also already knew me. We'd built up trust. They knew I'd been with MTG from the beginning and was not about to go spilling their secrets around the district. I hadn't done it before so the chances of me starting were slim. But still, discussing feelings, desires and experiences with me was going to be new territory for us all.

I knew that messages rained down on the girls, especially in school, that they shouldn't have sex, or even get too close to boys, until they finished their education. Salma told me, 'We've been told in class about what to do if you get the feelings [sexual feelings]. Our teacher said, "Keep yourself busy by reading books or do hard physical work and then the feelings will disappear." My mum tells me, "Just learn to ignore the boys. Study with them just as you would study with a brother. Avoid those who are not serious and stick to those who are serious."'

Michelle Fine[33] writing about adolescent girls, sexuality and school observes that in the United States underlying sex education is the assumption that girls have to learn to protect themselves from boys, to say no. Here, too, it is the girls' responsibility to make sure they don't get involved with boys, that they ward off the sexual advances coming from men and boys.

But, of course, I knew that many teenage girls in Kilifi were sexually active. They weren't refusing the sexual advances that were coming their way. Even if they weren't discussing it, the number of pregnancies among them was evidence enough. I wanted to find out more: what did they think of the messages they were exposed to? Did they take them seriously, or ignore them? How did they react to their own desires, to the attention of boys?

But my first big question was how was I going to get them to talk about their experiences? I called on my colleague Priscilla, who at that time was the peer education coordinator in MTG.

She'd finished secondary school and was the last-born in a family of ten, an intelligent and beautiful young woman. She was also a fantastic football player, slim with long legs and breath-taking speed. She'd scored a B plain in her KCSE but had missed out on a government place in university by 1%. Eventually in late 2006, with financial help from Friends of MTG, Priscilla became the first in her family and MTG to go to university when she took up a place on the parallel programme[34] at Moi University, Eldoret. But before she went off to study we got together to discuss the conundrum at hand: what would be the best way to get the girls talking about their sexual feelings and experiences?

Priscilla had been through her teenage years in the same setting as these girls. She suggested two questions to get the conversation started: 'Have you ever received a love letter?' and 'Have you ever been in a secret place with a boy?' I would never, in a million years, have thought of these questions myself and I still felt uneasy heading off to the interviews with them as my icebreakers. Would they really work? I wasn't sure I'd ever received a love letter, and I certainly hadn't as a first step in courting. But when I went to see the girls I couldn't believe how much information this question elicited. If they didn't have stories of receiving love letters themselves, they had stories of letters found in textbooks belonging to others. Love letters were delivered by friends, brothers and sisters, kept, put in secret places, ignored, returned, burned. I had an image of torn love messages blowing across school football pitches, evidence of spurned advances, unrequited love. Had any of them sent a love letter? Not one. So love letters were a one-way street? How did they reply to the sender? Responses were sent back through the messenger, and according to the girls it was normally a negative one. What the love letter question did was kick-start our discussions and open up the world of the girls' perceptions of their sexual being, their relationships, their position within those relationships and the decisions that they made to have sex, not to have sex, to 'control' their feelings or to explore their sexuality.

I found Mercy by far the most difficult girl to talk to. She was very shy and she found it hard to open up to me, to talk to me. I wondered about the place where we used to sit and talk, whether she didn't feel comfortable there. It was a disused classroom, private, away from the rest of the school buildings but it was dark, dingy and empty apart from us and the two chairs and the desk we had carried there. I didn't like it much but I'd asked the school for a private place and that is what they'd provided. I later reasoned that it wasn't very different from the places where I chatted with the other girls and I couldn't, with any certainty, say that it was the root cause of our sometimes torturous interviews. After I'd visited Mercy's home and met her mum she opened up to me a bit more. Once she went on to secondary school she became even more confident in expressing herself to me.

But the long silences in that classroom told me things about Mercy's life. And a lot of what she didn't say told me more than what she did say. She didn't tell me that there was stress at home between her parents until the fourth time we met, when a crisis had hit. She had alluded to it by saying her dad had no work. He would leave in the morning to go and be with his friends. She didn't know what he did all day but he didn't contribute much to the family budget. She had few positive things to say about him. During that fourth interview she told me that their domestic difficulties had been compounded during the very heavy rains in May 2006. The house they were all living in fell down in the rain. Juliet and Kanze also told me about their homes being destroyed by the rain. Each time I was told 'our house fell down' I felt a sense of despair. It made me feel cold, scared, as I pictured them during the downpour, the torrential rain beating down, watching their house disintegrate.

What do you do? Isn't your house everything? Isn't your family struggling enough as it is? Can it really rain so hard that the mud house begins to collapse and the roof over your head is no longer? It can and it does, and it inspires a resiliency I'm not sure I possess. You move in with your relatives or your neighbours, you get a roof over you and your children. People help, your neighbours help, you're not left to suffer alone. And then you start to work out how you're going to rebuild.

When we met in September 2006 Mercy told me that they had moved into their neighbours' home and had started to look for the money to build a new house. She said that this had caused a problem but that she had 'forgotten' what this problem was. I asked her if the problem was with her neighbours, thinking that overnight they had agreed to accommodate another eight people and that it might have proved a little stressful. No, it wasn't the neighbours, they were fine. In fact, they were really helping them. Eventually she remembered the forgotten problem: her parents had been arguing because her mother wanted to build but her dad didn't. In the end, her grandfather, her mother's father, had given them money and they had built a new house. The father moved in with them but by the middle of 2007 her parents had separated and her mum and her siblings had moved into a rented room nearby.

Mercy's grandfather was a bishop and she was a regular churchgoer. She'd been exposed to messages from her teachers when they brought girls together for a lecture once a term about abstaining from sex and not having boyfriends until the right time. She told me that older people say it's sinful to have sex before marriage but I wasn't convinced she also believed it. She told me, 'It's normal for boys to approach you and say, "I love you".'

I was fascinated by the use of the phrase 'I love you' in the girls' stories. It was the first communication, the chat-up line, and they, as girls, had to decide how to respond to a boy saying 'I love you'. When I was growing up it was a phrase that my friends and I loaded with meaning. We burdened it with so much weight that in a relationship if either you or your partner said, 'I love you', it was an indication of a deeper feeling that had evolved over the course of time in the context of a serious and trusting relationship. I agonised over whether I loved my boyfriend and whether I should tell him I loved him. Wouldn't that expose me to hurt? What if he didn't love me? Did I really know what love felt like? Was I in love? What was love anyway? I can remember discussions with friends; we would ramble on for hours about whether we loved our boyfriends. Such discussions would rarely end with any certainty. We would continue musing about the meaning of love and end up asking ourselves, 'What is love, anyway?' In the girls' stories, 'I love you' has an entirely different meaning and is a first step in a relationship rather than any sign of a strong feeling towards a partner. Boys would tell girls 'I love you' and then it was up to the girl to decide how to answer. A positive response would be a green light to sexual intimacy.

Mercy remained adamant that her response to 'I love you' would always be a negative one: 'I tell them I don't want them, not until I complete school. And then they leave me alone, they don't try again. I got a love letter. He wrote that he loves me but I tore it up. ... I've been approached[35] by five boys. I mean I was seduced by five boys, some from school and some from outside. But I don't want them. It's my decision. Older people see it as a sin if people have sex before marriage and it's not good because our time has not come. Maybe when you have both finished school and you have your own things, then you could marry. It is mainly teachers who tell us this and they say it to all the girls and boys in school. But sometimes I have feelings and when I want to study I can't concentrate.'

There was a time when I went with Mercy to visit her home—the new home that had been built after the old one fell down. We walked out of the school compound, along a sandy path. I remember noticing a change in Mercy from the shy, quiet Kilifi student to a more savvy and chatty teenage girl, out of the school environment, heading to her home with her 'guest' and a swagger. The way she was walking reminded me of how I was as a teenager. She was kind of strutting and it was making me laugh as I remembered the different walks we used to develop and then spend hours perfecting: Out with the girls: pout, head up high, swing the hips, flick the hair, laugh out loud, pout again. Out with the parents: pout, head down, scuff your shoes, toes pointed in, pout again. Mercy had transformed from monosyllabic schoolgirl to confident young woman. Everything she could hide from me when we talked 'officially' in the classroom, in the interview, was more difficult to conceal when she became Mercy, the girl out of school.

Two teenage boys were walking towards us. I looked at Mercy. She'd seen them coming and she was looking down, but with a smile on her face. They obviously knew Mercy and asked her about her guest, 'Hey. Who's your guest, the white person, where are you taking her?' She told them we were going to her home. She gave them a smile, a demure, shy smile but her body was tall and in control. I wondered if this really was the girl who rebuffed every sexual advance that came her way.

About six months later I heard a rumour that Mercy was one of a group of girls who were telling their parents that they were going to play football when they were actually going to visit their boyfriends. The story was that Mercy had become pregnant and had had an abortion. By that time Mercy had sat her KCPE and was just starting at secondary school. When I went to visit her at her new school I decided to ask her for her side of the story. I told her the story I'd heard and she told me this:

'There was a girl, a friend of mine. A friend of mine called Josephine. She had a boyfriend, and since she was my friend the teachers thought that maybe I also had a boyfriend. It was Josephine who had a boyfriend but not me.' Her friend Josephine had asked Mercy to help her abort her pregnancy but then Josephine's mum took her to Mombasa. She gave birth and, as far as Mercy knew, she was still in Mombasa with her new baby. Mercy kept up the story: she had never had a boyfriend and she had never had an abortion.

What does this episode teach me about teenage girls in Kilifi? Mercy had been approached by a number of boys to be their girlfriend. Teachers and church leaders were telling Mercy and her agemates that their time hadn't come for having sex. Mercy's body and mind were telling her that the time *had* arrived. I don't know for sure what Mercy did when faced with this situation. But she was in a dilemma that many girls face. The questions girls asked during peer education sessions, all of which have been documented, also illustrate the concerns and dilemmas girls have about their own emerging sexuality.

A selection of the questions girls asked about their sexual feelings and desires during MTG peer education sessions

o   Why is it that if a boy approaches you, you can spend the whole night thinking about him?

o   Why should a girl laugh carelessly, fidget and flutter her eyes when approached and touched by a boy?

o   If a girl loves a boy but the boy has no interest with her, that is, he has not yet seduced her, what should the girl do?

o   What does a girl feel that makes her go to bed with a boy?

o   What can we do to stop girls' desires?

o   What can someone do to stop from having sex, even if she feels like having it?

o   Why is it that some girls can't do without having sex?

o   How can a girl refuse a boy's request if she feels like having him?

o   Why don't boys get seduced by girls?

Juliet's story was a complete contrast to Mercy's. The first time we talked she told me of the first time she had had sex, when she was 13 years old. She then, over the two years, took me through her experiences, her dilemmas and her decisions, around sex. It was a fascinating story of a girl gaining control of her sexual self yet still constrained by her circumstances.

Her first sexual encounter was a troubling story: 'This guy was joining Standard 8 and I was in Standard 4, and he sent someone to me to tell me that he loved me. I didn't talk to him but he kept on insisting until I joined Standard 5. One day he came very close to my home as I was fetching water. He followed me there, and wanted to know my reply to his message that he loved me. I told him to stop disturbing me and to leave me alone but he insisted that he loved me and he continued following me. So I explained this to my mother and she explained to his grandmother because his mother had passed away. His grandmother talked to him and explained that following me was like him being interested in his sibling. But he didn't give up. He followed me and said, "Are you still not interested in me?" I didn't want to talk to him because one day as I was coming from Bamboni, where I had been sent by my mother, I had a handkerchief in my hand and in the handkerchief there was money and he took it, he snatched it from my hand, and I told him that I won't take it back. When I arrived home my mum asked for the balance and I lied that the balance was lost. I didn't tell her the truth.

'Later, on another day, I was coming from my grandmother's home with my friend and she was with her boyfriend, who is still her boyfriend now. The other boy who had taken my handkerchief was also with us. My friend and her boyfriend went into the bushes to make love. Then this guy said now your friend has agreed to have sex with her boyfriend, but you, you are still dodging me. We must make love today. So we ended up making love, on the way, in the bushes. He took his trousers off and he told me to lie down and I said, "You mean on the ground?" and he said, "Lie like that, I will spread clothes for you." So he took his clothes and spread them on the ground. I kept my clothes on. It didn't take long. I was still young so it was hurting and I was crying. He told me to be calm, "I am doing it slowly." I said I don't want this, I am leaving, so he stopped and we went home. That was in 2003. When he sees me now he can't greet me, he just passes me.'

He had eventually got what he wanted. He had pursued Juliet for over a year, telling her he wanted her, hassling her, taking her money, forcing her into a situation over which she had little control. Juliet told me the story in her soft voice, with little drama or emotion. He had been told to stop following her by his grandmother because they were related, but on that day, he had managed to coerce her into having sex with him. Had he planned with the other friends, to take advantage of Juliet, to force her to have sex with him? How powerless was Juliet in that situation? She was 13 years old; she couldn't shake off his advances. So was it inevitable that he would have sex with her? And she said she just got up after it and walked home. She didn't talk to anyone about it. I was the first person she had told, two years later.

During the same visit when Juliet told me about her first,

forced sexual experience she wondered aloud what she should do to 'control' her feelings. She explained it like this: 'Sometimes you can have feelings of wanting to have sex, sometimes when you have slept and you wake up you don't feel good. Like, you are asked by your mum, "Why are you not happy and why did you not say 'hi' this morning?" and you cannot say why you are angry. Maybe, you just had a dream, or just a thought, and you wonder how you will control your feelings if you dream or think of boys like that.'

Tolman writes that 'even to acknowledge the dilemma of desire, we have to be aware of our strong, embodied, and passionate sexual feelings and of the limited and oppressive ways these feelings are discussed or ignored in our own communities and cultures. It is crucial that girls understand that their desire *feels* like a dilemma as a direct result of social constructions of gendered sexuality.'[36] Juliet acknowledged her own desire and half-heartedly wanted to control these feelings because that was what was expected of her. Others, like Mercy, Mariam and Salma, felt these social constraints much more strongly, either resisting their own desires or making sure that people believed they were not acting upon them.

Later in the year, when Juliet was 16 years old, she talked about her new boyfriend, with whom she had made love. He'd been showing an interest in her for a while. She described how they ended up having sex: 'I was coming from school. He went one way and I went another and then we met further ahead. He said that he wanted to talk to me. I was with my friend, so my friend said that she was going. Now we talked and he said to me, "Just let me touch your breast," so I let him, and he kissed me. I felt good. I felt comfortable, I mean, I enjoyed it. He said that he loved me. I hadn't yet answered him so I also told him that I loved him too. We continued like that for a while until we did that, I mean, we made love.

'I love him because of the way he is. I love him because he is handsome. He attracts me with his body—it's a bit big. His hair is black and I like his face, his clothes. He's always smart. And eh, his words ... for example, when he says something, it does things that can make one love him more. I can't explain, I mean I can't explain clearly to someone. It's like sometimes he says, "I love you because you are beautiful. I haven't seen someone like you before." I feel I should stay with him. But now he has gone to Malindi to work and it's a long time since he left.

'Sometimes I dream about him as though we are together, we are standing together talking, me and him, but when I wake up he is not there.'

Juliet was talking about her boyfriend, Brian. Since he had left she'd been fending off a number of men, saving herself for him: 'There are many who have tried to seduce me, but I haven't accepted them. I say I know what I am waiting for. They are men, some are married, but my friend tells me I should never leave Brian. She says I won't find another boyfriend as nice as him. She told me, "That Brian is very good, the way he loves you. I mean if it was me, I wouldn't leave him."'

It looked to me like the stakes were high for teenage girls in Kilifi if they started acknowledging their sexual feelings. They are told that they must wait, that if they do have sex they will get pregnant. Having sex is bad. Start playing around with boys, the next thing you know you are pregnant and out of school—then what? It stops some girls from responding to their own desires or to advances from boys. The girls talked often about pregnancy. This was their main concern, their fear of getting pregnant and what this would spell in their lives. The dangers of having sex, the fear and the sinful nature of the act were pervasive in the girls' narratives, particularly the girls who claimed not to have been involved with boys. For the girls who had had sex there was an air of ambivalence and often an insistence that they weren't acting on their own desires but responding to interest a boy had shown in them. Only Juliet spoke openly about her own sexual desire when she told me that, yes, if her boyfriend was living nearby and she felt like having sex she could go to him and have sex.

It made me think of my own early sexual experiences and the similarities and differences. As a rural girl in Essex, UK, my first kiss was also out in the open air, in a cornfield, just before the harvest, a perfect private place. I used to go with my first boyfriend into the field behind his house. We would carefully stamp down the corn, make enough space for ourselves and have some fun, nothing very much; we were 12 years old just kissing, touching each other and rolling around. In the next five years I had other boyfriends with whom I started to explore my sexual feelings. Among my girlfriends we talked a lot about our boyfriends, boys we liked, boys who liked us. We would sit around, discussing what had happened at the weekend. There were school discos that we'd look forward to for weeks that provided a chance for you to 'pull' the guy you liked. We had a number system, which I don't think was unique to our group in any way but it provided a language in which we would talk about our experiences. It went something like this: 1) snogging, or deep kissing, 2) touching tits, or breasts, 3) fingering, 4) oral sex, both ways, 5) penetrative sex. Most of us would go through the base system, passing through each number with a boyfriend. The amount of time it took to get from 1 to 5 could vary—days, weeks, months or years depending on you, your partner and what your friends were doing.

After the weekend, you might have a conversation with your good friends, which would start something like this: 'So did you get off with him then?' 'Yeah, I did.' 'What number did you get to?' Often you might not get past 3 or 4 with a boyfriend before one of you 'dumped' the other. But it was important to have a boyfriend and I remember feeling real pressure to have one. At one time I was in a group of friends who had hooked up with a group of boys from another school: Emma's boyfriend was Jack, Sally was with Tim and Lucy with Matt. That left me and Andrew. We had to get together to be part of the gang, whether we liked each other or not. So he became my boyfriend, I became his girlfriend and we hung out for a few months. My memories of those years have been overlaid with later sexual experiences, longer relationships, heartache, confusion, love and disappointment. So I'm finding it hard to see my teenage years without those layers of experience. As a teenager, yes, I was exploring my sexuality, but I look back on it as a difficult time, when conforming was important to me, being part of the gang, feeling pressure to do what other girls were doing.

In Kilifi it looked as if there was no such thing as a number system and not much need for it either. If you were going to act on your sexual feelings or respond to being approached by a boy, you had as good as decided to have full penetrative sex. You might get a bit of 1 and 2, but 5 was where you were heading. Runganga and Aggleton found a similar situation in Zimbabwe where 'penetrative vaginal sex is "real" sex for the majority of young people interviewed ... in sexual seduction the goal of most young men is vaginal intercourse.'[37] It wasn't so surprising because where could you have sex, or start exploring your sexuality? Juliet had sex in the bushes and in a room behind the shop where her boyfriend worked. Carol in the half-built room of her boyfriend, late at night, snatched moments of responding to sexual desire.

One can always have complaints about one's partner. My biggest gripe with my husband is his inability to throw anything away, and worse still, the migration of his things onto the one small, sacred space in the house that can truly be called mine, my desk. This issue, though, can sometimes have an up side, which it did when I recently found a folded bunch of papers there. As I huffed and puffed, ready to 'have a go' I had a quick look (surely my right?) and saw it was the minutes from the latest meeting of the village school committee, of which Collins is a member. My eyes were drawn to the first AOB: what could they do about people having sex in the classrooms? It was a menace. So I asked him what they'd discussed. He told me it's been going on for years—sex and drug taking at night in the school. Once the children went home from school people from the village were using the school for all sorts of extra-curricular activities. I thought of the hard concrete, sometimes dusty mud floors, the rickety desks, the rough coral block walls, the vast open spaces that are the windows. Not the most comfortable or private place to have sex; you might have to be quick.

Girls knew that having full penetrative sex meant risk: risk of pregnancy and risk of HIV. They knew it as well as their teachers did. That's why the teachers kept telling them to hold back, don't act on the feelings, do something else, read, play football but *don't have sex!* And that is the reality in which young girls in Kilifi chart their adolescent sexuality.

Mariam was adamant that she hadn't had sex and that she wouldn't until she was much more secure in her life. She talked about living in a place where all around her people were having sex, especially her agemates at school, but her religion and her own convictions and confidence would keep her away from such trouble. She couldn't see anything good in thinking about having sex or getting involved in a relationship.

'If I'm passing on the road and a person says "tsk" I just leave him alone because I know what I'm doing. I know if I do such a thing [have sex] I won't learn any more because many girls are dropping out of school and mostly they are the good ones, those who are bright in class but ... I'll be forced to avoid it. If God wants me to do good things, but then I go and do it [have sex], I will have sinned against him.'

She laughed when she told me, 'I want to keep my virginity until marriage. I will try and I will manage. Life is hard nowadays. You start making love secretly. Your mum is not aware. Then if unluckily you get pregnant you have nobody to come to your defence. The boy denies doing it with you. ... I think it's bad. I want to finish my education, get a job. Then maybe I can get married later. I don't have time to think about boys. Seeing them means nothing. They just want to deceive you while you are in primary. Then you get pregnant and they abandon you.'

Mariam was very good at articulating what she observed in others, while I struggled to get her to talk about herself. She could tell me a long, convoluted story about another girl, but when I asked her about what she did, or what she felt, she would have little to say. Her stories about others, which were often sad, or shocking, or both, displayed a harsh social environment, with limited choices for girls. But she portrayed herself as above this; she wouldn't succumb to the 'vices' she saw around her. She often disapproved of the behaviour of her peers. She wasn't sympathetic to some of the decisions they made or towards the families from which they came. She told me, 'The girls themselves, some love money. When they see money they quickly follow men; they don't protect their bodies. They know they have reached adolescence and if they follow men they can get pregnant, but they don't care. It all depends on the way a person was brought up and the environment, if her parents are not strict. As you know some parents here are not educated so their children don't respect them. Sometimes a girl is told something, she ignores the advice, then later she gets pregnant.'

Her strategy to abstain and stay away from boys was informed by advice she had been given by her elder sister: 'A girl is not controlled by anyone. She must control herself.' So she had to take responsibility for her actions. That meant suppressing any sexual feelings, thoughts or desires she might have. There was a time before Mariam had received her first period when we were talking about being an adolescent, what happens to your body physically and how your thoughts might begin to change. She talked about how she'd developed breasts and that her mind was opening up. Because of the MTG peer education sessions she'd attended she now had a better idea of the changes that would take place and about menstruation. But she still said that she should control any thoughts she might have about boys: 'I don't think about boys because my time hasn't yet arrived. You might think a lot in class until your brain stops working. It can spoil you if you keep thinking about boys. It might destroy you, your lifestyle. You can be rude to your parents because you think you know everything and understand it all.'

❖   ❖   ❖

In August 2007 I held group discussions with girls who were attending the MTG training camp. The discussions were organised as we developed our strategic plan for 2008–2010. The training camp was ideal for getting the views of the girls in MTG. Over 100 girls were at Chumani Secondary School, girls from across the district selected for different training courses: Coach the Coach intermediate and advanced, Refereeing and First Aid. MTG United players had also been invited: the first team, the under-16s and the under-13s, to be trained by the intermediate and advanced coaches.[38] The peer educators and trained counsellors were also at the camp, providing information and services. I drove up to Chumani from Kilifi on the main Mombasa–Malindi road, a straight drive up the coast, dodging the obligatory potholes. As I turned into the schoolgrounds, a group of girls was slowly walking down from the football pitch towards the dining room. It was a great sight. Over 40 girls, all girls, teaming over the field, some carrying boots, others with balls, some with their arms around others, telling stories, discussing the practice, heading for a well-deserved lunch. Down at the school buildings the referees were ensconced in theory of the Laws of the Game in one classroom and the first aiders were tying slings on 'broken' arms in another. They spilled out of their sessions, running to the dormitories, meeting with their friends from other groups, sharing tales of the morning's training sessions. The camp was run by our VSO (Voluntary Services Overseas) volunteer, Cocky, who had arrived in Kilifi two years earlier to set up the Coach the Coach programme; Priscilla, back from university for the holidays; and Rose, the football coordinator.

I dipped in on three afternoons. My visits also gave the volunteers in the monitoring and evaluation (M&E) team a chance to lead these group discussions. One question we wanted girls to look at was what they saw as the main problems girls in Kilifi faced. The first group we sat with consisted of coaches and players from MTG United. We knew that as a small programme with limited resources we wouldn't be able to deal with all the problems they came up with. But as a responsive, participatory organisation we needed to hear from the girls what they saw as their own issues. The M&E team divided the coaches and players group into four groups of five each, distributed flip-chart paper and asked the girls to discuss and write down what they saw as the main problems they as teenage girls faced. We were in the classroom they'd been using for the referees training, and I sat on a desk near the door and looked around. Graffiti was scratched into the back wall, the paint was peeling off the walls and there were enormous cobwebs in the rafters. The wooden desks and metal chairs were an assortment of different shapes, sizes and ages, some looking like they were on their last legs and others looking not much better. A drab, uninspiring place; not an environment I would have found easy to learn in. I thought for the millionth time about the difference between here and where I'd come from, but it didn't really get me anywhere. That was there and this is here—just get on with it. I focused back on the job in hand and looked at the girls in their groups. Some as young as 13 and 14 were becoming coaches of their teams, starting to express themselves, thinking critically about their lives and being a part of a big group of girls who'd come together because of football. Each group selected one girl to write down their ideas and another to present their ideas at the end. They were quietly discussing the question, encouraged by the M&E team to write down everything they came up with as this wasn't a class—there was no right or wrong. The topic was bringing up a lot of discussion and the exercise gave the girls the chance to provide further insight into the more challenging parts of their lives.

A number of groups mentioned that girls received money after having sex, as Mariam, Juliet and Carol had also discussed with me. Girls wanted to afford sanitary pads, soap, clothes, and many said that, because of poverty, their parents could not provide for these basic needs. As teenage girls, some were taking control of the situation, using the one asset they had.

During one meeting of the M&E team the girls had a heated debate about how girls got money for buying sanitary pads, lotions, and so on, and the rural-urban differences. On one side Jackie was arguing that girls in town were less likely to have sex for money because there were more opportunities to get money through other activities such as washing people's clothes, selling chapatis and doing other odd jobs, whereas in rural areas the only work you might be able to get was on the shamba. Her argument was that girls in more rural areas are more likely to consider getting money to cater for their needs through having sex. On the other side, Margaret was saying that in town you need more money to survive. There are more men with money around, so you are *more* likely to sleep with someone and be given money. What these discussions and the girls' interviews told me was that girls have sex and are given money in both rural and urban areas. They talk about it among themselves. It's happening, and it's not seen as anything particularly newsworthy.

Juliet, so in love with Brian before he went to Malindi, had not seen him for over a year when he came back on December 23rd 2007. They'd been in touch through his brother and she knew he was coming home.

'I wasn't there. I had gone to see my sister in Kilifi. But I came back home on the 24th. When I was getting out of the matatu at the stage Brian was there. He followed me and he told me, "I have come, I wanted to see you, I wanted to talk to you, but I couldn't find you. We haven't been together for so long." I said, "When did you come? You left a long time ago, last year?" He said, "I came yesterday and I came to see you. If it hadn't been for you I wouldn't have come here." I told him, "That's OK, I'm just on my way home." And he escorted me to the tap close to home and then he went, saying we'll meet tomorrow.

'The next day was Christmas Day. We did our chores at home as usual. There was an all-night celebration at the church so when it got to evening we went there. When I got there I saw him. He told me he had only come there because of me. He told me, "I've been away, but I haven't found another girlfriend. I just want you." I told him, "You're lying to me. You've been away for so long and you say you haven't found another girlfriend." He said,

"I'm not lying to you, I'm telling you the truth." So I said, "Well, if it's true, you wait for me because we're still singing and this is our church." So he said, "OK, I'm just waiting here outside, when you're going home come and tell me."

'So we were singing and singing until around 4 o'clock in the morning when I left. When I left he was sitting there. He followed me, he told me, "Now I want to make love with you." I told him, "I can't." So he said, "Don't tell me you can't, I need to make love to you today." So I said, "OK, we can do it," but he used a condom. We went into the bushes ... It was good, because we hadn't been together for long. It was just good. Then he went back to Malindi to work. Recently he called me and he said he would be coming back again on February 2nd.'

So there Juliet had been, singing her heart out at the all-night celebration at the church while Brian waited for her outside. He'd waited patiently until she'd decided to leave the church. After telling me about Brian's return Juliet had more to say. She hadn't been waiting patiently for him to come back from Malindi: 'There's another guy I've been having sex with. He recently left here but he was working in a shop near where we live. But I still love Brian more. I like his colour. I like the way he is with me. He can help you, he can even help with money. But with Paul, you can go and have sex and he'll only give you 50 shillings. With Paul, we would have sex in the room behind the shop. I'd leave home at night and go to his to have sex, normally once a week. On a Saturday, I would go. He's not bad but if you compare him and Brian, Brian is way ahead. We would use condoms every time; he could take them from the shop. It's important he gives me money, because you could be having your monthly periods and you don't have money to buy sanitary pads. He'd always give me something, money, skin moisturiser cream, soap. I wouldn't say I love him. But with Brian, we love each other. When he came recently he gave me 400 shillings [US$6] for Christmas and before he had come he had given me 200 [US$3].'

Love and money are so very closely linked. Mills and Ssewakiryanga's work with students in Kampala led them to conclude that 'within an intimate relationship emotions and things are not as separate as an observer might imagine: they do each other's work and are never easily reducible to the   other'.[39] A student in their study said, 'You are buying love, by using money you are strengthening the relationship, it shows you are responsible'.[40] Much is written about transactional sex, particularly in poorer settings, but I wonder if when we all engage in sex an exchange of some sort doesn't always take place.

When my first serious boyfriend bought me flowers, it made me feel more in love with him, it showed me he cared for me, he wanted me. I felt closer to him, I wanted to be physically close to him, I wanted to make love to him. When, out of the blue, he gave me a book by Albert Camus, his favourite author, it showed me he was sharing himself with me, he wanted me to understand him, to be with him. It affirmed our relationship. It was exciting, it made me tingle, it made me feel so loved, needed, desired, that we had something that was between us, our secret, sharing things about ourselves that no one else was party to. It felt good.

And it goes on and on like that, through different relationships with different dynamics and different gifts, tokens of love, needs for sex. It's intimate, sometimes safe and sometimes dangerous, peppered with transactions. Why, when it's money and not books or flowers, does it become transactional? All the gifts I've received and given for love had nothing to do with my basic needs, but that's because they were already covered. As Mills and Ssewakiryanga point out, things and emotions are not very separate.

I wondered how Juliet felt about Paul and Brian. She talked about a real love for Brian and his attractiveness, not just his looks, but his character, how he helped her with money, and how, importantly, her friend had advised Juliet to stick with him because there weren't many like him around. With Brian she was in love, with Paul she needed the money.

But Brian disappeared off the scene, to work in Malindi, and she had her needs and her desires. Juliet liked having sex. She also knew that having a boyfriend could help her cater for some of her needs. But I don't think she was exploiting him, she was just doing what she needed to do. She was feeling desire, a need for closeness, a need to respond to her sexual feelings. I tried to put myself in her shoes: you wake up early, you cook some breakfast if there's any food but normally you go to school on an empty stomach, you study all day, you come home, you collect firewood, you collect water, you cook, you wash your younger siblings and put them to bed. You're 16 years old, you have enormous domestic pressures, pressures to find money—for your exam fees, for the fees of your siblings—and you have your inner sexual desire and a need to explore it, to experience sex, love, physical closeness to somebody you have chosen to be with. Is that calculating, is it exploitative? Or is it just sensible? Isn't it what many teenagers, many of us, would consider doing in Juliet's circumstances?

She's made a judgement; she's decided to sleep with Paul regularly, the guy in the local shop. She says they have protected sex. He helps her out financially so when her period comes round every month she has the dignity to be able to use sanitary pads, rather than cloth. She can afford skin lotion, washing powder, and she gets a chance to feel good, to have sex and satisfy her sexual desires. It's too complex to be categorised; it's a relationship that was working for Juliet, catering for both her basic and her sexual needs.

You might be wondering if we ever got beyond heterosexuality, to explore other sexualities. We did, during the discussion after Asya had had us all in stitches with her impression of the old man at the local disco. I was asking them whether the disco was a good place to find a partner:

ASYA: We don't seduce. It's a boy who seduces a girl. But some girls in what they wear, they seduce boys.

KADZO: And there are girls who seduce their fellow girls, don't you know?

JANET: That one is there.

KADZO: A girl and she is seducing a fellow girl. There is this thing where a girl needs another girl …

ASYA: A girl for a girl?

KADZO: I heard about it on ___ FM [a local radio station]. Every day you will hear a certain girl ...

KANZE, ASYA, CAROL (in unison): But it's not OK.

KADZO: Now how can a girl seduce her fellow girl? You will ...

ASYA: Maybe a girl will seduce a boy, some do.

JANET: And there's a boy and a boy too.

ASYA: But the right thing is a boy to seduce a girl, but for a girl to seduce a fellow girl ...

SARAH: I want to ask you, why is it not right? It's OK for a girl and a boy, but not a girl and a girl even if they love each other?

At that point Asya reverted to Kigiriama and said something I couldn't understand. It made all the others laugh. She then said boys and boys and girls and girls are just not possible. The consensus was, yes, homosexuality might exist but it just wasn't right; a bit like girls seducing boys just wasn't right. These things might happen but it was better to conform, to be seduced, not to seduce, and to want to be seduced by a boy not a girl. Kadzo, who was enjoying the discussion, decided to take it further, with more stories she'd heard on the radio:

KADZO: Then there are boys who pretend to be like girls. In Mombasa there is a guy who puts on a bui bui [burka—the loose, normally black, long garment worn by many Muslim women outside the home], and then he changes his voice. He talks like a girl.

ASYA: Is he tying Ninja fresh?[41]

KADZO: No, he doesn't tie Ninja.

ASYA: But if you look at him you say that's a babe?

KADZO: Yeah, it was on ___ FM. He was being interviewed. He says, everything that I do, I do it like a girl. I mean, I put on make-up like a girl. And, I mean, even if I try to control myself to be a man, I can't, so I am a girl now. So he was asked have you accepted that you are a girl? He said yeah I have accepted that I am a girl because I want to be one myself. Now he doesn't know what to do if he talks. I mean, you hear a girl's voice but it is a man. He talks just like a woman. He says everything that a girl does he must do too—putting chemicals on the hair, applying lipstick, I don't know, eye pencil. He hides because when the police know about him they will arrest him. He was asked, 'Now, who will marry you?' He answered, 'I will be married by a man. I mean, who normally marries girls? In fact, I already have a husband; it's only that he has to hide, because I am a man.'

SARAH: And with a boy and a boy or a girl and a girl, isn't it his or her right to love somebody?

KADZO: Is it their right?
           Asya clicked her tongue disapprovingly.

KADZO: Is it their right for a boy and a boy to be in love? The correct thing is a boy to fall in love with a girl. Like, I love all of you here but ...

ASYA: But that's not loving the way they love.

KANZE: It's not good.

ASYA: It happens to other people but for now we can't.

SARAH: Why not?

OTHERS: It's our tradition, our culture.

So they recognised that there were alternatives to heterosexuality, but they'd been socialised to believe that this was not for them. It was something for other people.

Back at the camp on the second last day the MTG United team, a select team of the best players from all the MTG players in Kilifi District, hosted a Kenya Football Federation league match against the Coastal Queens from Mombasa. The camp had been the first time that MTG United had been together for a sustained period. After five days of intensive training they trounced the Queens 13-0 in a one-sided affair. They played brilliantly and their coaches said it was the best the team had ever played. There was a huge buzz about the place when Margaret, the programme director, and I arrived for the closing evening's entertainment the next day. Preparations were ongoing in the dining hall where a huge banner saying 'MTG— Empowering girls through football' was being strung up across the stage. A new style of dress had been invented by Priscilla, wearing a *kikoi*, a Kenyan cloth, as a skirt, tied at an angle with a triangle slit at the front. She'd been copied by the girls who had kikois, making them an exclusive club within the group. When each went up on to the stage to collect their certificates they got the loudest cheers and wolf whistles as they strutted up to the stage. Girls were given prizes for all sorts of things: best first aider, best coach, best player, best referee, most improved, most hard-working. There were T-shirts and radios for everyone. There were songs, some of the girls performed a drama skit. By the end of the evening Cocky, Rose and Priscilla looked exhausted after nearly two weeks at the camp, which was now to become a regular fixture in the MTG calendar.

7

Caught offside: Reproductive choices, pregnancy, abortion, and HIV and AIDS

When I was in Form 1, there was a girl called Eunice Kahindi. She wasn't a footballer, she didn't do any sport. Every day she used to wear a pullover and she was quiet. She didn't talk to anybody and when the teacher left the class she used to sleep a lot and cry. So we wanted to know why she was sleeping and crying so much and she said she was pregnant. When she joined the school in January she was already pregnant and her parents weren't aware and they bought her everything for school but she didn't tell them not to send her to school because she was pregnant. When she was at school, her legs started swelling. She had to return home. I don't know if she will come back to school after delivering or whether that will be the end of her education.

Janet

When Janet told me this story she did so with little empathy for Eunice. She wondered how Eunice could have not told her parents while they were spending all that money on getting her to school. Not only was she pregnant, she had lied to her parents, kept the truth from them, and let them spend thousands of shillings for nothing because she'd soon be back at home, pregnant and out of school. How could she? But I couldn't help thinking what a difficult dilemma Eunice must have been in. When she was getting ready to come to secondary school, while her parents were finding the money to buy her uniform, her lockable metal box, or *sanduku*, her school fees, she knew she was pregnant and unlikely to get through the first term before being 'found out'. She couldn't possibly tell her parents before they could see with their own eyes that she was pregnant. Going to secondary school was, for most girls, a big and important step when less than half of those who finish primary school in Kilifi got to go on to secondary school. For those that did, it was a massive achievement. I remember the day when two of the girls who'd got football scholarships to secondary schools through MTG passed by the office on their way to school for the first time. They'd come with their mothers to say goodbye, to show us all what they looked like in their starched uniform, pleated skirt, white shirt, green tie, black shoes, white socks. There was such an aura of excitement around them that they would be going to school, that they had got to secondary, that they had done what most of their friends would never do. What an accomplishment.

Poor Eunice would have had to go along with all the preparations for secondary school, knowing that later she'd have to face the consequences of her hidden pregnancy. Having been pregnant twice myself, I'm always astounded by the resilience shown by the girls I know who've become pregnant. If I think of all the worry, fear and panic I experienced through each pregnancy while regularly visiting the obstetrician and having a husband who would listen to my every complaint, I wondered how they coped. Most hide the fact that they are pregnant for the first few months, until there's no way they can hide it any more. They just get on with it, it's normal, people get pregnant, and if there is a problem, well, that's when people will help out, mothers, aunties, traditional healers, medical professionals, whoever the family turns to at such times.

❖ ❖ ❖

At a lecture on HIV and AIDS in South Africa, J. Head says we need to challenge the conventional wisdom around sexuality and some of the assumptions embedded in the work. She states, 'Part of problem with the dominant approach is that it is sexually reductionist. It discounts what most young people know only too well, and what most older people tend to forget. Youthful sexuality is about exploration and pleasure, but it is also about love, trust, and respect. These are complex feelings and emotions that lie at the heart of our humanity. As human beings we are impetuous, self-justifying and prone to make mistakes. Unless we acknowledge the complexities of our humanity when we talk about HIV and AIDS prevention I suspect we will always miss the mark.'[42]

When we talk about adolescent sexuality too, we need to recognise this and think of how we can assist teenagers to chart a safe and fulfilling passage through adolescence when there are many obstacles in the way. The more I spoke to girls in Kilifi the more insight I got into their experiences of discovering their sexuality. On the one hand it was the same as for any other teenager, with pressures of what to do and what not to do, and with messages coming at them about what a teenage girl is supposed to be. It was an exciting time for them but also a time when they were told to control themselves. On the other hand, there were risks: sex was mostly penetrative, often unprotected, often resulting in pregnancy, and then abortion or teenage motherhood. Unprotected sex also meant risk of HIV and other sexually transmitted infections. But they are teenagers, they are human, and they have complicated emotions and feelings that they want to act upon.

They are living in a time of social change and flux. Their grandparents and great grandparents had lived in the rural homestead in relatively cohesive social units, adhering, or not, to the rules and cultural traditions of that setting. There was, of course, change during those times, but the last 100 years has brought much greater influence from outside and now education, Islam, Christianity, migration, AIDS, poverty and politics were all working together to create significantly different social circumstances in which girls are living their adolescent lives.

Traditional routes for learning about sexuality for girls were from grandmothers or aunties. I'd been told that girls shouldn't really talk to their mothers about such things until they were getting ready to be married. But many of the girls no longer live with their grandmothers or their aunties and the traditional lines are blurring. Education has also greatly affected the traditional social structures. Many grandparents and even parents, especially mothers, have not been to school. Those that have may have had limited education, having been lucky to finish primary school. The younger generation respects their elders because that is what you have to do, but the respect can often be limited. As Mariam once said, 'As you know, some parents here are not educated, so their children don't respect them.'

In a small study we did with 50 girls to evaluate the use of the wind-up or solar radios that were distributed in collaboration with the BBC World Service 'Kimasomaso', a Kiswahili programme for adolescents on reproductive health and HIV and AIDS, we asked girls whom they talked to about sexual issues. The following table illustrates their answers, with most girls talking to more than just one person about these issues. Their friends, mothers, sisters and grandmothers were the most consulted, combining traditional routes of grandmother to granddaughter with more modern support from peers and their mothers.

To whom do I talk about sexual issues?	No. of girls
Friend	22
Mother	21
Sister	18
Grandmother	18
Teacher	5
Aunt	4
Brother	3
Grandfather	1
Father	1

❖ ❖ ❖

Universal primary education is the second Millennium Development Goal. It has universal benefits for communities, but in individual lives, striving for an education has caused tension and friction in the family that create challenges for both parents and children. Carol told me that she could never give letters from school to her dad because he didn't want anything to do with school. He told her once, 'I didn't go to school so what's so big about school?' School, too, is supposed to be the place where young people learn about adolescence, growing up, their reproductive health, and HIV and AIDS, but in reality most girls turn to their friends and their family when they want to discuss such issues.

But the relationship between education and a girl's evolving sexuality is central to their sexual experiences. For me, growing up, my education and my sexuality developed in parallel; they really didn't have much to do with each other. I knew if I had sex I could get pregnant and I worried about that but I didn't relate it to dropping out of school. Girls in Kilifi explore their sexuality against a confusing backdrop with education at one end and marriage at the other. What should you be? I never had to deal with those perplexing and contrasting routes: it was school, work, marriage, children—that was the path my friends and I would take. School and work were the drivers. Getting married and having children were ideals that my parents wanted for me. But for me and my friends other routes were OK: being in a relationship, not being in one; same-sex relationships; wanting children, not wanting children. But these were our choices, we could decide. Or so we thought. There were still social pressures to conform to the patriarchal norm.

But in a place like Kilifi, what are your parents telling you? Your aunties? Your friends? Your teammates? Your teachers? Religious leaders? What do you hear on the radio? In schools, generally, the message is this: wait, your time hasn't arrived yet, get your education first, then think about having a relationship, having sex. This is the message girls in Kilifi are getting at school, and it's a similar story from the religious leaders. Some of the girls also told me that their mothers were telling them not to have sex.

The girls have developed a perception of the limited options that face them if they do dare to explore their sexual feelings. If you do decide to start having a relationship the consensus was that you were looking at having penetrative sex and that came with risks. It could be protected sex, but it was much more likely to be unprotected—and that's where the fear kicks in. Their number one worry was pregnancy: will I get pregnant? If I do, what can I do? Have an illegal abortion and return to school? Have the baby, ask my mum to look after the baby and return to school? Or have the baby, forget about school, go to the boyfriend's home and get married. HIV and AIDS barely registered on their personal radars. Janet, Kadzo, Mariam, and in the last interview, Juliet, mentioned HIV and AIDS when discussing their sexuality, long after our lengthy discussions on the consequences of becoming pregnant.

❖ ❖ ❖

The realities are more complex, less clear cut than the perceptions and fears of becoming sexually active. The worries were driven by messages they received from adults and were in black and white: have sex, get pregnant, life's over. But the reality contained more flexibility in the decisions being made, more support from family and friends, and less judgement of the teenage girl who does get pregnant. These stories, in this chapter on pregnancy, abortion and HIV, follow the strategies the girls employ in negotiating the messages they are exposed to and the decisions they had made regarding their sexual behaviour.

In her work on teenage pregnancy in research in South Africa, Mkhwanazi comments that 'teenage pregnancy occurs as a result of social relationships. It is also managed through and affects social relationships. These relationships occur within changing circumstances and are influenced by local ideas of how to be and act. An approach which places emphasis on understanding the social context in which actions concerning reproductive health are taken by youth, and how they and others make sense of the consequences of these actions, is critical.'[43] These stories told to me about the girls' own pregnancies and pregnancies of their friends and acquaintances paint pictures of the social context in which the girls make decisions, listen to advice, take or resist advice. They also portray teenage lives where pregnancy is managed and discussed, contrasting viewpoints are aired and decisions are made.

Janet's stories were an intertwined narrative of her own sexual abstinence surrounded by the sexual activity of others. She had so much to say about relationships with boys, how she negotiated through the advances that came her way and what others did when faced with similar dilemmas. I was captivated by her tales, spiced with the views of her friends, religious rhetoric, and her own questions, contradictions and judgements. They were often repetitive. To make certain points, she'd tell a story one way, change it a little in the retelling, adding a little, leaving a bit out, but telling it nonetheless in her breathless style, as if constantly sharing a secret with you.

When we first met she knew I was coming and had prepared for her guest by applying a thin layer of talcum powder on her face. It made her look soft and dreamy. This was the cosmetic many girls in Kilifi used, not too expensive and good for hiding any signs of oily or sweaty skin. Later on, when she had moved away from home to study at another secondary school, I went to visit her and this time she had on powder, eye liner and a very sweet, overpowering perfume because, she told me, she'd got so bored waiting for me that she and her cousin had decided to put on make-up to look good for my arrival. I felt privileged, even as the smell knocked me back when I entered her sister's coral block house.

During that first meeting, Janet said she and her sister went to church every Sunday. This, she said, helped her to know how to live her life, and to keep away from men for the time being: 'I have not yet thought anything about making love as long as I'm in school; God has kept me as a girl and so when the time comes for me to get married, then I will make love. But now I could do it and then get pregnant, and I would miss out on my studies. The father of the child wouldn't marry me, so I would remain useless.

I tell those girls who are doing it that they are making mistakes, but they say it's for their own pleasure. So when someone tells you that, what do you do? But right now I am going through this period. I am in a group of girls. When they talk about boys I feel tempted, so when they start talking about boys I don't stay there to listen to them. I go a bit far from where they are because it is very easy to be tempted. I don't know why when my friends talk about it, one gets tempted and some end up getting pregnant.'

Janet said she hadn't yet thought about making love, but she had. She'd already started making decisions: She could have sex, but then she'd get pregnant and, as she must have seen through the experience of other girls it was unlikely that the father of the baby would hang around. In her mind that would render her 'useless', with not enough education, on her own, with a baby. So her decision was don't have sex.

She'd had two incidents in her first year at secondary school of possible seduction but she was adamant that she wouldn't let these advances get in the way of her education. 'I received a letter from a certain boy. He'd written I love the way you walk, you walk nicely, you're always smart, and many other things that I have forgotten. After reading the letter, I tore it up because I didn't have any interest in this boy.' The next time Janet was warned by a friend that she could end in bad company because some girls in school who were trying to befriend her had bad behaviour. 'Bad behaviour', *tabia mbaya,* has many meanings, from rudeness to drunkenness. It is used when someone disapproves of what someone else is doing. In this case there was no mistaking that this girl was advising Janet to stay away from these girls because they had boyfriends and that this was not good, this was 'tabia mbaya'.

Janet's experiences of seduction began before secondary school. As we talked more she uncovered a past at primary school where various boys had shown an interest in her. Each time she went to her friend for advice and each time the friend told her to stay away from these boys. 'When I was in primary school I was seduced by another boy. When he seduced me, truly, I didn't know what to do. I told my friend Pendo, there's a certain boy who has told me several things. What should I do? She said, "Wait, I'll tell someone," and she went and told Beatrice Kahindi, the prefect. After telling her she told me that the boy has so many girls and that I should stop seeing him. The story spread and when the teachers heard about it, we were asked to go to the office, the boy and I, so they advised us to stop the relationship, so we stopped it.'

At the beginning of this story Janet says she didn't know what to do when the boy approached her, yet at the end she had gone to see the teacher with the boy and agreed to 'stop it'. She never divulged what the 'it' was, but it was she and the boy who had agreed to stop it, not the boy agreeing to stop following her. I wondered to what extent the story was filtered for me.

It wasn't long after this that she told me, 'I went to the shop and I met another boy. The shop was closed; it was just the two of us. He told me he loved me but I told him that I would answer him later. When we'd been alone we just talked. He didn't touch me or kiss me. Touching and kissing come later, after you've agreed.'

There's a ritual here: a boy will tell you, 'I love you' and will then wait for your reply, for your answer, your agreement. 'I love you' is more of a question, an advance and in this context needs a response—a rebuff or a green light. The answer could be a *sawa* (OK), or an outright refusal but an answer is needed.

Janet continued, 'I told Pendo everything and she advised me to stop seeing him, to stop being involved in relationships with boys. So I went and told him that I didn't want to be with him. I didn't give him a reason why and up to now he hasn't approached me again.'

Pendo was Janet's friend and chastity belt. At every turn her advice was sought. And every time Pendo told her to say no to the boys who were showing an interest in her. Janet, meanwhile, was in a dilemma, part of her telling herself to just try it, see what it's like. She was likely to have other friends too who were saying the same. It was a lot of pressure on her. At the same time she was determined to finish her education. She was caught in the sex versus education war because if she tried to do both she thought she'd end up in a mess.

❖　❖　❖

In August 2006 I sent out the letters to all the girls, through their schools, for our next meetings. Word came back from Asya's school that she was no longer there. She was six months pregnant and had left her home to go and get married. On my way back from visiting Mercy I stopped off at Asya's school to see the head teacher on the off chance that we would be able to have a chat about Asya. The head teacher was a man in his fifties with wild grey hair, balding in the middle and a paunch protruding over his khaki green trousers. We'd met a few times before but had never talked much. I was nervous about discussing the issue with him. I didn't know if he knew anything about Asya or how much he knew about her home life, whether he was one of the teachers who would want to blame someone or something for the situation. I was particularly concerned that he might want to blame the pregnancy on Asya's involvement in football. This was happening in two other schools at that time and we were engaged in delicate discussions with teachers, parents and girls on the issue.

I told him what I knew: that Asya was pregnant and had moved out of her grandparents' home. He filled in some gaps, telling me the grandparents had come to see him, to explain the situation to him. I found him reassuringly engaging. He'd been a teacher in rural Kilifi for many years. He must have come across such scenarios hundreds of times before. He talked with real empathy towards Asya. There was no judgement, no blame, just a desire to help me to get to see her. He called a young female teacher and Asya's younger sister, Husna. Husna said she could take me to her grandparents, to her home, so that I could talk to them, so we set off with the teacher. We started chatting and I quickly found out that the teacher was a saved Christian, recently out of teacher training college and very talkative. Husna was quieter and seemed much more streetwise than the teacher.

We wound through the bush on a narrow, rocky path towards the main road, a red dusty stripe that cut through the valley. We walked, and talked, and walked and walked and walked some more. My feet were caked in dust, my neck was burning red while

Husna loped effortlessly along, assuring me that it wasn't far now as we branched off down another small path off the road. I asked her if this was the distance she walked to school every day. At this point she told me, 'I'm not taking you to my grandparents place. We're going to where Asya is.' Ah, OK. I realised that Husna had taken control of the situation; she'd decided to take us to Asya, not the grandparents. She'd been quiet most of the way but she was a big girl, much bigger than her older sister, strong and determined. I was to meet her again twice at meetings we held in Kilifi. Both times she was sociable and bright. She had a confidence that allowed her to say what she wanted to say in front of people she didn't know.

It wasn't long before we came across the compound, nestled near the base of a long, slow, undulating slope. There were a few rooms, one large one, of grey mud and makuti roof, and three smaller ones. Asya was sitting, chewing cassava, in front of the kitchen hut, from which smoke was seeping out of the makuti roof. There were two other girls there, sitting, but no one else in the compound, no sign of any elders or men—just the young women of the home.

Asya wasn't very different from Mercy when it came to conversation. She was hard work and difficult to read. Before I knew she was pregnant she hadn't said much about sex. One time she'd said: 'Sometimes I hear our neighbours, like when they are making love, and the woman, she makes a noise like she is excited. Then I ask myself, the person who is doing that thing and is excited, what does it mean? But if I ask them what that thing is, they tell me if I don't know then that's my own problem, they don't want to tell me the truth.'

On the day we went to see Asya, she explained to me how things had developed until she was sitting here, six months pregnant, in her husband's home. It was a story during which she showed a level of control over her life that I hadn't known she possessed. I knew her home situation was difficult. She'd never known her dad, her mum had passed away a number of years earlier and she was staying with her elderly grandparents. I once asked her about missing her mum and she told me, 'Ah, I miss her, I miss her every day, but we can't talk about her. If we do my younger siblings cry and it's too painful.'

Asya and her siblings had relied on their uncle for everything and he was finding it hard to provide for everyone's needs. For Asya the final straw had come when he had refused to pay her exam fees at the end of Standard 7. To her that showed very clearly what he thought about her education. It wasn't important. She didn't need to stay in school. Education wasn't going to be her way out of a difficult home life. She would have to find another way.

As she was contemplating what to do, her future husband started to show an interest in her. 'I saw him, he explained his problem to me; he said that he wanted me. I refused the first time, and the second. I was not in a hurry to say that I was interested, but I took his words. By that time I had already been denied money to pay for my school exams, so I waited to hear what he had to say next and then it happened. He proposed to me and I said yes.

'He was the first person I had sex with. The first time he knows but you don't. He was touching my body, but because I didn't know anything, I did what he asked me to do. You have to obey even if it means tears will come out.

'I wasn't expecting to get pregnant. My grandmother asked me what was wrong; I was sleeping all the time and being sick. So she thought maybe it was malaria and she gave me 150 shillings [US$2] to go to be tested. When I went to the hospital they told me I was pregnant so I didn't use the money. I thought I would tell my grandmother, but when I got home I decided not to tell her. My grandmother asked me, where are the drugs? So I told her I'd been given an injection. I took the money and put it all back where I had taken it from.'

❖ ❖ ❖

'We had a home wedding. But it wasn't that simple. He paid my grandparents dowry but they had a problem. They wanted me to stay in school. But my uncle had refused to pay my exam fees. How could I stay in school if I couldn't do the exams? To me the pregnancy was a small issue, but my grandmother was saying that I should have an abortion. But I said no, I will give birth because many girls have given birth and still continue with their education. She said I was shaming her if I was going to go to school with a baby. So she said I should leave and I left.'

At that point Asya moved to her husband's home. He was working at a cement factory in Mombasa. He later got a job working in western Kenya as a turnboy[44] on a lorry. He had completed primary school but he didn't get school fees to go to secondary. She told me, 'He buys everything for me. I don't even ask for clothes, he brings them by himself.'

I have not met her husband; he's never been there when I've visited Asya. The last time we met, in Kilifi, Asya told me he was still working away from home and she was at home looking after her baby, who was nearly one year old at that time. So Asya, similar to Carol, had got away from home through marriage. Within her restricted confines she had made some bold choices: to say yes to marriage, to say no to an abortion, to move out of her home, and she was ready to accept the life she had chosen.

As an organisation we have had many issues in the peer education programme in dealing with discussions on condoms with girls in primary schools. Mr Wanje from the District Education Office told me that condoms were mentioned in the primary school syllabus, that they were 'touched on very lightly' in health education. Some teachers and head teachers were not happy with peer educators explicitly talking about condoms with girls in school. Some told peer educators that they could talk about condoms if they were asked by the girls but that they shouldn't initiate the discussion. Of course, all peer educators during a session on HIV and AIDS were asked about condoms, and condoms were discussed. Condoms, in this setting, are still the only contraceptive available to teenage girls. Any other methods, such as contraceptive pills, injectables and implants, are more often than not seen as family planning and not for girls and women before they have had their children.

Mr Wanje said that, in his opinion, condoms had in some places encouraged more sexual activity among young people. He told me, 'In some of the more rural, far-off places, girls were abstaining from sex. Then they were told about condoms and this gave them the green light. Condoms were there and they started having sex. Some of the boys were making jokes about them, blowing them up like balloons. But the problem is when the condoms are not there, when they run out, they are still having sex.'

Both Carol and Juliet told me that when they had sex they used condoms. It was always the first thing Juliet said when telling me about her sex life, I never had to ask her. It was always, 'We made love … we used a condom.'

Janet talked about a shop close by that sold condoms, but she said you didn't need to buy them because you could get them at the dispensary a few kilometres away. It had been announced at a local meeting that whoever wants to get condoms should go and pick however many they like from the dispensary. Two others, Kanze and Mariam, told me how they had heard that condoms can have holes in them, that they weren't safe, and that it's difficult to get the man or boy to wear a condom. Janet said that the boy you have sex with might spoil the condom: 'It's OK to have sex using a condom but he might make a hole in it without you knowing. He will make a hole and as for you, you think he used a condom … and then you will say a certain day I made love with a certain boy and we used a condom. Now you won't even understand what's happening to you. You don't know where the pregnancy has come from because you used a condom.' This story was more evidence of the many tales, rumours, truths and untruths about condoms that continue to circulate.

There's no doubt that girls and boys know that condoms exist. If you ask any primary school pupil in Standard 5 to Standard 8 about condoms they might not know exactly what they are used for but they know they are available. Carol's description of the first time she had sex with her boyfriend, Eric, illustrated her confusion of what exactly a condom did. I had wanted to know whether they had used any form of protection so I asked her: 'Did you protect yourselves or …?' She cleared her throat and said, 'Protect from what?' So I said, 'from pregnancy'. She told me, 'He protected himself but I didn't protect myself.' I was confused so I probed her: 'What did he do to protect himself?' and she replied, 'He used those things—Trust [a local brand of condoms].' I left it there, taken aback that she may have thought that in using a condom he was protecting only himself.

Salma, a staunch advocate of abstinence for girls, explained to me why girls just need to control their sexual feelings: 'It's hard to get a boy to use a condom. He will use it for two days or three days and the fourth day he will do without. It's true he won't want to continue using it because there is a saying … or people are saying, you can't eat a banana with its peel on, you have to peel it. So the only thing a girl can do so that she doesn't get pregnant is to restrain from these habits. They are not the only ones with such feelings. Many people have such feelings but they restrain themselves.'

Women and men were asked about condom use in the national Kenya Demographic and Health Survey. The figures in the table show the percentage of women who had sexual intercourse in the previous year who used a condom during their last sexual intercourse with spouse or cohabiting partner, with non-cohabiting partner or with any partner, by background characteristic (age and rural/urban).

Background characteristic	Spouse or cohabiting partner		Non-cohabiting partner		Any partner	
	%	No.	%	No.	%	No.
Age						
15–19	2.8	349	22.1	293	11.4	627
20–24	1.7	952	27.0	256	6.8	1,192
25–29	1.7	1,035	25.7	153	4.4	1,180
30–39	2.2	1,553	23.0	177	4.2	1,718
40–49	1.5	899	15.7	102	2.8	987
Residence						
Urban	3.7	1,043	32.7	324	10.3	1,355
Rural	1.4	3,745	18.9	657	3.8	4,349

Source: Central Bureau of Statistics, 2003

These figures show that condom use is not the norm for Kenyan women, particularly not for rural women. Other forms of contraception, such as implants, injectables and pills are even less widely used among younger women and girls in rural areas. These contraceptive methods are seen as family planning, that is, to be used once you have had your children, and are not readily available to young women. So condoms, really, remain the only viable protection available to teenage girls to avoid pregnancy or HIV. But they need to get hold of them, either free from the local clinic or bought from a shop. In rural areas the girls are likely to know people working in either of those places and may feel reluctant to go there, not wanting people to know that they are planning to have sex. Then, if they can get a condom they will need to negotiate its use with the person they are going to have sex with. It is, therefore, not particularly remarkable that many young girls who become sexually active become pregnant. It's also not so surprising, then, that abstinence messages rain down on girls when realistic alternatives, if you want to continue with your education, are so limited. How can girls explore their sexuality safely? If you're going to start responding to your feelings, you're going to have sex, which more often than not, will be unprotected sex.

Janet's story of a good friend captures the issues faced by sexually active girls in relationships: 'Some convince you, even when you don't want to do it, they convince you to do without a condom. I had this friend while I was in Standard 8 who had a boyfriend. The boy told my friend that because they had known each other for a long time, they should have sex without a condom. He loved her in the first term, second term, and then in the third term he thought the year is almost ending while I'm with her, I will impregnate her then find another girl. My friend didn't know that he wanted to make her pregnant and then just leave her, and she accepted. She missed her periods for two months and she came to me, I advised her to talk to her mum. She went and told her mum who was very angry at first and told her she should go to the boy's home. Afterwards her mum decided to help her daughter abort and took her to her brother working in a certain hospital[45] where she had an abortion. She is now back in school.'

Most of the girls mentioned abortion in passing, normally related to someone else in the same way Janet described the experiences of her friend in a 'so-and-so got pregnant, she had an abortion and now she's back in school' way. Nothing particularly unusual about it, it just happens.

It wasn't long after this conversation that I received an invitation from the Kenya Human Rights Commission to an abortion mock trial in Nairobi, to address the question of unsafe abortions in Kenya. Unfortunately by the time I, in remote Kilifi, had received the invitation, the tribunal, dubbed 'Abortion: private decision, public debate', had already taken place. And it had hit the headlines in the local media as pro-life supporters had hijacked the event. The invitation letter stated that a recent study[46] in Kenya revealed that 320,000 unsafe abortions[47] are carried out every year, of which over 2,000 result in death and another 20,000 in long- and short-term injuries. The mock tribunal was organised to look at whether there is a problem of unsafe abortion in Kenya, and if there is, the tribunal was obliged to ask, 'What can be done about this problem?' It also wanted to 'create a forum for women to be heard, create awareness to the larger public and underscore the negative impact that results from the lack of dialogue between 'pro-life' and 'pro-choice' groups on the issue of reproductive rights of women.

According to Susan Anyangu, writing in the *East African Standard* the day after the tribunal, 'Trouble started when the protestors, who had sat quietly among the audience, suddenly shot up in unison demanding audience to air the plight of the unborn babies. The activists shouted: "This forum is one-sided, who is speaking for the children? We have heard the testimonies of the mothers, who will speak for the children." "Kenya is a failed state, how will legalising murder help this country? We already have too many deaths in our society, we do not need to legalise more," they chanted. ... Health assistant minister, Dr Enoch Kibunguchy, who was the keynote speaker during the proceedings, said unsafe abortions are a reality and the issue needed to be discussed. "The whole topic of abortion is emotional and moral but we should talk about it," Kibunguchy said. He said while Kenyans may wish the issue away, the reality is that 300,000 spontaneous and induced abortions occur annually in Kenya.'[48]

Abortion is illegal in Kenya, except in extreme circumstances. If a woman or girl has been raped and becomes pregnant there is provision in the law for her to have an abortion, if two medical professionals agree that her health and well-being could be at risk if she went ahead with the pregnancy. In such situations the abortion can be carried out in a hospital.

What the girls told me about abortion caught me completely unawares. I started digging a bit deeper about what they knew, what they thought, when we met up soon after this tribunal in the middle of 2007. I began by talking about how the issue of abortion was being debated by leaders in Nairobi but that, by all intents and purposes, abortion was illegal in Kenya. Did they think it should remain that way? I couldn't believe the extent to which they could talk about the issue: what they thought about it, the choices that were available to a girl in Kilifi if she got pregnant, the steps she could take. The girls they knew who had had abortions—sisters, friends—talked about it like any other incident in their lives with scant regard for the fact that Kenya has very restrictive abortion laws. It looked to me like abortion was normalised in their lives.

It began to dawn on me that abortion was being used as a form of contraception. They knew more about abortion than they did about condoms; they certainly talked about it in more detail and with more knowledge. It was a reality, the option in dealing with unintended pregnancies. But let me make one thing very clear here. In many of the stories about abortion the girls talk about what they have heard, what other people have experienced, and these tales get distorted and embellished in the memory and the retelling. While their stories might not accurately describe exactly what happens, in using traditional medicines or in procuring an abortion in a hospital, they do reflect the knowledge they have and the pervasiveness of the practice in trying to look for options when you accidently get pregnant.

Mercy, interestingly, had strong views against abortion, despite being the centre of a rumour I'd heard about her having had one. The views she expressed, illustrated her knowledge, her exposure to rumours, myths and truths, and the arguments put forward about abortion. She had known a girl who had died as a result of an abortion gone wrong, although quite what caused the death was not clear from Mercy's recounting of the incident. She knew that abortion can lead to later complications and that religion plays a central role in how people see the issue of abortion.

'It's bad and dangerous. You can die. There is a girl who died near our home, she aborted, then she died. They gave her pills that she swallowed, the drugs reacted with her body, she went to the hospital. When she reached there she was told that she was doing an abortion then she was given an injection and she died immediately. If you have an abortion you can end up not having any children. Maybe God had only given you that one child and you aborted it. You won't get a child again or you might end up not able to get to give birth at all. You can be infertile. If a schoolgirl gets pregnant she can go and have the baby and return to school.'

Salma also felt strongly that abortion was not good. She argued that 'if you get pregnant you should give birth because maybe there is someone who wants a baby badly but she doesn't get a baby. But when you get pregnant and you plan and abort it, there is someone who is really in need of that baby. If you are in school you will be forced to have the pregnancy until you get a baby. Because if you abort it won't be good, you better keep it and look for help to keep the child alive.'

Carol talked about what she would have done if she'd got pregnant while still in school: 'If I tell you the truth—maybe if I had got pregnant by bad luck when I was at home and still at school, I would have aborted.' She went on to explain to me the process of what you might consider doing if you wanted to abort:

'Maybe if I say you go to the hospital, you need money and maybe the man who impregnated me has no money to pay the bill. So I would have used herbs. Because another friend of mine who gave birth, we went to the same school, she was three months pregnant and she took some herbs and boiled them. They were very bitter. She boiled and then drank it. She also took a razor blade, boiled it, then took the water.[49] She took many things but she didn't succeed. She had the baby. It's three months old now.' Her friend had failed to abort using these methods but Carol insisted that she would have tried it, so she must have known others who had succeeded using such tactics. But she said, 'If I had money? I would go to Kama hospital. But, no, I can't go to Kama because my uncle works there. I would go to Mombasa. I know the hospital, but I don't know what happens inside there. I would ask when I got to Mombasa because my sister-in-law who is married to my brother when she was three months pregnant, she went to Mombasa to do an abortion. She was taken to the hospital by my brother.'

Carol's description of what one would do when faced with an unintended pregnancy was typical: try local medicine first, then hospital, preferably a hospital where no one knows you. Others said that if you needed money you would go to the boy's family first. Only if he refused to help out would you turn to your own family. Juliet, Janet and Mariam said much the same as Carol. All four came from very different parts of Kilifi. Carol and Janet in the more rural, interior areas both talked of using traditional methods first. All four talked of the need for money and the responsibility placed on the boy or man's family to provide the money for an abortion.

Juliet started by talking about what she would do if she got pregnant and finished off with a story of how a friend got pregnant and aborted without her mother ever knowing: 'If unluckily I get pregnant while in school, even my parents will not know that I am pregnant, especially if the boy who impregnated me has money and is able to pay for an abortion. I would go to the hospital; there is one around here that does abortion. If you are three months pregnant I heard you pay 3,000 shillings [US$47]. And then you are admitted for a day. You are given medicine. One of my friends did an abortion. She said that she went there, to the private hospital. When she arrived she was given medicine then she left. She had gone to the boy's place to get money. She didn't go to her mum's because she felt that if she goes there, maybe they can discover what has happened. So her mum didn't know she was pregnant. It's the boy that paid the bill.'

A school friend of Mariam's got pregnant: 'When she got pregnant her mum came and told the senior teacher at school what had happened. When she was at home she vomited after eating food. She was told let's go to the hospital, to see the doctor, to know what illness you have. That's when she ran away. She went and did an abortion at the home of the man who got her pregnant. Then she went back home and now she is continuing with her education.

'You can get an abortion if you have money. You talk to the doctor secretly, and he'll do it. The doctors who help in abortion are there, they take the instruments and use them at home and they do the abortion. In the beginning she was affected. She lost weight but now she is OK.'

Janet, as was often the case, had the most to say: what the authorities would do if you had an abortion, judgements on who could and couldn't abort, and plenty of detail on how girls who she knew, including her sister, had gone about having abortions.

'If one is raped it's OK to abort because she didn't intend to be pregnant. If you are raped and get pregnant you can abort but if you agree to have sex and get pregnant you should not abort at any cost. Some girls agree to have sex and when they get pregnant they abort; it has become their game. At our home it's not easy to do an abortion, though, because if you are living there and people find out they will report you to the police, chief or anybody and you will be accused of murder. You will be asked, "Why have you killed your child?" but if you say that I was raped, they will say fine. But if you had sex willingly and you got pregnant and now you have aborted it you will be accused of killing the child.

'Even close to home people abort in the hospital, but if you don't want to be known you will come to Kilifi or go to Malindi or somewhere else. If you want to abort it at the hospital they first get rid of it. I don't know how they do it. I don't know what they use—instruments—I'm not sure.

'There are girls who take herbs to help them abort. They take *mwarubaini* [from the neem tree]; they take its bark, boil it and drink the bitter herb. Eh, they drink it and then they get rid of the pregnancy or they boil tea [concentrated black tea without sugar] and other herbs, I don't know, like *madzaji* [a fruit]; they eat the madzaji, which is bitter, and then they get rid of the pregnancy.'

I asked her: 'Does madzaji really cause a miscarriage?' and she told me about her sister: 'Yeah, it gets out. I have a sister, when she was in primary school she tried to do an abortion. She used madzaji, she was two months pregnant, she had the madzaji, then she got rid of the pregnancy. We told her that it's very bad. Then she played the same game again and now she has a baby and she is at home. She aborted when she got pregnant the first time. The second time she tried to abort again but she didn't manage. She took the herbs but she didn't get rid of it. She boiled tea leaves and mwarubaini. She boiled a lot of tea leaves but the child remained inside. That's when she started thinking what am I doing? Why did I drink the herbs? The pregnancy was still there. She was in a dilemma. All the time she was thinking deeply, she was confused; she didn't know what to do next. The father denied that he was responsible when he was approached. When she told him he said, "I am not the father." What was she to do? He told her to stop following him. Now she had to leave that place. She came and stayed with her mother at Jaribuni, and this is where she had the baby, a handsome baby boy.'

So Janet believed her sister successfully aborted her first pregnancy, although she may have miscarried, as many pregnancies do in the first trimester. Her sister's second pregnancy, despite her attempts to get rid of it amidst denials by the father that he had anything to do with it, went to term and in the end there was enormous relief, a beautiful baby boy.

Agnes Odhiambo from the Africa Woman and Child Features Service pointed out in the *Standard*,[50] about a week after the mock tribunal, that the Kenyan government is a signatory to the Protocol on the Rights of Women in Africa. The protocol affirms reproductive choice and autonomy as a human right and provides protection for women's human rights, including sexual and reproductive ones. It unequivocally articulates a woman's right to abortion when pregnancy is a result of sexual assault, rape or incest; when continuation of the pregnancy endangers the life or health of the woman; and in cases of foetal defects incompatible with life.

What the girls in Kilifi said about abortion makes it very clear to me that it happens and that it happens in a backstreet way. It is normalised, it's talked about and it looms as an immediate concern for girls if they get pregnant. Asya chose not to have an abortion, she wanted to have her baby, while Carol said she would have had an abortion if 'by bad luck' she had got pregnant while still in school. Juliet and Janet recounted vivid descriptions of a friend and a sister having abortions. Kanze's sister had also aborted but was now pregnant again. Where were the options, I wondered, for girls and boys to explore their sexuality in their teenage years without coming up against such difficult issues? How could they experience safe sexual intimacy if they wanted to? For a boy, you get her pregnant, you run away, you claim it wasn't you. Or you help out, give her drugs, find the money somehow, take her to the hospital, get rid of the pregnancy, the evidence, and pray she'll be OK, that there won't be any repercussions, that she won't die. You stay in school. And for the girl, you're pregnant, keep it, get rid of it, take drugs, pray you miscarry, look for money for an abortion? What are you going to do? These are very hard decisions for young women. I don't believe that these girls are any more sexually active than any other group of teenagers. But they have unprotected sex, penetrative sex, snatched moments in the bush, behind the shop, in a room, with little time to negotiate using a condom.

❖ ❖ ❖

On my way home from a day spent engrossed in writing at the office I popped into an internet café where, as I checked my emails, I was greeted by a friend, who was a teacher. I had some photographs I wanted to show her so she sat down next to me as we continued chatting. She came from Mombasa and was in her late 30s. As I opened the folders on my flash drive to find the photos she said, 'Sarah, you've got a file called pregnancy and abortion. What on earth is that for?'

I wasn't entirely sure where to start, having heard the shock in her voice. But I began, 'Well, you know as part of my job. ... I'm writing a book ... girls' stories ... young people having sex ... they don't have many alternatives when it comes to safe sex ... well, there are condoms, but ...'

'Oh, Sarah, please don't tell me you want them all to be given condoms?' Me again: 'Well, you know, they are having sex ...' Her again, 'My daughter's 15. You know she's very beautiful, she has big breasts, not like mine. Please, no.'

I felt for her; she told me more about how difficult she finds it to talk to her daughter about sex, how scared she was for her daughter. She had tried. She'd bought her daughter a book from a Christian bookshop in Mombasa on growing up, but she wondered aloud what else she could do. Then she told me, 'Well, if she got pregnant, a child, a child we could manage. But HIV? That's another thing.' She went on to tell me how as a teenager she was kept in the house when not in school, her parents were so fearful of what might happen to her out there, with boys around. Those experiences had rubbed off on her but she couldn't keep her own daughter locked away from danger.

It was interesting that HIV was her main worry. As a mother and an older woman, she knew about having children. A child, a grandchild was something she, and her daughter, would be able to handle. She was less concerned about pregnancy, more worried about her daughter becoming HIV positive. Her concerns were quite different from the concerns of the girls around their growing sexuality. For them, the number one worry was the pregnancy, the immediate time bomb ticking, counting down nine months to motherhood. HIV was something seen as far off, the future, altogether less tangible.

❖ ❖ ❖

There's no doubt that these conversations with the girls in Kilifi go along with what Motsemme observed in her work with young women in Kwa Zulu Natal in South Africa. Motsemme 'found the socio-cultural milieu in which they are remaking themselves and their futures—redefining what constitutes risky and normative intimacy, and what remains joyous about relationships, sex and love in the age of HIV/AIDS—to be highly contradictory and complex'.[51] In Kilifi though, it is the axis between unintended pregnancy and education, more than HIV and AIDS—although this is a significant issue for young women in Kenya—that is shaping their complicated experiences of sex and love in their everyday lives.

I found it difficult to get very far in talking about HIV and AIDS. They all knew about HIV and how it was transmitted but it didn't register as something to be too worried about—just yet. That's how I interpreted their monosyllabic responses. While discussions on boys, sex, pregnancy and abortion elicited long, twisting tales of their own dilemmas and experiences, the stories of their sisters and their friends, stories from the here and now, mention of HIV threw us back to 'what I know about HIV', pulling it away from the personal and back into the classroom, onto the billboards, standard public health messages for everyone, ... but not for me.

Was it that they had more immediate concerns: doing OK in school, work at home, finding money to cover their basic needs, friends, boyfriends, family, football, pregnancy—and HIV was appearing a lot further down on the list? Or was it more than that? Were HIV and AIDS just more troubling or difficult to talk about? Or did they see them as distant, for an older generation, not something affecting them directly, just yet? But I knew that AIDS has a negative impact on all of our lives, from my husband's family, from friends: we have all lost mothers, fathers, aunts, uncles, friends, daughters, sons, cousins to the disease. Orphans are absorbed into families and maybe that's what was making it difficult. AIDS was all around them, touching their lives, but related to their family situations, not their own sexual experiences. National figures show very clearly that HIV infection should be an immediate concern for them because young women in the age group 15–24 years are more than twice as likely to be infected with HIV as men in the same age group.[52]

Mariam, though, was one girl who was worried about HIV infection: 'A girl might think that she is OK when she has sex with a boy and gets pregnant. It's better to get pregnant. What if it was HIV?' The implication was that a pregnancy could be managed. People were used to doing that, but how would a girl who became HIV positive live? She then said, 'Wouldn't you be a burden to your mother?'

Kadzo learnt a lot from the sessions her teachers would call: 'At school you are told not to have sex carelessly. If you have unprotected sex, you can get pregnant or infected with AIDS. We are called together by one teacher in a gathering and she tells us not to have sex because you may get pregnant or contract dangerous diseases.'

The first time Juliet mentioned HIV was the last time we met, when posing a question and answering it herself, about what she should do about her two boyfriends: 'Now, I have a question. You know I have two boyfriends and there's one I love more than the other, but what do I do? They both love me. I should just have one or …? And there's one I like more. Paul has gone to Kilifi and he wants me to go there, to visit, to stay for a day and then come back but I don't even know where he lives there. I think I need to struggle to choose one because to have two is not possible. You know these days, it is not good to have more than one. There's a disease out there. It's better you're faithful to one person.'

When Carol first told me her mother had passed away she said she'd died of TB. But later her dad told her something different: 'Dad said she didn't die of TB, it was AIDS. Mum used to sell cassava and coconut in Mombasa, so he claimed that it was AIDS, not TB. I didn't say anything because I didn't know what was going on, because when she was sick she was at our uncle's place. She wasn't at our home. When she came back home she didn't even finish a week before she died. I was at school.' It is in these circumstances that girls are coming up against HIV and AIDS: ailing parents, orphans coming to stay in their homes, attending funerals of older siblings, aunties and uncles. They all know that HIV exists and how it is transmitted, but relating it to their own first steps into sexual activity remained problematic. Pregnancy was the worry; anything else would be dealt with later, much later.

Janet told me what she thought should be done for people who were HIV positive: 'People with HIV are supposed to be taken care of, especially when both parents are positive. In our area some neighbours take the responsibility of taking care of the family, knowing that if they discriminate against them they will die more quickly. I know there are some drugs to prolong the lives of people with HIV but I don't know their name.'

Gollub states: 'Instead of the public health community worrying about insulting, demeaning and confusing women with too many choices, why don't we just "tell it like it is" to the women who desperately need protection and let them decide.'[53] In MTG the peer educators are desperately hungry for accurate information, for details, for knowledge. They want to be more and more informed, and they are not content with just scratching the surface of an issue. These are young women with a thirst for knowledge that, if provided, can be disseminated very effectively to others. They want to be empowered to protect themselves, not to rely on others. This supports Chege when she writes: 'Instead of looking at young people as part of the problem of the HIV/AIDS pandemic, we need to look for strategies and solutions for the malady from among them. One way of doing this is to engage young people in the process of HIV/AIDS education, not just as consumers of information but also as generators of relevant knowledge that is responsive to their needs, aspirations, anxieties, fears, hopes and dreams.'[54] This is where MTG can stand out. Young women and girls on the verge of adolescence or going through it, as members of a collective group, can be strengthened by their involvement in sport and the solidarity their teams provide. Mbeyu is one of these girls who's taken it upon herself to use the skills she's learnt within MTG to help others.

Mama Mbeyu: It's not just about football

MTG has helped Mbeyu with many trainings and seminars. She's learnt about things she didn't know before. She's learnt about how to protect herself from AIDS. She goes and tells the older people, 'You know lots of people are dying because of this thing. Do you know how to use condoms?' And then when she demonstrates, how a condom is used, they laugh. She doesn't laugh. You see she has that feeling that if there weren't such attitudes, people wouldn't be dying. It's not something to laugh about. She doesn't laugh, she feels bad that people are dying. There's this woman here, our neighbour, and she likes making fun of Mbeyu when she shows them how to use a condom. But Mbeyu has been touched by this thing that people are dying and they don't know why. Then I saw this child of mine, she understands about these problems.

Mbeyu is someone who talks, so she says if I'm helped through school and to play football I will make sure I help others. Lots of children don't have anyone to look after them, some girls don't go to school, others don't have enough food, maybe a girl has her periods and her dad can't afford to buy sanitary pads. They need to be helped. But now those girls are given money by boys, they can't support themselves. Now a boy gives you money to buy sanitary pads, at the end you sleep with him and you get pregnant. That's the end of your life. So Mbeyu, if she is helped, she will help these other girls, she says she wants to be a counsellor. You know she is friendly to all people, boys and girls, and the way she talks she has a vision for her life.

8

'They think it's all over'[55] ... but is it? Motherhood and marriage

Whenever I went to see each of the girls, as part of our typically long greetings, they would ask me, 'How are your children?' Always, without fail. They wouldn't ask about my husband, that would be far too intrusive, but they could always ask about my children. By the end of 2007 I was asking Asya the same question. She'd given birth in January while Carol was heavily pregnant. Both were married.

That December in 2007, we'd planned to meet up at Chambai. When I arrived at around nine in the morning, the time the meeting was to start, only Carol and Asya, with her sister and her baby, were there. They were sitting out on the wall, swinging their legs and taking in the sea breeze. I was amazed to see Carol. I'd thought there was no way she'd make it to the meeting because I knew she'd be heavily pregnant. But there she was with a nice big bump under her T-shirt, chatting with the others. I said to her, 'Wow, you're here, you've made it.' She said, with a completely straight, and slightly annoyed, face, 'Why did you think I wouldn't be?' Asya's beautiful daughter was starting to crawl, a gorgeous little bundle, who looked just like her mother. I picked her up, startled her with a big kiss as we all agreed to go inside and have some *mahamri* and tea.

Over tea we started talking about Carol's pregnancy, joking about what was in store for her. Where was she going to have the baby? Who would be there? I suggested to Asya that she give Carol some advice about the whole thing. Asya told me, 'Hey, I can't tell her about what giving birth is like. For everyone it's so different. There's no point telling her, it won't help her at all.'

I thought about the last few months before I had my first baby.

I read book after book on childbirth, I went to antenatal classes, I asked my good friends who'd recently given birth to recount every single detail of their own deliveries. I soaked up as much information as I could; it was mind boggling, it made me feel even more nervous about this impending event over which I would have no control. In the end, I had to agree with Asya—it seemed as if all that information counted for nothing at the actual moment when push came to shove in the delivery room. I had my first child, Flo, in Cambridge, in the UK. After a long, painful, drug-assisted labour, I ended up having a Caesarean section. It was a world away from Asya's delivery at home, about which she did give us a snippet, when giving Carol a small piece of advice: 'When you give birth, people will hear the news that you have gone into labour. They'll all come to your place, where you are and they'll give you advice—do this, do that, take your clothes off, get naked … no, keep your clothes on. But you, ignore them, just do what you need to do. You'll have someone there who knows what they're doing. That's a must. Listen to her.'

I thought I'd see what they thought about their husband's being present at the birth. My husband's eternally grateful to our first daughter for arriving early. He was on an overnight flight from Kenya to the UK when I gave birth and he was driven straight from Heathrow airport to the hospital to find me with his angelic, sleeping baby. So I asked Carol, 'Will your husband be there?' She told me, 'No way, what use would he be?' I demonstrated that maybe he would be stroking her back, giving her encouraging words and she just said, 'How will that help me?'

Asya butted in: 'They don't want to see the baby coming out; they just want them later, in their arms.' As young, married, rural women, that separation of a man's world and a woman's world is stark and clear. Birth and child care, this is the domain of women. There's no place for a man there. The man should provide financially. He can hold the child, play with the child, but the responsibility for its day-to-day well-being belongs to the women. When bigger decisions are needed to be made, for instance when the child is ill and money is needed to go to the traditional healer or the hospital, the man is involved. Both Asya and Carol had married into a traditional rural Kilifi homestead where the woman's role is reproductive and domestic. Carol had finished primary school, fully aware that her chances of going to secondary school were nil. Asya had left school before finishing Standard 7. Both were living in their marital homes as wives who were not bringing any money into the family.

Asya and Carol's married lives were significantly different from their previous lives. What they told me concurred with the observations of Otoo-Oyortey and Pobi when they wrote 'young married girls are under more pressure on a number of fronts: to show evidence of their fertility, to be responsible for the welfare of their children and to do a disproportionate share of domestic chores'.[56] They had both made conscious decisions to change what was happening in their lives, to get married, to get pregnant, to get away from the family situation in which they lived. They were making decisions about what to do in their lives; they were not being forced to do anything by members of their families. In my mind, the world was not their oyster. They had very limited options, but they both weighed up those options and made choices. They were young women who had decided to move away from their family home to a new life, maybe not very far away, but with new people, new rules, new roles and duties, and a new excitement and happiness with their new husbands.

Asya had passed the test of being a fertile young woman: 'I got pregnant the first time I had sex. Lots of people have asked me about this and they tell me that if you get pregnant that easily you are the type of person who will have many children and you will give birth in quick succession. I don't know if they are telling me the truth.' This must have given her status in her marital home. This was a young woman who would provide many children for the home.

I liked Asya because she was a mix of rural tradition and attempted cool. When I first started talking to her she would speak with a kind of twang, trying to sound like someone from Mombasa, from town, rather than someone from rural Kilifi. At that point she wanted me to know that she was exposed, that she knew about the world out there. This changed dramatically over the two years and at the end, when we met up in December 2007, all her jokes in the group were said in Kigiriama. She was entertaining the other girls, using cultural nuances to make them laugh; she was being the joker. They could all see that she was a mother, but she was still a girl, still the funny one, still a part of the gang, trying to show she was not really very different from the rest of them.

She also knew how she saw herself when it came to sex with her husband: 'I cannot want to have sex. I'm a woman. I can't, it's him who wants it. He should want it and tell me to want it, if he wants it. Understand, I am telling you, for example, if he comes to me, it's usually in the evening. And he tells me, now, we shall do this, then if I am ready I will tell him it's all right. If I am not ready I will tell him it's not possible. And he keeps quiet.'

So she says she can't actively want to have sex because she is a woman. This was different from all the other girls. They'd all said they had feelings, desires and that they were the ones who chose whether to act upon them. Most said that they chose not to respond to these sexual feelings but they did acknowledge that the feelings existed. I wondered whether the women Asya hung out with in her husband's family compound were influencing what she said. Was this submissiveness towards sex with her husband something she had been told she should exhibit, to be a good wife?

Her husband wasn't around much but he looked after her needs. She told me that she couldn't yet reflect on married life, because she hadn't been married for long enough: 'He buys everything for me; I don't even ask for clothes, he brings them by himself. But I don't see my life as better or worse. Now I am not at our home, I'm now at someone else's place [her husband's home]. In the evening I go and look for food like vegetables and then firewood and then I cook for people. But at our home [her grandparents place], I could even complete a week without cooking because my grandmother would cook. Now it's a must that I cook here. If it comes to your day, you cook.[57]

'But every day has its time and this is a different time. I would be able to talk about married life if I'd been here for a year but since I haven't completed a year yet I can't really say what married life is like.'

I was taken aback by her pragmatism. I'd known about the situation she had come from and the one she'd married into. Neither looked very good to me but her analysis that 'every day has its time and this is a different time' seemed to me accepting, passive, a way to explain a new and different stage in her life.

But as I was asking myself whether that was really enough for Asya I realised I was laying my own assumptions and expectations of my own life on to hers. From my materially privileged position it looked tough, it looked like Asya was jumping out of the frying pan of life with her poor grandparents and into the fire of married life with a mainly absent husband. But why couldn't I just respect the decisions she had made, the control she had taken of her life? I was judging her, asking myself how this could be good enough, how could she just quietly accept it? But am I really in a position to judge her decision and her acceptance to wait and see what married life was like? By this time I'd been talking to these girls for over a year, but I hadn't lived the lives they'd lived. Maybe she was being more sensible and mature than I would have been at that age, biding her time, waiting to see what might happen. It might not have looked so good to me but to her, that was the way it was at that time, full stop.

And, as she told me later, it didn't necessarily have to be forever, despite her belief that she should try to follow tradition: 'Even if it's not good [to become a mother when young], it happened. They [the elders] don't usually want you to give birth while you still live in your maternal home. They want you to go! I mean you should go to get married. You can give birth but if you give birth in your own home, for that child to grow up in that home, it's not accepted in our tradition. But even now, if I were at home [grandparents' home] I think we could stay together there.'

Asya says that in their tradition a girl is not supposed to give birth in the home where she was born. Yet her own mother, before she died, was living in her maternal home. Asya had grown up in her mother's home and had never known her father. But she still talked of what was and what wasn't allowed, regardless of whether people followed that path. Asya had made a conscious decision to follow tradition, to move out of her maternal home, to go and live in her husband's home. But, even more interestingly, she twice mentioned to me that she could, might, go back to live with her grandmother.

One time soon after she'd given birth, I went to visit Asya. She told me she thought that if she ever needed to go and stay back at home, if things didn't work out where she was, she would be able to go back and her grandmother would accept it. And here she says it again. If she had to go home, she thinks it would be OK. When she came for the meeting in December she had come with Husna, her sister. In the previous meeting she had also come with a woman from her husband's place. The husband had insisted that this woman come with her. When I asked Asya why she had come on her own this time she said her husband's family knew what she was coming for and her husband had agreed she could come alone.

Carol moved to her husband's home in March 2007 and got pregnant soon after. Similar to Asya, she had made what looked like a sensible decision given her situation at home. There was no chance of her going on to secondary school; her father wanted her to stay at home and work on the shamba, and she had no money to cater for her own needs. Then this guy shows an interest in her and asks her to marry him. When she came to the meeting in December, I asked her how her husband had allowed her to come on her own. Her response gave me insight into her married life and how her husband, despite having no objections to her travelling to a meeting in Kilifi, still maintained some control over her: 'My husband had no problem with me coming here for the meeting. He was the one who was given the letter because I'd gone to fetch water. When I got home, he had already read it.

Then he told me about it and I read it again. And he said I don't have to go with another person, I could just go alone.' The letter had been addressed to Carol but it was his right, as her husband, to open it.

Carol was eight months pregnant and was far from her usual open self. When I asked her about her life in the future she was particularly reticent. I put it down to the pregnancy and worry over the impending birth of her first child. She told me, 'Life's not bad, it's just normal. My husband says he wants me to give birth safely; he's happy, he wants a child. At the home where I'm married I haven't noticed problems. But I don't know about the future. Problems will always be there, like food—you can have food today but you won't eat again until tomorrow evening. We don't cook at lunchtime, because at the moment there's no maize left. We have to buy it, as much as four kilos a day. My husband's mother gave birth to many children and some are still in school. So sometimes you have to go to bed hungry. I tell my husband and he gives me money and I go to buy bread and soda at a hoteli along the road. I eat, then I sleep. At the moment we don't sleep together. He sleeps on the floor while I sleep on the bed. Because the bed is narrow, when we sleep together he squashes me. So now he sleeps on the floor while I sleep on the bed. He has no problems with it. He says it's normal because when one is heavily pregnant you can't have sex.'

Carol's plan was to give birth at home but her sister called me just before Christmas. She told me Carol had been taken to Kilifi District Hospital with chronic pains and that she had no money for bus fare to go and visit her.

If you're like me, and you've heard too many anecdotal stories of mothers dying during childbirth in Kenya and you have no medical skills or knowledge, any news of possible complications in a pregnancy can fill you with a terrible sense of foreboding. I was worried for Carol and went to the maternity ward to see her. I bought a few things on the way—juice, bread, soap. When I got to the hospital I found her resting on the concrete veranda outside the ward, sitting with her back leant against a metal post. Her hair was neatly plaited, and she wore a pink and green leso wrapped around a loose dress and blue flip-flops. We greeted each other and had a small chat. She said she had terrible back pain and that it had been going on for a few days. She was with an older woman, a relative of her husband's. We sat for a while in the quiet morning sunshine. When I got up to leave, she walked very slowly with me, carrying the black plastic bag of things I had brought for her. When we said goodbye she started to give the bag back to me and looked shocked when I told her it was hers—as if she couldn't believe I had brought anything for her.

The days passed, Christmas, and then the disputed election. As the violence escalated in other parts of the country and we sat tight in Kilifi, I kept thinking of Carol. I hadn't heard anything. She must be back, with her baby, in the safety of her rural home by now? I would have heard if anything else had happened. But it wasn't until January 2nd that she called. She was still at the hospital and she had had a baby girl that morning.

I went to visit them, Carol and her baby, the next day, when they were supposed to be leaving the hospital. Carol looked exhausted and bewildered. She said she didn't have any breast milk yet and she was worried. We talked about the next few days. I tried to reassure about how the milk can take time, that breastfeeding can take a while to get used to, how your emotions can go crazy, about postpartum bleeding. I was sure she could cope but I just wanted to give her as much information as possible, all the things I had never dared to say before she had given birth.

❖ ❖ ❖

Three tales of teenage motherhood

Both Asya and Carol were very new to motherhood. But a number of the older girls in MTG already had a great deal of experience with it. I'd worked alongside three of them without ever knowing much about their experience of pregnancy, childbirth and the hard work of looking after young children. The time had come to find out more.

❖ ❖ ❖

Teenage mother 1, Lilian Mbeyu:
Giving birth, going back to school, getting a job

Lilian Mbeyu is 22 years old and works for MTG as the divisional coordinator in Kaloleni. She ensures all football and health peer education in the division takes place, that matches are played, trained referees and first aiders are present, and peer education sessions are held. She also coordinates with schools and parents, dealing with any issues that come up regarding the girls who play football.

Lilian was 16 when she found that she was pregnant: 'I was very scared because my parents were very strict, especially my father. I was in Form 2 in secondary school. I decided not to tell them until they noticed because I didn't know how to approach them. Only my boyfriend and his mum knew about the pregnancy. He wanted to marry me but I was still in school and my parents wouldn't have agreed. I stayed in school for six months with no one noticing that I was pregnant.

'I went home for a two-week holiday and my mum noticed I was different and she asked me if I was pregnant. I told her that I was but that I'd been too scared to tell them. She was annoyed that I hadn't confided in her and when she told my dad he was angry because he had already paid my school fees for the whole year. He wanted the boy responsible for my pregnancy to pay for it. If my parents had chased me away I would have gone to stay with my boyfriend because I didn't want to abort the baby. I would have left school and cared for the baby.'

Towards the end of her pregnancy Lilian said she started to get scared about giving birth: 'I wondered how the baby would come out. I felt a headache and back pains so I decided to go to the hospital without telling my mum. As I got close to the hospital I decided to jump the fence and enter the hospital that way instead of using the main road because many of my dad's friends used the main road and I didn't want them to see me. My mum, who really helped me, had followed me and she told me we should go to the maternity ward.

'By 7 pm I had given birth. It was really bad and I made a lot of noise. There was a nurse I knew and she told me not to make noise because everything was going to be OK. I was taken to the delivery room and I told the nurse that I wanted to go the toilet. She told me that I would just have to do it there. I kept insisting that they take me to the toilet but suddenly as I was pushing the baby came out. I was very happy when I saw the baby. It was a girl and I had wanted a girl. I called her Sharon.'

After a couple of months Lilian's focus shifted back to her education: 'My dad wanted me to go back to school. I had to get a maid to take care of the baby. My mum told me I had to stop breastfeeding so that she could get used to normal milk. It was very painful because the milk built up in my breasts but I had to stop feeding her.

'I went back to school the following year in Form 3. I had only missed one term. I went for the Form 3 interview and I passed. I didn't go back to the school I had left. I felt I was going to be the odd one out in the same school because I'd had a child. That school was also far from my home and I wanted to be close to my baby so that when I missed her I could just go and see her. My baby stayed with my mum and dad and the maid, and she got used to them. She would call my parents mum and dad.

'I had a neighbour who advised me a lot. She told me that getting pregnant is not the end of my life but that I should work hard and take care of my child. My mum also helped me. I knew I had to work hard in school since I had to take care of my baby.'

Lilian finished secondary school and began to volunteer for MTG. In early 2008 she was taken on as a full-time employee.

Teenage mother 2, Janet Karembo:
Family support and returning to the football field

Janet Karembo runs MTG's Coach the Coach programme and MTG United, the organisation's representative teams (first team, under-16s and under-13s). She's just over five feet tall (153 cm), slight in build but is one of the strongest football players I've come across, with speed, a never-say-die attitude and great skills.

I was waiting for her in the office when she texted me to tell me she'd be late. Her daughter, Fridah, had been up all night with a bad cough and she needed to get medicine for her before she took her to nursery. It was an ongoing problem that the doctors hadn't got to the bottom of. She looked stressed as she came into my office asking if I'd got her message, but when she sat down, she started to talk about her experience of pregnancy and now, motherhood. Janet was 19 and had finished secondary school by the time she found that she was pregnant.

'I felt like I needed to vomit. I was choosy about the food I wanted to eat and after going to the hospital I was examined and told I was pregnant. I was very stressed. I told my boyfriend about it. He said that I should wait until he told his parents. At that time I had only just found I was pregnant. We continued together but then when the pregnancy was seven months along he told me I should abort. He told me if I didn't abort he would leave me. I was shocked because I knew the baby in my womb had grown. I could feel it. I was worried if I aborted that I could die. I decided to tell my mum. My mum asked me why I hadn't told her earlier because no one had noticed the pregnancy. I was just wearing normal clothes and I was still playing football. My mum told me I should leave the boy alone because getting pregnant is not the end of your life. She said she would help take care of the baby.

'I felt very bad about what my boyfriend had said. I wanted to kill myself but I knew I had a mum who was ready to help. I loved him very much but if he could tell me to abort the baby then he is just like a murderer. Anyway, I thank God because now I have a baby and she is four years old. I may not give birth in the future but I already have a baby. When I was about to give birth my mum decided to take me to my uncle's place so I could give birth there. When I came back home my boyfriend approached me again but I refused his advances, knowing what I'd been through. He told me that in future I'd need him. I told him I wouldn't stop greeting him but being boyfriend and girlfriend again would not be possible. He doesn't help me with anything now.'

'I wasn't sure how the baby would come out. I thought the vagina would be too small so I went to see a friend who was a nurse and a counsellor and she explained everything to me. On the day I gave birth I woke up feeling fine but by the evening I felt my stomach aching. It would ache and then it would stop. I told my aunt about it and she told me that I would give birth that night. At night I felt worse. I woke my aunt and she told me the baby was coming. Suddenly my waters broke. I was taken to the nearby hospital on the back of a bicycle. I think the movement on the bicycle helped it along, as we were bumping along the road. At the hospital the nurse, who'd also been my counsellor, helped me. She was the one who'd explained to me how the baby would come out. I gave birth in the morning and I took a shower. Then I was injected because I had lost a lot of blood. I was told the baby was ready and I had to breastfeed her. It was my first time to breastfeed and it felt like the baby was tickling me. I was told I had to breastfeed her to get more milk to come out.'

'I started playing football again when the baby was three months old. Sometimes I would go with my baby for practice because she was very good, she wouldn't disturb me. I was then invited for football coach training in Nairobi and I had to leave the baby in Kilifi. I left her with my mum. My mum knew I was now happy because I was playing football again. Now that my baby is older I have to think of many things. She doesn't just need food, she also needs clothes and her education. So life is good and also bad at times but I want to thank God for giving me a child. I might not get married but I know I already have a baby. The baby may help me in future. I'll teach her about what life is like so she knows more than I did.'

❖ ❖ ❖

Teenage mother 3, Salma Ali: Struggles in love and life

'My dad passed away when I was 17. After that I stopped going to school because we didn't have money for fees. I met my boyfriend when he used to buy fish from me. Our home was near one of the bars that he used to go to and I used to cook and sell fish near that bar. He wasn't from Kilifi. He was a Luo[58] from Kinango and he worked on ships going to Saudi Arabia. One time the ship dropped them in Kilifi and that was when we met. He then went to work in Mombasa at the port. He became my boyfriend. I found out I was pregnant when I missed my period. When I told him he said I should go for a check-up to see if I was pregnant. I was 19 at that time. When I was six months pregnant he told me that his boss had transferred him to work in Saudi Arabia for three years. He told me he would send money to his mum who would send it on to me. He did send the money but after a while he stopped.

'My mum was working as a cleaner at the district hospital. She really helped me with my first child. I found a job as a waitress and I told my mum to stop working, that I should be the one to work. So she stayed at home and looked after my son and I worked. So we continued like that but unfortunately my mum suffered from TB and she passed away. She used to cook and sell fish and the smoke from cooking over a fire had affected her. My baby was one year old when my mum died.'

Salma has an older brother and five younger brothers. One younger brother is married and her uncle managed to get places for all four of her other brothers in an orphan support programme where they are given three meals every day and supported to attend school. Salma got a new job in a small factory that processed cashew nuts while her aunt or her sister-in-law looked after her baby.

It was at this point that she found out about MTG and joined up, playing football every Saturday. She began to sell charcoal, going round to local hoteli asking for orders. Together, her brother and Salma managed to buy a small plot of land and build a mud house. Her brother moved into the house while Salma rented a room in Kilifi town.

She had moved close to another bar, and she got to know the bar owner's son: 'We started to talk, I explained my background to him and he became my boyfriend. He told me he would help me look after my son. There was a time when my son had an accident. His foot was run over by a car. This boyfriend of mine supported us all the time we were in the hospital.

'We stayed together. We were using protection; I had an injection, the one for every three months and we used condoms too. I was losing weight using the injectables so I decided to stop. After some time we agreed to stop using condoms. Later, I got pregnant. Then his mum and his aunt told him he shouldn't be with a girl from Kilifi because girls from Kilifi have bad behaviour. His aunt told him if he stayed with me he should leave their house.

'When I went into labour he came to take me to the hospital. We were with my aunt and on the way to the hospital she told him, "She is going to give birth before we even get to the hospital, let's go back to the house." I was taken back home in the car he used for work. When I reached home I gave birth. Later on my boyfriend told me to go to their home but his mum told me to leave him alone. He doesn't give me money any more so it's like we are separated. My aunt, who works at the survey office, helps me to pay rent.

'I loved him very much because he had taken care of my first son. But he changed his mind later. I think his mum forced him to do that. She told him I was no good for him.'

Lilian, Janet and Salma provide a snapshot of the differing experiences of single mothers in Kilifi. All three have been trained as peer educators by MTG and Lilian is one of MTG's 20 counsellors, who were trained to certificate level by the Kenya Association of Professional Counsellors. Here I gave them a chance to give a small piece of advice to other young girls:

Lilian, Janet and Salma: Advice to girls

I would advise girls that getting pregnant is not the end of their life, so they should not abort the pregnancy. They should look for experienced people to advise them. To avoid pregnancy they should abstain from sex, but if they can't then they should use condoms. The boy, if he understands, will agree to use a condom.

Lilian

I would tell them to abstain but if they can't and they do get pregnant, do not abort. The baby will teach you a lesson that you will never repeat. You can always agree with your mum to care for the baby and you go back to school.

Janet

I would advise girls to stay with a boy for at least two to three years. We used protection but then it reached a time when we decided not to because, if I got pregnant, he said he was ready to take care of the baby. But in reality he wasn't ready. You should get to know his behaviour and also get to know the parents well.

Salma

9

Kenya, women's world champions in 2019? Our hopes, dreams and aspirations

KADZO: *You, Sarah, you've changed… because you now have two children.*
JANET: *And you've become old.*
ASYA: *And you've got grandchildren now.*
SARAH: *You've started giving me grandchildren?*
ASYA: *And you will get another one, I can see it coming …*

There were seven of us, six girls and myself, sitting around a square table in the meeting room at Chambai. Looking out of the rusted louvre windows that had been battered by the salt-laden sea breeze, I could see the calm Indian Ocean, low tide, shallow over rock pools where three young boys were fishing with homemade rods. I'd been looking at them for quite some time, drifting away amidst the silence that had greeted my question. I'd just asked how we all thought we'd changed over the last two years. It wasn't an easy question to answer with just a few seconds to think, and I was trying to think of how I could probe them further. Luckily Kadzo broke the silence. She'd focused on the change in me, and the change in me as a mother.

I had two children, having given birth to my second daughter in March 2006. Her observation made us all laugh and set the agenda on where we'd go with this question. Janet pointed out that I was now old. We laughed again as Asya said I had grandchildren. It took me a second to work out what she was implying—that I was their mother and now a grandmother to their children. It was interesting that our reproductive role as women was the focus, that was how you could see real change—a new baby, something significant, a landmark in the life of a woman. Having children was something they all, unreservedly, aspired to do.

They were playing with both facts and their own imaginations, to make each other laugh. They were teasing me that I was a mother to all of them. I couldn't be their friend. I was too old, but through this work we'd become close and I'd been told things about their lives that they might never have told anyone else. I hadn't seen myself as a mother figure to them. I hoped maybe I was more of an older sister. Here we were joking that their children, who were pretty much the same age as my own children, were my grandchildren. I'd thought a lot about it, and it made me reflect again on what I was to them, what they were to me. I wondered what being a part of this 'life stories' thing really meant to us all?

In November 2005 I started talking to nine girls, who were all in school. I doubted that I would still be in contact with all nine by the end of the project. Surely one or two would drop out, maybe because they weren't enjoying it, they weren't interested any more or they just didn't want to do it. Every time I went to see each of the girls we would talk about whether we would meet up again. I gave them the option to stop, but none said they wanted to. Mercy once told me she wanted to continue with the interviews 'because I tell you things I don't tell anyone else'. Mercy, the girl who said so little, saw me as someone she could discuss secret things with. It made me realise that the first time she released those tiny snippets of information about her parents and their problems she must have felt that she was offloading an enormous, heavy burden.

Others said they had learnt things during our talks. I'd tried to let the girls talk, let them lead the conversation, not teach them anything, not during the interviews anyway. I remember one time when Kanze was trying to explain to me what she knew about the menstrual cycle, ending up in a confused mess of day counting, miscalculation about 'safe days' and with her telling me that ovulation took place during menstruation. I told her we could discuss it in detail after the interview, which we did, with me drawing the menstrual cycle and explaining it, slowly and carefully. I wanted our chats to flow. I corrected things that they may have said that were factually wrong only after we had stopped talking. By being given a chance to talk, a chance to air their stories, their experiences, the girls were benefiting from adult support outside of their family that they wouldn't necessarily have had otherwise. I was a trusted ear who would listen to their problems, their dilemmas, let them ask questions and expose their confusions, and I wouldn't judge their decisions. Although they said that they learnt a lot, it was more that they were given a chance to talk about what they thought and knew. They often posed questions about their own dilemmas that they ended up answering themselves.

❖   ❖   ❖

By 2005 I had been in Kilifi for over four years. I'd got used to finding out very little about people from what they said. When meeting people I had always wanted answers, information, detail, clarification, which I rarely got. Instead my enquiries would be met by silence, one-word answers, ambiguity.

I remember a discussion I had with Collins about this. I told him about my frustrations at how little people would talk to me. It was early on, when I was fresh from the UK, I couldn't speak Kiswahili and I was desperate to get this MTG project up and running fast. I asked him why people were so miserly with their words, so unwilling to open up and tell me what they thought. Instead of giving me the nice, succinct explanation I was looking for, his vague response further confused and frustrated me. He said that words were not the only way through which people communicate, to which I responded angrily that I wasn't a mind reader. End of conversation.

But it did make me reflect. I played with what he had said in my mind for a long time. It brought an about-turn in how I interacted with people. I stopped searching and digging and started looking and listening; I became more introspective and less arrogant that what I saw and my observation and interpretation of it was right. Having grown up in a middle-class British family I'd been conditioned to look for solutions, answers, to find the best way to do things and to have the confidence that I was the one who could fix it. I realised that if I was going to work effectively here I had to be much more aware of how people interpreted me and how I was interpreting them. More often than not, I didn't have the answer.

I'd previously never been a fan of silence in public places. I had always thought that if people weren't talking in a bar or a restaurant or a café there was no point in them being out and about with their friends. Spending time in Kilifi completely changed that. I still find it difficult to sit in silence myself, much to the exasperation of my husband. But if I see others doing it I look at them and think how nice that must be, to sit with a friend or a partner and be happy to sit and think your own thoughts in the company of others. How comfortable you must feel to be able to do that.

But I still needed to have an explanation for the cagey, detail-free, frustrating interactions I sometimes had. This made sense, that in this culture, communication was a whole different ball game. This and many other episodes in Kenya have taught me to be so much less dogmatic. I've realised that living somewhere as an outsider requires a humility that rubbed against my upbringing in the UK. I had developed a confidence in myself, my views, my ideas and my way of doing things that I took to be universal and applicable wherever I might be. Coming to Kilifi turned that on its head and made me question everything I thought and did—a painful and trying process, but one that, I hope, has made me more understanding, less sure that my way is always the right way and more able to listen to the views of others.

I'd had sneak previews into the lives of girls in Kilifi through working with MTG, snatched conversations at football practice, before meetings, in a vehicle on the way to a school, to a match. Many conversations were often more like me asking lots of questions and getting stock answers—what you should tell an adult, not revealing what was really going on in their lives. But the interviews with these nine girls opened up a new world to me of truths, half-truths and lies, of experiences and thoughts of teenage rural girls. Some of them kept up the veneer of a 'good Kilifi girl' who worked hard in school, didn't act on her sexual feelings, was making sure she finished school before thinking about getting involved with any boys. That some wanted me to see them as virtuous virgins reveals much about the pressures they felt from their families, their teachers and their friends. Others, though, shed any skin of shyness they might have had and exposed complex lives juggling responsibilities with ambitions and realities of what they might achieve in their lives.

Both approaches from the girls taught me about teenage girls' lives in Kilifi. I relished their latest instalments, which were at times breathlessly exciting, stupidly funny, boringly mundane or depressingly sad. Slowly we got to know each other. We had shared things about our lives, and I'd been given access through their stories to their lives. This had a massive and unexpected effect on me.

It's difficult, from a position of immense material and educational privilege, to be empathetic rather than sympathetic towards the girls and some of the stories they told me. Things sometimes look so bad that you can't see how they are going to cope, survive and move forward. There was a time when I was struggling to continue with the interviews. I'd been overcome by a feeling of despair but I couldn't put my finger on exactly why. By that time we had met twice. I knew quite a lot about their family situations that were so severely affected by poverty, illness and death. I felt heavy at the thought of all the balancing girls had to do: school, domestic work, farmwork, tradition, religion, before they had even started on puberty, menstruation and their sexual feelings and desires. I couldn't stop thinking about Carol and how her father had told her, when her mother had died of AIDS, that she should now go and find her real father because he was not her dad. Carol's resilience, her ability to deal with what he was saying, the concrete steps she was taking to finish her primary education were both depressing and inspiring. We knew each other a bit, we had built up trust but we were still relatively new to one another. What the girls were saying was shocking me, depressing me, yet they were just talking to me about their homes, their families, their schools. Should I really have been that surprised? Shouldn't I already have known about all this? It's easy to know the facts and figures about poverty in Kilifi but now I was getting an insight into the real stories, the people behind the figures, their lives and their challenges.

I don't think I'll ever stop being taken aback by some of the things I hear, things that are normal for girls in Kilifi, that they hide from older people but discuss among their friends. Just recently I was with four staff members on our way in my car to football practice. We'd taken the long dirt road behind our office and just passed the home of some girls from MTG. I stopped outside a small video den so that one of the girls could rush to her home to get her football kit. It was around 4 o'clock. Children were coming home from school. Fish were being fried at the side of the road, *sukuma wiki* (a leafy green vegetable like kale), shredded and stuffed into small plastic bags to be sold for 10 bob for an evening meal.

We commented on how the UEFA Champions League match between Liverpool and Inter Milan would be shown in the video den later. I wasn't a fan of either team and noticed that it would cost 20 bob to go in to watch. One girl on the back seat of the car then said, 'Did you see Halima just back there?' Halima was a very good young footballer but neither of her parents had ever been very supportive of her playing. Her mother sold mnazi, and drank a fair bit of it too, as did her dad. The mother had a temper that was legendary in that area and was often the butt of jokes told by the girls from around. I'd never heard anyone say a good word about either of them and remember a story of a stormy argument about a fish and a stolen 20 shillings that one girl retold one day as we were getting ready to play at the field. It was a story that was both hilarious and sad, spiced up in the retelling with impressions and actions of this ranting, fiery woman with a bottle of mnazi in one hand and a fish in the other, looking for her lost 20 bob.

The conversation about Halima continued, 'She's not at school these days.' Another girl said, 'She's married', and then, 'No she's not married, she's just, you know, living with a man.' 'She's pregnant', and someone asked quietly, 'What, again?'

There was silence. No one wanted to reply in the affirmative that she'd been pregnant before. It was as if they felt they had said too much, allowed me to hear too much, to hear things they didn't want me to know. I wanted to pretend that I wasn't shocked, that I also thought it was normal that Halima, at 14, was pregnant again. From the discussion in the car I'd found out she wasn't in school. She was pregnant, she'd previously been pregnant but hadn't given birth, and she was living with a man.

But all this wasn't what had surprised the girls. What they couldn't understand was what she was doing back in this area, where her parents lived. She had moved to be with the man, to have his child, so what was she doing back here, in her parents' home; what might have happened now?

I did take a break from the interviews, which conveniently coincided with my maternity leave. Looking back at our first two meetings, this was where we got to know and adjust to each other and settle into a rhythm. The girls now knew me and the kind of things we would discuss. When I went to meet the girls after that long break I realised that we had built something up, we had begun to develop relationships. I was more ready for what they might say, more relaxed. I got a sense that they began to look forward to our chats, that it gave them a chance to talk and let off steam. What I also realised was that we laughed more. They talked more about the everyday, the ordinary, the funny, small incidents, the slapstick humour. It took me back, too, to my teenage years and reminded me of my experiences, my decisions and the connectivity that we had, the universality of puberty and all its associated excitement, thrills, disappointments and dilemmas. By the time we met up that December in Chambai I looked forward to seeing them, with all their idiosyncrasies.

During the group discussion in the final meeting I had

spectacularly failed to get them to look and talk about how they might have changed over the last two years. They had focused on me. It had become a big joke. I wasn't sure it was the right forum to try to delve again, to try to get them to analyse themselves. I left it, but as we were coming to the end of the project I wanted to get a better idea of their aspirations for the future, in education and work and also their relationships. I wanted to get a sense of how they saw their choices. They were making choices: Janet was determined to stay in school, finish her secondary education and had not allowed her dad's lack of financial support and disagreements with her mother and stepfather to get in the way. Asya weighed up her options before getting married, as did Carol. Choices were limited, but they still made choices that could both expand and contract their aspirations.

Kanze had turned up to the meeting wearing a beautiful and stylish cotton dress, blue with red and yellow swirling patterns and intricate ribbon trimmings around circles on the neckline, which she later proudly told me was called 'binding'. She had made the dress herself, a complicated and fashionable design, that wouldn't have escaped the notice of the other girls. She was still quiet and shy in the group but she looked much more confident. When we sat, just the two of us, she spoke with such clarity, like a girl who knew what direction her life was going in. She had finished primary school and was now living with her brother in Malindi, who was supporting her to study at a tailoring college. This was the brother who had come with her to the previous MTG meeting earlier in the year, a man who was not just supporting Kanze financially but also providing her with guidance and advice. I had really liked him and could see that under his wing Kanze had a chance to gain a skill that would give her some independence. She told me, 'I'm at a tailoring college. I like it. I like the teachers there. When I get home at around 1 pm I get a good chance to study. Then, you know, there are other young people around who like playing football. There's a girl who wants me to teach her how to play. We practise there at home or we go to the field to play every day.

'I will do everything I can to be independent. I will buy myself a machine and finish my training so I know that if I get married and then maybe we divorce, I will be OK. There are others who buy a machine or maybe rent a machine for themselves and work from home. Even if she has to depend on the husband, she will not be completely dependent on him. He can go to work and maybe he doesn't get paid until the end of the month and at home there's no food. If the wife has a sewing machine, I know you can get money every day, that's why I like it. When I finish college I will go back to my rural home. I will buy the machine and I will go home and open a workplace at home so I can help myself.'

Kanze's ambitions were completely within reach and she was being helped to realise her goals by her older brother. It looked to me that his influence in her life was central to whether she would achieve that longed-for independence.

While she'd been in school she said she knew the family didn't have money for secondary school for her. But she had still hoped she would go, or she would look for a job, 'any job, anywhere' if she didn't continue with her education. Since moving to Malindi she had become more driven and focused in what she wanted. She wanted to be working, making money, being independent, before thinking about marriage. In a husband she wanted just two things: for him to have a job and to be understanding. 'I mean, the way to look for a husband, he should be working. He should be kind when maybe I have problems. I mean, the issue of understanding each other. It shouldn't be like you are together then you disagree every day. That's not good.'

Kadzo was still in primary school and unclear about her chances of going to secondary. Her priority, though, was to help her parents: 'I speak through my heart. Why don't I complete school and get a job so that I help my parents? Now I see they are suffering. They're sick and neither of them works.' She said she wanted to be a doctor and was expecting more advice from school when she went into Standard 8 next year. While getting a job was her number one aim she said that getting married was also a must.

When I asked her what kind of husband she wanted she came back to the neighbours who had become such an influence in her life: 'I have a good example, our neighbours. Her husband is very good. He will go to work but when it reaches 8 o'clock he is home. He doesn't take his food at a hoteli; he wants to have his food at home every day. Now when he reaches home he tells his wife, "Let me teach you to drive." She didn't know how to drive. He taught her slowly until she knew how to drive. He tells her, "Say what you want and I will do it for you." Actually, he loves her. She told him I want you to open a shop for me and he opened a shop for her. If I get a husband like this, won't we develop our lives well? Because if I tell him I want to help my home, my parents, he will accept because we will both work. Now he will have to tell you OK, take some money and help your family, and some we shall use here. So life will be good like that.'

Both Carol and Asya, as young married women, had more difficulty in looking ahead. Asya seemed to be living day to day, trying to work out what married life was really like. Her husband had a level of control over her and she wasn't quite sure how things would work out because the marriage was too young. When I asked her about maybe looking for work she said, 'Now this thing of work, I can say I want to, but my husband may not want that. According to my heart I might want to, but for him he could say what is the job for? What work is it anyway? But I will reason like this: He might come back from Kakamega [the town in western Kenya where he works] today or maybe not until next year in August. What will I do in between? If I have no money I will have to work so I can get money.'

Remember that Carol was eight months pregnant when I asked her about what she wanted in her life. I couldn't have expected her to think any further ahead than the birth of her child but it was worth a try. I had never known her to be tongue-tied before but this time she was stuck. There was nothing I could do to get any more than this out of her, when I asked her about her aspirations, about her life in the future: 'That's a difficult question, I mean, I don't know what to say. Now I'm married, I don't know what to say. ...' No elaboration, no detail, she just didn't have anything to say.

By this time Mercy, Janet and Salma were all in secondary school. Salma had told me she wanted to be a TV or radio broadcaster or a nurse. I could imagine her in the media. She was a confident young woman, she was her form leader in school and she had a way with words when retelling stories. She'd be great on radio, but I wondered if she knew how much hard work was needed to turn the dream into reality. Who could advise her? Who could provide that lucky break? So much would depend on things she didn't know. I hoped that she might have a teacher at school who would help her out.

Janet told me boldly that she wanted to be a 'mass communicator' or a doctor. I wondered what she meant by a 'mass communicator'. She answered that she wanted to work with wires and mobile phones, that there were opportunities there. The doctor ambition, I worked out, had come from her dad, when he'd advised her on what subjects to take in Form 3. It seemed quite typical that parents would have ambitions for their children, ambitions that might not necessarily correspond to their talents or capabilities.

Mercy had her heart set on the army, something she'd looked into and been advised on by a teacher. She also wanted a good, Christian husband. She said: 'I don't know what work I will do. It depends on the grade I get but I want to be a soldier. The teacher told us to work hard. If a person needs that job, they need to work hard to get a good grade. If you look for a job with the school certificate to show you have finished secondary school, you can easily get a job. You need, let's say like a B– to get a job. When I think of a husband, he needs to have a job, his behaviour, yes, his behaviour. The place he is living, it should be nice, and those people he lives with must also have good manners, good behaviour. For example let's say they should be Christians, they should not be drunkards, they should not drink.'

Juliet's ambitions were so grounded in her reality as a 17-year-old rural girl from a poor family with one parent, struggling her way through primary school, twice repeating years because she had failed the exams. Her mum worked away so she was the head of the household most of the time, responsible for feeding and looking after her younger siblings. With limited horizons she had limited ambitions: 'About my future, I don't know. If I look at my mum, she can't pay school fees for secondary school. Maybe if I finish primary school I can maybe get a sponsor or just get someone to give me work, any work, I don't know which work I could get.

'The issue of getting married—I haven't yet thought about it. But if you ask me about a husband, I'd want a husband who has work, who would be able to help me, maybe even to take me to college so that I would be able to help myself. I'd want him to be faithful to me, know about my problems. And I should know about his problems. I should be able to tell him anything and he will understand me.'

All the girls' aspirations were impressively realistic. There was no wild ambition that might never be achieved, just possible scenarios that they hoped to realise. They were not asking for much, a bit of independence here, an understanding husband there. And for me, that's the crux of it. Girls in Kilifi might not have very high expectations because they know and understand the environment in which they're growing up. They've played it out, they have a good idea of the possibilities.

Those limited horizons got me thinking about MTG and my aspirations, and the aspirations of others for the organisation. In the beginning, when I first came to Kenya, MTG was pretty much just about my hopes and ambitions. There was a supportive committee in the UK that was hoping the project would work and a few football coaches, players and friends in Kilifi who had some expectation. But at that point whether MTG sank or swam depended on me. While I was still in the UK, just before coming to Kenya, I didn't exactly feel the burden but I did get tired of being asked, 'So what will you do if or when it doesn't work?' I didn't see that as feasible; it wasn't going to fail. Quite what the 'it' was, was still open to interpretation: 'an innovative pilot programme' or 'an irrelevant waste of money', depending on where you sat. Thanks to a programme officer at the British Council in Nairobi who liked football, we got £3,000 to kick-start MTG. Fast forward through seven years, struggling for funding, support and recognition, and MTG is now a small but established community-based programme with ten staff members that reaches out to close to 3,000 girls who play football in the district.

❖ ❖ ❖

Mbeyu's selection to represent Kenya at the Youth Conference at the All Africa Games in Algiers, Algeria, in 2007 reaped unexpected dividends for her family. Her mum explains how her daughter came back with more than just memories of North Africa.

Mama Mbeyu: What use is football to girls?

Mbeyu was given an allowance in Algiers. That money helped us so much. It was almost 150,000 Kenya shillings [US$2,240]. My dear, I'm telling you, this money, we got electricity connected to the house, we connected water, we bought a TV and a DVD player. I told her, this money that remains will help you go to Form 1, to secondary school. She told me, 'Mummy, that money is not for sending me to school, it's for you to do with it what you want. The money for me to go school, I know you have it or have you not been planning for me to go to secondary school?' So, Sarah Forde, if you come to my house, the lights will be on, you can watch TV and a DVD. So imagine if I'd kept Mbeyu in the house, not allowed her to go because she was doing her KCPE exams that year? But she went and she came back and did her exams and she passed better than many who didn't go to Algeria. So this thing, it was planned by God, not by people. So we were happy. If I say the truth, if it wasn't for MTG, there would be no profit from her talent.

Mbeyu's story is important for MTG. For a start, she's getting national and international recognition as an excellent young player, but also for the organisation, because without MTG, Mbeyu would not have had such opportunities to showcase her talent. She wouldn't have played in Nairobi, Mombasa and all the other places she has been where people have been entertained by her footballing skills. MTG opened doors for her in football and in accessing information on reproductive health, HIV and AIDS, and child rights. She's now a trained coach and leads some of the best training sessions in MTG. She commands respect from other players and adults, who are amazed by her ability to talk with confidence and show that girls in Kilifi have the potential to become effective leaders. Importantly, her family has also benefitted from her talent. Not only did Mbeyu's trip to Algiers open her eyes to a different world but it brought back a financial windfall that has developed her family's home in ways they could have only dreamt of before.

But what next, what are the organisation's aspirations? It's no longer just about my aspirations, but also about those of everyone in the organisation: our management board, staff members, peer educators, referees, coaches, first aiders and players. Aspirations differ within the organisation, depending on where you are. Listening to all aspirations, giving them the consideration they deserve has made MTG the organisation it is, rooted in the community in which it works. In 2007 we held a number of discussions and meetings on our expectations as part of the development of the next strategic plan. Interestingly the girls' hopes focus on four main areas.

The first was materials, equipment and assets. Girls wanted vehicles, motorbikes for staff and a bus for teams with, of course, a girl driver. This would partly deal with one of our main challenges of getting around in such an enormous rural district. They wanted football boots, football kit and, most importantly, our own pitch. Currently MTG begs to use the fields of schools and other institutions. When sharing football fields with boys and men the negotiations can become quite heated. Despite our best efforts a group of teenage girls will still find it very difficult to stand their ground to use the field ahead of a group of around 20 older men.

The second hope was for recognition, wanting people to know about MTG, with MTG participating in football tournaments outside Kenya.

But the bottom line was money. Their third and fourth hopes were for money for individuals and money for the organisation: MTG should help girls find employment and start businesses, MTG should provide sanitary pads at a reduced price. These are sensible, realistic hopes articulated by rural girls searching for a way out of poverty. They wanted MTG to be much more self-reliant, with its own headquarters in Kilifi town and offices in the divisions.

The board members, meanwhile, mentioned three main aspirations. Again recognition, that MTG should be better known for its work. Their second focus was education, that MTG could do more about keeping girls in school for longer. Third, they wanted sustainability and a diverse funding base.

While the board consists of professional women and one man and most players and volunteers are teenagers and young women from disadvantaged backgrounds, their views and visions for the organisation are not so far apart. When their hopes were discussed at a joint meeting of board, staff and volunteers, it was clear that these aspirations were not so significantly different. They collided, they merged, they were discussed and debated and finally linked together, locating our hopes closer to each other than it might, at first, have seemed. Board members suggested that in five years MTG should be the leading African girls' football programme and the leading African girls' social programme—big ambitions for a small project.

The girls hopes focused more on *how* this might be achieved, the process of achieving this: by exporting coaches and providing the national coach of the Kenyan women's football team, developing a profit-making activity, playing in tournaments outside Kenya.

Not only did girls want MTG to be famous, they wanted it to be able to pay its players in the MTG United select team. This may seem an unrealistic aim, but in Kenya sports people have often been employed by companies or by the government. You'll find that many of the best international Kenyan athletes are in the police force or in the army. Within their job they're given time off to play, for example, volleyball for the company team, or to go and represent Kenya in athletics. In the Mathare Youth Sports Association their Mathare United men's and women's teams get some payment. In return they play and they are active in their community development programmes, as HIV and AIDS peer educators or in environmental clean-ups of the slum. That way your top players can put food on the table at home and also become role models to younger players.

As for me, what do I want for MTG? Of course I want it to grow, I want it to be known, but what do I want it to be known for? The issues girls face in Kilifi are more complex than I ever imagined. One slip-up can knock you back, take the wind out of your sails, just when you thought you were on the right track. Things can look OK from the outside. School goes some way to protecting you from the harsh realities of rural life in Kenya. But one event over which, more often than not, you have no control can disrupt the life of any individual. The death of a parent, a lost job, a failed harvest, illness in the family, inflation, price rises, all can exert too great a pressure on families and can snuff out the hopes of the most promising girls. Or when you get your period you start missing days of school. Your periods are heavy, painful, you can't afford pads, you're frequently absent and your performance in class starts to deteriorate. In the end, you stop going to school.

I'm cautious about what MTG can achieve when there are so many other factors that affect the lives of girls. It is a small development project. But I'd like to see it stick to its core principle of girls' participation as it grows, employing girls from Kilifi if possible, building their skills and building a collective power that can give young rural women a voice so they can participate more actively in development in their community and in Kenya.

I want Mbeyu and other girls from Kilifi to play for Kenya in the Women's World Cup finals in 2019. Mbeyu will be 26 then and in her prime in football. It may seem a ridiculous idea, but it's possible, if the political will is there to get national structures in place to seriously develop women's football in Kenya. The talent is there.

I want our peer education programme to become a stronger social support network, to give girls the peers with whom they can talk, who have relevant information and knowledge to share. I want us to have a football academy at a girls' secondary school in the district, known for its football and academic excellence.

I have many other wishes, but my last is that MTG successfully develops the production and marketing of sanitary pads, made from local materials as a social enterprise, so that girls can have a bit more dignity when they menstruate, young women can be employed and the organisation can put its profit back into funding activities. This will be a whole new venture and may take a long time to get off the ground but it could, ultimately, be one of our most effective: responding to a felt need, providing jobs and improving sustainability.

Afterword:
Adjusting our tactics

My objective with this book is to improve the general understanding of the sexual and reproductive health experiences and needs of rural girls. All too often policy and programmes are developed and implemented without being grounded enough in the real-life context and experiences of the recipients. What I wanted to do was use the experience of living in a rural coastal village and working for a number of years with young women to shed some light on their complex lives.

Essentially this book has been about listening to stories and retelling them to an audience that might not speak Kiswahili and is unlikely to have the time or access to listen to the intimate stories that girls tell. It has been a deliberately subversive project. Plummer says that 'stories become more and more likely to challenge authorities and eclipse one standard telling.... Once stories become more self-conscious, recursive, and are told to distinctive audiences, then the stories from on high are seen to be artefactual. The foundation collapses, and authoritarian stories are only one amongst many.'[59] It is my sincere hope that these stories challenge adults, decision makers and those working in policy to consider what these young women are saying about their own lives and how they see their own experiences, options and choices.

In reflecting on what I've heard and learnt, I realise that many issues stand out for me as ones that deserve a second look by policy makers or service deliverers concerned with enabling young women to reach their full potential. Many are beyond the scope of my expertise, but they include a cluster of issues that make school particularly difficult, such as the medium of instruction being English, which for most of the girls in this study was their third language; such as the effect of a flexible policy that allows the repetition of years in school if a student 'fails' a year—which I can't help feeling has few benefits for a young, learning adolescent.

The tales of the burden of domestic work on the shoulders of rural girls in Africa don't come as a surprise. It's a universally recognised reality. But the domestic role that they fill, and the added weight of engaging in informal work to contribute to the family income, reduces the amount of time they have to concentrate on schoolwork and ultimately their chances of excelling. It does a very good job of sustaining gender inequality.

Interesting is the mix of Islam, Christianity and traditional religions in Kilifi and the girls' balancing acts in dipping in and out of one, two or all of them, and how ultimately they use religion as a source of hope, inspiration and entertainment.

These girls face internal struggles in adolescence—how to deal with menstruation, their own feelings of desire, advances from men and boys, and the over-riding fear of exploring their own sexuality because of the chances of an unintended pregnancy or HIV infection.

Four main policy issues could do with more creative thinking and action in Kenya: 1) menstruation and its impact on school and sexuality, 2) the relationship between school and sexual activity, pregnancy and abortion, 3) the fluidity of family situations, 4) alternatives to secondary education such as vocational careers and sports.

I don't have answers to these complicated issues, and I fully appreciate that many individuals and organisations are taking them on. But in drawing this book to conclusion, I want to bring out more clearly some of the things that this project has made me think about in relation to each of them. They are offered in the spirit of partnership, recognising that complex problems do not have silver-bullet solutions, but that the starting point to solving something is understanding it more fully.

Much has been written about the effect of menstruation on the education of girls, less so about its effect on their sexual activity. Toilets in school are not adequate. This is a national problem, as Elimu Yetu Coalition's work in Nairobi confirms: 'In Kibera[60] some of the girls' toilets had no doors. The facilities were dirty and faced the front of the school. Girls felt embarrassed to use these toilets.'[61] Kadzo and Mercy told me how they missed days off school because of their periods and others elaborated on the ways in which they managed their flow, with cloth, cotton wool or, if they could find enough money, sanitary pads.

In Kenya the Girl Child Network, an NGO in Nairobi, and UNICEF have spearheaded campaigns to make sanitary pads available to girls in school, to keep them in school. These have done much to highlight the issue but a national strategy is needed that ensures that *all* girls who go to school will have access to sanitary pads and adequate toilet facilities. Isn't such a strategy as essential for keeping girls in school as the feeding programmes in many schools in Kenya? Whether these pads should be free or subsidised needs further deliberation. They need to be affordable, but what is affordable? Thirty shillings (US$0.45) for a packet of 10 was the figure mentioned most often in MTG's feasibility study on producing sanitary pads as a price rural girls could afford. How to dispose of pads is a real issue, particularly in rural areas and urban slum areas, where toilets are in short supply. Incinerators could be installed in all schools, but girls are not in school all the time so what do they do with the pads when they are at home? Throw them in the bush? The priorities are to make pads affordable, provide adequate toilet facilities in schools and ensure girls can dispose of the pads in an environmentally sustainable way.

What I found surprising and a little shocking from the conversations I had was that there seemed to be a direct link between not being able to afford sanitary pads and a girl's sexual activity. Mama Mbeyu, the girls at the football camp in Chumani and Juliet all mentioned scenarios where girls would have sex to get money to pay for pads. It was something I'd heard anecdotally on other occasions. It was told to me here with a complete lack of drama—it's just something that happens, another coping strategy for girls. It's a rural reality, as is the likely follow-on pattern: unintended pregnancy, then abortion or early motherhood. The implication for the reproductive health and well-being of young women is massive and gives further weight to the urgent need for a national plan to ensure young girls and women can deal with menstruation without putting themselves at unnecessary risk.

❖ ❖ ❖

Education for all is an MDG and a national goal. Free Primary Education, introduced in 2003, and Free Secondary Education, launched in 2008, are evidence of the government's commitment to making education more widely available. In the family too, it often has high priority. When Lilian became pregnant while in secondary school, her family did all they could to make sure she returned to school and finished her education. She missed just one term of her second year to have the baby. But for others it is more complex; there is a national policy for re-admittance of young mothers but it's weak because of social factors that affect girls. As Mr Katana mentioned, stigma is still attached to being in school while being a mother. A young mother will need to find someone who can look after her baby while she is in school. So, if it's not easy to enforce the policy, what are the alternatives? Are there vocational alternatives? Or schools specifically for young mothers? If we don't look at workable alternatives the policy won't stand for much and the majority of school-going girls who get pregnant will continue to see their education ended by the pregnancy.

This battle of education versus sexual activity haunts girls. If they do accidently get pregnant, the options seem simple—have the baby, education over or abort and continue in school. Their long, detailed, normalised stories of strategies employed by friends and sisters when confronted with an unintended pregnancy caught me unawares. Too many women's lives are put at risk by their attempts to procure illegal abortions. The Reproductive Health and Rights Bill 2008 drafted by FIDA (Federation of Women Lawyers) and COVAW (Coalition on Violence against Women) has further stirred the heat of debate around abortion in Kenya. Abortion disproportionately affects women under the age of 25, women like the ones in this book. Therefore, in such debates we should hear their voices loud and clear, not just the polarising noise of politicians, religious leaders and pro-choice campaigners.

❖ ❖ ❖

Sex for young people in this rural setting is just that—full penetrative sex, snatched moments in the bushes or behind a shop. So what implication does this have for policy? How can girls and boys explore their sexuality safely? We need to peel back our fear and not see teenage sexuality as an enormous uncontrollable beast that needs to be bashed into abstinence. That approach doesn't work, and young girls and boys are putting themselves at risk. We need to confront the issues. Girls and boys need to learn about points at which they should stop, to negotiate these stopping points so that it's not always full penetrative sex, so that they can develop relationships in which girls do not get pregnant before they want to get pregnant, so that girls have some control over their reproductive health. At the moment their options are abstinence or condoms.

Juliet and Carol both talked about using condoms and said it was their boyfriends who initiated the protection. Research carried out by Family Health International in Coast Province found there was evidence to suggest that young people are more likely than older people to use condoms.[62] Condoms might be more effective among the younger generation, who have grown up with HIV and AIDS around them and may be less encumbered with entrenched ideas about what is acceptable sexual behaviour. Could these small signs of progress be built on? Could there be a more sustained approach to promoting safe sex among young people as part of a wider reproductive health and HIV programme?

While the girls had knowledge of HIV and AIDS they rarely related it to their own sexual activity. This calls for HIV information to be more integrated into general reproductive health services. It is just one of many sexual and reproductive health issues young women face—menstruation, puberty, relationships, knowing your body, experimenting with sex, safe sex, pregnancy, abortion, STIs.

How young people find out about all these issues needs a more holistic approach both in and out of schools.

The problems girls face in Kilifi are not just about poverty. The nine girls were all from Kilifi District, all between 14 and 16 years old and in school when we started, and from the same socio-economic background. But their experiences of poverty were diverse and complex, illustrated by where they all were at the end of 2007, aged 16 to 18. Salma and Mercy were sponsored in a boarding secondary school; Janet was with her brother, studying at secondary; Kadzo and Juliet were still at home and in primary school; Asya and Carol were both living in their husband's homes; Kanze was at tailoring college, staying with her brother in town; and Mariam had just finished primary school and was living on her own. This provides a significant problem as to where to target initiatives. To educational or training institutions? To health facilities? The mass media? Hotlines? Traditional healers? The family? Whom would you target in that family? Grandparents, parents, older siblings? How many rural girls will slip through the net?

It is recognised in the 'Adolescent reproductive health and development policy'[63] that families are changing. We know that close to 80% of young Kenyans do not go to secondary school, so what other channels can we use? Rani and Lule in looking at demographic and health survey data for 12 developing countries, including Kenya, concluded that 'poor adolescents may be overlooked by current service delivery modes that rely on mass media, clinics or schools. Alternative strategies, such as community-based outreach programs must be implemented to serve the needs of poor young women.'[64] Hotlines don't go far beyond Nairobi, yet 90% of Kenya's population live outside the capital city. Community-based approaches that rely on well-trained individuals can be much more effective in reaching out in rural areas. We need creativity, innovation and multifaceted approaches in getting to *all* young people. Since 2007, MTG has run a programme, funded by APHIA II Coast, specifically aimed at out-of-school girls aged 15 to 24, a notoriously difficult group to reach. It mixes football and health peer education at MTG's football fields and beyond, where peer educators can impart information to anyone, anywhere. Peer educators are key to its success. They recruit players and encourage their friends to come to the field and bring their friends with them. Lidya Kasiwa is heading the MTG programme: 'When girls see their peers at the football field they are more willing to go along themselves. Many rural girls are still unaware of some of the risks they might be exposed to and gaining information through peer learning at least gives them the chance to make informed choices. We've been asked by girls in neighbouring Malindi District to take the programme there. It makes me believe this can work well for out-of-school girls in other parts of Kenya.'

According to official Ministry of Education figures, only 22% of the eligible age group is studying in secondary school. That means 78% of young Kenyans do not go to secondary school. What are their current options at the age of 15, 16, 17 when they leave primary school? What realistic apprenticeships are available? For girls there's tailoring and little else in Kilifi. But most people in Kenya have at least one or two ideas of possible business plans in the informal sector. With such high unemployment rates they are greatly needed, as a strategy of hope if nothing else. How do these ideas become realities? The Ministry of Youth and Sport launched the Youth Enterprise Development Fund in 2007. One billion shillings (close to US$15 million) has been set aside to support groups at the constituency level and provide loans to youth-owned businesses. But what of the rural girl who wants to sell chapati or fried potatoes at the side of the road but who lacks even the skills or confidence to register her business. How can she secure a loan of even just 5,000 shillings (US$77) to start her business? How does she learn to keep good records? She needs training, as do many in a similar situation. An obvious potential initiative that can fill this gap is micro-finance, a booming approach internationally. But as others have pointed out, it is still not easy to reach girls who are this poor. How flexible can loans from institutions really be? What happens when they can't pay the money back? Do their struggles become greater? These are issues people working in micro-finance are dealing with, and it appears that there is no simple solution.

❖ ❖ ❖

The Kenyan runner Pamela Jelimo, just 18 years old, won the gold medal in the 800 metres at the Olympic Games in Beijing in August 2008. She brought back one of 14 medals won by young Kenyans on the track in China. Sport is inextricably linked to youth and national pride, as the pomp and ceremony led by the president, vice president and prime minister that welcomed the returning Olympic champions demonstrated. But how many equally talented Kenyans are not afforded the opportunity to work hard to turn their dreams into reality? Football administrators in Kenya have, to be blunt, brought the sport to its knees. If there isn't significant change, Mbeyu will end up living in one of the slums in Mombasa or Nairobi, scraping together a living, playing football at weekends, maybe playing for the national team, squabbling over allowances and feeling demoralised by the game that she loves so passionately. Organising sport needs strong, well-managed institutions run by committed and skilled people who want a fair system that gives all young players the chance to represent their country and play at the highest level. The Minister for Youth and Sports, Professor Hellen Sambili, spoke at the FAWE (Forum for African Women Educationalists) Kenya General Assembly in July 2008 on the role for youth and sports in community advocacy for girls and women's education. She concluded by saying that there's a need to identify effective strategies for increasing girls' mobility and visibility in their communities through sports. This is happening right here in Kenya, in Kilifi, through Moving the Goalposts. Girls are showing that through football they can be strong, public, communal, voluntary, successful; they can support each other to try to reach their goals, be they on or off the football pitch.

❖   ❖   ❖

My life in Kilifi with Collins and our two young daughters continues: I'm hoping that I can contribute to changing the context in which they, and all other young Kenyan girls, will grow up. This is not the last publication using Asya, Carol, Janet, Kadzo, Kanze, Juliet, Mariam, Mercy and Salma's stories. MTG is planning to present them in other ways too: a shorter, simplified version in both English and Kiswahili for girls, and boys, in East Africa, so they can learn more about the struggles, dilemmas and decisions that face young people. Scenarios from the girls' stories are currently used in MTG's peer-education programme, as role plays and as 'what would you do in this situation?' discussion topics. I'd like to build on the relationship I've developed with the girls. I'm fascinated to know what their lives will be like in 5, 10, 20 years and believe it could shed much more light on women's lives in Kenya in the 21st century.

Notes

1   *Daily Nation,* January 16th 2007.

2   Tolman, 2002, p. 188.

3   These girls were in school before free primary education was introduced in Kenya in 2003.

4   My family (the family I was born into and grew up with before leaving home) consists of my mother, elder brother, three younger sisters, my stepfather and two stepbrothers. My father died when I was 12 years old. My mother remarried when I was 15.

5   Mbilinyi, 1992, p. 35.

6   Temple and Edwards, 2002, p. 16.

7   Silverman, 1985, p. 157.

8   Silverman, p. 171.

9   As quoted in Plummer, 1995, p. 5.

10 As listed by primary school players during evaluation of 2005 football tournament.

11 Kenya. Ministry of Finance and Planning, 2000.

12 Kigiriama is a dialect of the nine Mijikenda tribes. Other Mijikenda tribes can understand dialects such as Kichonyi and Kiduruma, which are similar.

13 There are many cases when children who have finished primary school return to Standard 7 at another school. The reason given is that, because of poverty, they have failed to raise the fees to go to secondary school and rather than staying idle at home they would prefer to go back to repeat two years in school. Now that primary education is free they can return to primary school while planning how they might get enough money to go on to secondary school.

14 Kenya. Ministry of Planning and National Development, 2005, p. 38.

15 Juggling a football with your feet.

16 A chorus from a popular contemporary Kenyan song.

17 MTG girl coaches selected 'super teams' to represent their divisions to play against other divisional super teams. This tournament pitted Ganze, Kaloleni, Vintengeni and Bahari against each other in a one-day competition.

18 Fasting during the month of Ramadhan is to go without food or water from dawn until dark.

19 Each of the girls was given a wind-up, solar-powered radio; 300 radios were distributed to girls in MTG through collaboration with a BBC World Service programme,' Kimasomaso'.

20 These 'things' could be a string around the waist with specific beads or knots of medicine and perhaps grains or herbs tied into the string

as a protection against evil spirits.

21 A matatu doesn't run on a fixed schedule but waits until it fills with passengers before leaving.

22 Motsemme, 2004, p. 913.

23 Two of the three in secondary had been helped by MTG to get scholarships.

24 As reported by the Kilifi District Education Office, February 2008.

25 In Kilifi District there are some education bursaries dispersed through the local members of parliament, the District Education Office and the Constituency Development Fund (CDF). Other small organisations, such as KESHO [Kilifi Education Support KuHitimu Organisation] and Northern Magic support needy children through school.

26 Personal communication, District Education Office, May 2008.

27 ibid.

28 Mondoh and Mujidi, 2006, p. 58.

29 Fees for a secondary day school at that time, in 2006, were around 15,000 shillings (US$227) each year.

30 FIFA President Sepp Blatter, at the launch of an 'era of development' for women's football in 1995.

31 A bath in this context is water in a basin, which you use to wash your body.

32 Plummer, p. 5.

33 Fine, 1988, as cited in Tolman, 2002, p. 202.

34 Parallel programmes at university are for privately sponsored students.

35 The Kiswahili word the girls use is *kutongoza*. There isn't one suitable formal English word for a direct translation. English slang fits better but in this context kutongoza means all of these things: to approach, to seduce, to court, to pull, to hit on, to tap, to tune.

36 Tolman, p. 199.

37 Runganga and Aggleton, 1988, p. 75.

38 MTG United is the organisation's select team. The best players at the fields are selected for their field 'super team'. The best players from the field super teams play in their division's super team. The best from the divisions are selected for the MTG United teams, which play in tournaments and leagues outside Kilifi.

39 Mills and Ssewakiryanga, 2005, p. 91.

40 ibid., p. 93.

41 'Ninja fresh' means wearing a bui bui with the head and face covered and just the eyes showing.

42 Head, 2005, p. 5.

43 Mkhwanazi, 2006, p. 103.

44 A turnboy loads and unloads goods on and off the lorry.

45 A hospital can be any health facility: a private clinic, a government clinic, district hospital.

46 2005 study on the magnitude of abortion in Kenya, by the Ministry of Health.

47 WHO definition of unsafe abortion: 'A procedure for terminating unwanted pregnancy either by persons lacking the necessary skills or in an environment lacking the minimal medical standards or both'.

48 *East African Standard,* June 27th, 2007.

49 In following up this method, which I had never heard of, I was given this explanation from three different girls. You boil the razor blade to get the 'poison', or metallic salts, out of the metal. You then drink the water it was boiled in so the 'poison' can cause a miscarriage.

50 *East African Standard,* July 4th 2007.

51 Motsemme, 2004, p. 369.

52 Kenya. Central Bureau of Statistics, 2003.

53 Gollub, 2006.

54 Chege, 2007, p. 3.

55 Kenneth Wolstenholme, BBC TV commentary of the final moments of the match when England won the 1966 World Cup final, 'The crowd are on the pitch, they think it's all over … it is now…'

56 Otoo-Oyortey and Pobi, 2003, p. 44.

57 It's typical in a rural homestead that the female members of the family take turns to cook and do the other household chores.

58 The Luo tribe comes from the west of Kenya, around Lake Victoria.

59 Plummer, 199, p. 137–138.

60 A huge slum settlement in Nairobi.

61 Elimu Yetu Coalition, 2005, p. 112.

62 Family Health International, 2008, p. 33.

63 Kenya. Government, 2005. See both policy and plan of action.

64 Rani and Lule, 2004, p. 112.

Acknowledging the team

It's a wet, cool, dull and cloudy day—a rarity in Kilifi. I'm looking out of my office window on the first floor of Jakob's building, thinking about all the people who've had a part in this. But I'm distracted; at eye level two ripe, juicy-looking yellow papaya droop from the tree, inviting our neighbours to come and knock them down with their long, wobbly, thin stick. Further on, and much higher, are coconuts on trees swaying and bedraggled by the rain. The call for prayer is under way (is it that time already?) and the neighbours' buckets and jerry cans are lined up at the edge of their house, gratefully receiving the rainwater running down and off their iron-sheet roof. I thank whomever I should thank for this view, and the day-to-day Kilifi action I've observed through it—which is another story altogether. It was a welcome distraction from the process of writing.

My greatest debt of gratitude, though, must go to the nine girls who have so openly shared their lives with me since we started this project at the end of 2005. They've made me laugh and cry. They've given me much to think about and even more to challenge the many assumptions I've made about life, both mine and theirs.

Many people have listened, advised, helped and cajoled me as I've tried to make sense of the stories I've heard and the experiences I've had. The two people who were the reasons I came to Kilifi, my husband, Collins Owuor, and my best friend, Sassy Molyneux, might not realise quite how influential they've been. Always there, they are my rocks, keeping me grounded, listening to my endless tales and interpretations, providing other interpretations and sometimes, not often, telling me to just let it go for a while.

I thank Carla Sutherland of the Ford Foundation because she took a risk in recommending MTG for funding at a time when we were still young and relatively untested. She had the vision to sow the seeds for this project, this publication; she's a woman with more ideas than can ever be implemented and I'm indebted to her for seeing the potential in us.

It was a grant from the Ford Foundation that kick-started this project and kept pushing it along. Without the financial support from Ford it would never have come to fruition.

I was lucky to have the support of a bunch of brilliant women in an advisory group: Dayo Forster, Nduku Kilonzo, Martha Mwangome and Sassy Molyneux. They all gave their time to meet, discuss, twist and turn the initial ideas for the book, read the whole manuscript, and meet again to provide the kind of encouragement I feel privileged to have had. I can hear Dayo's enthusiasm and laughter as I write and her innate ability to know what works and what doesn't. Nduku, never one to shirk from saying it as it is, always posed the most difficult and direct questions and dilemmas, making me think and critique in more depth than I'd done before. Martha's phenomenal understanding and experiences of growing up rural in Kilifi clarified much and tested what I thought and felt, while her own story-telling abilities came to the fore. Sassy is an immense support, always professional, always thinking and questioning.

Jane Bennett, Charmaine Pereira and all my fellow participants at the Gender, Sexuality and Politics seminar at the African Gender Institute at the University of Cape Town in 2007—Agnes, Aisha, Bantu, Beatrice, Bibi, Gertrude, Helen, Nancy, Ndeshi, Nkoli and Shereen—provided a safe, supportive and thought-provoking space for three weeks. You all listened and advised and gave me the confidence to stop procrastinating and start writing. Thank you.

Many people within MTG and in Kilifi with whom I've worked over the last seven years have been instrumental with their contributions, stories and ideas. Margaret Belewa, with her direct, no-nonsense style, insisted that I had my own space, away from the rowdy day-to-day goings-on of MTG, in which to write. Thanks to Priscilla Munga and Reuben Jemase for discussing, transcribing and translating, and to Lidya Kasiwa, Cocky van Dam and Mr Mbaji, who all read drafts. Among the many staff members, volunteers and players are Harriet Chea, Mr Mwaro,

Janet Karembo, Betty Mapenzi, Salma Ali, Lilian Mbeyu, Rose Konde, Grace Werikhe, Mbeyu Akida and any peer educator who might have been passing the office when I was asking for opinions, who fielded my questions and tolerated my musing. I'm grateful to you all. You have provided me with a huge, rich resource of information and ideas about girls' teenage lives in Kilifi. Thanks to MTG's management board members, Betty Bundotich, Damigott John, Dorcas Kamuya, Florence Kitsao, Cleo Mugyenyi and Edna Ogada, who have midwifed MTG as it has grown into the strong, confident and transparent institution that it now is. To all the teachers and people who work for government and in NGOs and CBOs in Kilifi I owe a debt of gratitude.

Al Davies, Caz Lightowler, Tabs Mwangi, Trudie Lang and Britta Urban have been there in Kilifi for me with friendship, support and suggestions throughout the process, as have Sally Theobald, Helen Derbyshire, Catherine Locke and Claire MacKintosh from the UK. Special thanks to Heather Beresford who, as someone who had never been to Kenya and didn't know me, read the manuscript and gave invaluable insight from an entirely new perspective. Helen van Houten and Dali Mwagore did a great editing and typesetting job and were a pleasure to work with. Thanks also to Phillip Miyare for designing the cover.

Thanks to my mum for supporting all the decisions I've made and to my very special daughters, Flo and Bella, who've made sure I haven't spent every minute of the day working, for taking me away from this and for making me laugh.

Finally I express my gratitude to the game of football for being such a big part of my life. I've played it, coached it and watched it in many different places, from the fading chalk-dust touchline in Ganze, Kilifi, with 20 other spectators to the press box at the 1999 Women's World Cup final, alongside 90,000 others packed into the Rose Bowl stadium in Pasadena, USA. Football might not matter to everyone, but it has introduced me to places and people I would never have come across without it, and for that I am grateful to the beautiful game.

Appendix 1
Team selection

Eighty-eight girls filled in the forms to volunteer for the Life Stories project. In the end I chose nine, three from each of the divisions of Bahari, Ganze and Kaloleni in which we were working at the time we started. I knew most of them to some extent. From the 88, I selected 21 for the first interviews. I looked at where they lived, religion as Christian or Muslim, and their level of activity in football. I wanted to get a mix in geography, religion and football activity. When I interviewed the 21 girls, we talked about family, home life, domestic work, things they liked to do, problems in their lives, menstruation and football. I analysed how open and chatty they were in the interviews and selected nine, trying to get a variety of quiet, shy ones and more open girls. I then wrote letters to the girls who'd been selected and those who had not, to give them the news. I also wrote letters to the parents or guardians of the selected girls, which they had to sign to give their consent for the girls to take part. This is standard practice in MTG for girls to play in the football leagues, attend training courses, go on trips, and so on, and I felt that this project was no different, as it would take their time and energy.

All of our conversations were held in Kiswahili. Transcribing, translating and interpreting was a team effort. Although I did the interviews I was helped in the transcriptions and some of the translations by Priscilla and in the other translations by my Kiswahili teacher, Reuben. So we were a mixed bunch in gender and race: white British woman, black Kenyan woman and black Kenyan man, all with our own histories and locations.

Temple and Edwards comment on the social location of the interpreter and their own assumptions and concerns that they bring to the interview and the research process.* I knew both Priscilla and Reuben very well. My first concern in the team was

---

*   Temple and Edwards, 2002, p. 11.

confidentiality. I knew I could trust them not to talk about the identity and names of any of the girls with anyone other than me. Priscilla was particularly impressive in this concern because she and I were both working day to day with the girls, but I never, not once, felt worried that she had discussed with other people anything she had transcribed or translated.

This was easier for Reuben as he did not know any of the girls. I'd known him for over five years when I first asked him to do the translations. He had taught Kiswahili to many people in Kilifi and was a good friend. He lived in Mombasa; he was a socio-political commentator, with considerable in-depth knowledge of Kenya's political history and strong views on corruption and impunity. He also loved football. We had some great discussions once he'd got my Kiswahili to a respectable standard.

Reuben and his wife, also an experienced Kiswahili teacher whom I had never met, did most of the translations and provided me with more insight. Reuben was used to translating written documents from English to Kiswahili, and vice versa. He hadn't come across transcriptions of teenage girls, written as they had spoken. He commented to me on the way in which they talked: broken sentences, mixed tenses, a switch from the personal to the abstract and then back again, exactly as they had talked to me, the way teenagers, or anyone else, can talk when getting into personal narratives. Reuben had also been shocked by some of what he'd read. He said it was a learning journey for him, that the stories had taught him about teenage lives, and that it had helped him prepare for the looming adolescent years of his sons.

❖   ❖   ❖

The girls knew from the beginning that we would not use their names and that I would also change the names of any of the places they specifically referred to. I asked them to choose their pseudonyms, to imagine what they would want their names to be in another life, at the meeting in July 2007. But I later felt that I needed to take more control of this process. By the time the book was written the nine girls had met three times in meetings, and I wanted to reduce the chances of them being able to piece together each other's stories. In writing the book I changed their names again so that none of the girls could know anyone else's pseudonym. This didn't fully resolve the problem within the group, but in subsequent meetings their maturity and understanding of this complex issue allayed my fears to an extent. I felt that there was a solidarity that had built up within the group. They knew that individually they had opened up to me, told me 'secrets', and they deduced that the other girls had done the same. I got the impression that they would try to work out who was who but that they wouldn't do so with the intent of using that information in a negative way. I felt there was an understanding that they were all in the same boat and needed to protect each other.

My greater concern was protecting their identities from other people who knew them and might read the book. I was worried about whether I could fully protect their identities while keeping the essence of their stories. We discussed this in detail at a meeting with the girls in May 2008 where I took time to explain confidentiality. Despite their names being changed, the risk in this type of work is that someone reading the book who knows a particular girl could piece together her story. As the girls had disclosed thoughts and actions that they might not have shared with others, it might be difficult to know whether people would take their stories positively or use the information against them in some way. It was a long discussion but I felt that they had all contributed to the conversation and had grasped the concept.

I also wanted them to be comfortable with what I had written about them. I gave each her own copy of the final draft of the book and a list of every page where she was mentioned. I asked them to take the draft with them and to read all the parts that concerned them so that we could meet again individually and discuss it. I wanted to make sure they understood it and that they were OK with what had been written. If there was anything they were uneasy with they had the option of asking me to remove it. We scheduled the individual meetings at their homes or schools for July 2008. When I went to visit them in July they'd all taken the time to read the parts of the book that concerned them and some had read much more. They were very positive about it, they liked it. A couple wanted clarification on some issues and they all wanted to know when it was going to be ready, when they would get their own copy of the published book. I was nervous when Kanze told me that her older brother had read it until she told me what he'd said. He told her, 'Eh, this really is your story. But you could even be any of these girls in the book. This is how your lives are. I hope that more people in Coast Province will get to read it. It can teach us a lot.'

At the time my final draft was ready three of the girls were still under 18. All their parents or guardians had given the girls permission to take part in the project at the beginning, but I had considered going back to the parent or guardian of the girls who were still under 18. That, however, could have compromised confidentiality. It would be hard for the parent or guardian to consent for their daughter's story to be used if they hadn't also had the chance to read through and make sure they understood it. I was faced with a dilemma: involve the parents again, taking control away from the girls, or, as all the girls were at least 17 by the time the book would come out, treat them as adults who had understood the issues well enough to consent to their stories being used. In the end I decided to go with the second option, believing that the girls had understood that there was still a chance that someone might be able to deduce that the story belonging to so-and-so was hers.

❖ ❖ ❖

From the start I had a firm agreement with the girls about this project. It was voluntary. They didn't have to do it. They knew that, and had agreed to it, knowing that they would not receive anything material from me or MTG. But as we moved along and the girls told me so much more about their struggles I became increasingly concerned. I felt that as an organisation we should show some appreciation towards them, to recognise that they were, through their stories, providing information to help MTG and, we hoped, others outside the organisation.

At the same time, I was expecting the girls to ask me for things, just because that would have been normal. It was an occupational hazard for a white person working in a poor district that relies to a great extent on the tourism industry. But they hardly ever asked me for things. Mercy once asked if I could buy her a pair of glasses. Asya wanted a sewing machine for herself and a phone for her one-year-old daughter. Carol, at the time we met just before she was to give birth, half-heartedly told me that her husband was wondering if I could buy her a mobile phone. But the rest never asked me for anything, ever.

We did eventually, as an organisation, give them all something for their contribution: a solar wind-up radio. We had 300 to distribute through collaboration with the BBC World Service Kimasomaso radio programme. The radios went to girls who were active volunteers or whose teams had done well in MTG leagues and tournaments. So they received something small and tangible for the time they'd volunteered to tell their stories.

One thousand copies of this book are being published with funding from a grant from the Ford Foundation. We have specific target audiences: 1) people working for NGOs and donors in East Africa, with a focus on adolescence, 2) international, regional, national and provincial policy and decision makers, 3) national and local government ministries and 4) sports organisations. These copies will not be sold. Neither I nor MTG will receive a shilling for the book. We are producing them to bring girls' stories to a wider audience, to get their stories out into the open, not as a profit-making venture.

Appendix 2
Not a level playing field:
Kilifi District facts and figures

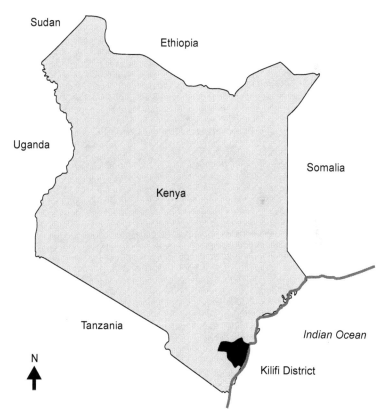

Sudan

Ethiopia

Uganda

Somalia

Kenya

Tanzania

Indian Ocean

N

Kilifi District

Source: KIM Epi-Dpp
VIS a Cartography by Census Department

Table 1. Demographic indicators, 2002

Population	597,354
Number of males	283,702
Number of females	313,652
Female-to-male sex ratio	100 : 95
Primary school population (6–13) years	143,085
Secondary school population (14–17) years	56,575
Number of youthful population (15–25) years	118,304
Labour force (15–64) years	294,754
Population growth rate	3.05%
Rural population at start of plan period, 2002	411,417
Urban population at start of plan period, 2002	189,227

Source: District Statistic Offices, Kilifi, from Kilifi District Strategic Plan, 2005–2010

Table 2. Socio-economic and health indicators, 2002

Total number of households	90,311
Average households size	6.6
Number of female-headed households	14,296
Number of disabled	59,653
Children needing special protection	26,014
Absolute poverty (rural and urban)	66.8%
Income from agriculture	80.6%
Income from rural self-employment	1.85%
Waged employment	6.2%
Urban self-employment	11.4%
Number of unemployed	231,978
Crude birth rate	49.2/1000
Life expectancy	56 years
Infant mortality rate	85/1000
Under-5 mortality rate	141/1000
Total fertility rate	6
HIV prevalence rate	7%
Doctor-to-patient ratio	1 : 100,000

Source: Various, including district medical officer of Health from Kilifi District strategic plan, 2005–2010 (Kenya. Government, 2005).

Appendix 3
If you let me play: The growth of MTG in Kilifi, 2001 to 2007

	Total number by:		
	2001	2004	2007
Girls' football leagues	0	7	17
Girls' football teams	20	106	146
Girls' football players	392	1,672	2,316
Girls' football matches	12	864	2,545
Primary schools tournament	1	4	6
Secondary schools tournament	0	3	6
Coaches trained	20	59	287
Referees trained	0	75	136
Peer educators trained	0	10	128
First aiders trained	0	3	33
Committee members trained	0	25	97
Evaluators trained	0	0	18
Counsellors trained	0	0	20

A few notable moments
○ MTG United Under-13 champions of the MYSA 'Women Unite for Peace and Reconciliation' football tournament, Nairobi, April 2008
○ Hosted Manchester United Under-15 boys' team in 2004 when they visited Kenya. Rose Konde from MTG was an assistant referee during United's match against a Mombasa Youth boys' team
○ Two MTG projects selected in the 16 finalists in the Nike Changemakers Global Sport for a Better World competition
○ MTG United Under-16 winners of the Mombasa Show tournament, 2007, in front of a crowd of over 5,000 people
○ Mbeyu Akida selected as one of only two young Kenyans to represent the country at a youth summit in Algiers, 2007
○ Priscilla Munga the first girl from MTG to go to university in 2006

Appendix 4
A game of two halves: Income and expenditure for teenage girls and their families in Kilifi

I knew that the profit margins in Kilifi for small-scale, informal work were minimal but it still surprised me how small they really are. The amounts of money the girls can earn through hard labour out in the fields or through selling snacks in the hot sun is extremely little. You can work for two whole days in a shamba to afford sanitary pads, up to six or seven days to pay for your end-of-term school exam fees. If a girl is out selling things on behalf of her family, any profit will be used to cover the basic needs of everyone in the family, not just those of the girl who has been doing the work.

Income

Work, activity	Income	
	Kenya shillings	US$
Selling half cakes, mabuyu (baobab fruit), peanuts, mahamri, sunflower seeds, mangoes, cashew nuts	1–10 per piece or packet	up to 0.15
Selling vegetables, such as mchicha, mnavu [leafy green vegetables], door to door	5–10 per bunch	0.07–0.15
Working in the shamba (for a day)	30	0.45
Making brooms	15	0.22
Collecting water (per 20 litre jerry can)	10	0.15
Washing clothes (per item)	5	0.07
Selling firewood (sold depending on size of stick)	10 for 20 sticks	0.15
Plaiting hair into lines	10, 20, 30, 40	0.15, 0.30, 0.45, 0.60
Looking after children (in school holidays)	800–1,000 per month	12.50–16

Expenditure

Item	Price	
	Kenya shillings	US$
Food items		
Sugar, 1/4 kg	15	0.22
Tea leaves, 5, 10 g	3, 7	0.04, 0.10
Bread, loaf	38	0.60
Unga, the maize meal staple food, 2 kg	71	1.10
Unga, 1 kg	36	0.57
Omena mkebe, tin of small dried fish that can last a family for 2 weeks, if not eaten every day	100	1.50
Papa, dried shark: number of pieces depends on the size of the family	10, 20, 30, 40	0.15, 0.30, 0.45, 0.60
Salt, 1/4`kg	5	0.07
Royco cube, flavouring	1.5	0.02
Water, 20 litres, 4–6 a day	2–3	0.03–0.05
Cooking oil for one day	10	0.15
Onion, 1	3–5	0.04–0.07
Tomatoes, 2–4	10–20	0.15–0.30
Egg, 1	10	0.15
Blue Band margarine, 25 g, 50 g	5, 10	0.07–0.15
Milk, 1 litre, unpasteurized, sold door to door	40	0.60
Milk, ½ litre, unpasteurized, sold door to door	20	0.30
Milk, 500-ml packet pasteurized	30	0.47
Milk, 1 cup from the cow (in rural areas)	10	0.15
Non-food and personal items		
Sanitary pads, pack of 10	45, 55, 67, 80	0.67, 0.82, 1.06, 1.25
Cotton wool, packet of 50 g, used instead of sanitary pads	20–35	0.30–0.55
Washing powder, 200 g	32	0.50
Panga, hard soap for washing clothes, size depends on amount of clothes to wash	5, 8, 26	0.07, 0.12, 0.41
Soap for bathing	10–26	0.15–0.41
Hair braiding or plaiting—cost depends on size of braids; could be free if a friend or sister does it	20, 30, 40, 50	0.30, 0.45, 0.60, 0.75
Hair oil—can be free if made with own coconut	50	0.79
Coconut oil for skin—can be free if made from own coconuts	10–12, 25	0.15–0.18, 0.37
School		
Pen or pencil	10	0.15
Rubber	2	0.03
Geometry set	250	3.70
School uniform	450–500	7.10–7.50
Exam fees, every term	200–220	3.00–3.30
Shoes and socks	500	7.50

Appendix 5
The football season: Annual calendar for girls in Kilifi

Month	Home and shamba	Food security	School, games, rest	MTG football	Season
January	Buying *mapanga* [large knives for cutting trees] and *majembe* [hoes]		School opens	Practice starting, annual planning for leagues	
February	Clearing of fields in preparation for planting, cutting big trees, slashing grass at weekends		Ball games at school: football, basketball and netball in primary. Athletics, hockey, handball in secondary	Football leagues start. Sometimes too hot to play without shoes on sandy pitches between 11 am and 3 pm so have to wait until later in the day	No rain, very hot, becoming more humid
March	Preparation of the shamba, clearing and digging, planting if there is rain: maize, green grams, cassava, groundnuts, cowpeas, *mbaazi* (pigeon peas)	Some maize remaining from last year's harvest	Games ongoing	Secondary school tournament finals	
April	Weeding, planting greens: *mnavu, mchicha*, cabbage, *sukuma wiki* (kale), tomatoes		School holidays: weddings, burial ceremonies, remembrance ceremonies, discos	MTG United teams to Nairobi for MYSA tournament. Under-13 super team tournament. Rains affect participation. Girls working in the shamba during the holidays	Rainy, hot

Month	Home and shamba	Food security	School, games, rest	MTG football	Season
May	Planting more cereals—cowpeas, weeding at the weekends	Food shortage: hunger	School re-opens. Cross-country and athletics in primary	Labour Day tournament, Mombasa	Rainy, cooler
June	Harvesting fruits in season: mangoes, tangerines. Applying manure to crops— waste products of chicken, cattle, goats, sheep	Food shortage: hunger	Ball games in secondary school: football, handball, volleyball, basketball	Coach the Coach programme ongoing—girls raid mango trees at the side of the pitch during water breaks for ripe, juicy mangoes	Rainy, cool
July	Weeding. Starting first harvest	Roasting of the first crop of green maize	Preparing for second term exams	Primary school tournament finals	Dry, cool
August	Harvesting maize and cowpeas. The elders decide when to harvest but everyone knows when the maize looks ready. A small child can go to an elder and say they think the maize is ready, let's go and harvest. Maize drying in the fields	Roasting and boiling of maize cobs to eat	Schools closed, weddings, remembrance ceremonies, discos, Mombasa Show—the annual provincial agricultural show at Mombasa showground	MTG training camp: training courses in coaching, refereeing, first aid, peer education and practice for MTG United first team, under-16s and under-13s at a school in the district	Dry, warm
September	Second harvesting of dried maize, put into the granary, a small raised mud hut with a *makuti* roof. Maize taken off the husks, put into sacks and treated to stop weevils and other insects	If maize is plentiful, it is shared among neighbours	School opens	Football leagues ongoing	Dry, warm

Month	Home and shamba	Food security	School, games, rest	MTG football	Season
October	Maize is pounded and taken to be ground at the *posho* mill		Girls asking for cards to wish them success or good luck in passing their exams	Moi Day, Kenyatta Day—go to the field to play and for celebrations	Hot
November	Tangerine harvest, pounding maize	Enough maize	End of year exams: KCPE and KCSE	League closing ceremonies	Rainy, hot
December	Visiting family members—grandparents, aunties, uncles		Schools close, Jamhuri public holiday, weddings, discos, burials and memorials	Jamhuri Day tournament on Dec 12th, at Mombasa. Close for Christmas break	Dry, hot

Appendix 6
The team line-up: The girls from 2005 to 2007

Name	Age		Lives with ...		Religion		School	
			2005	2007	2005	2007	2005	2007
Asya	16	18	Grandparents, mother passed away, never knew father	Husband's family, including her 10-month-old daughter	Muslim	Muslim	Standard 6	No longer in school
Carol	15	17	Father, mother passed away	Husband's family, 8 months pregnant	Christian	None	Standard 7	Finished primary
Janet	15	17	Father, divorced from mother	Brother, close to school	Christian	Christian	Form 1, Secondary	Repeating Form 2 secondary
Juliet	15	17	Mother, father passed away	Mother working away from home. Juliet head of household	Christian	Christian	Standard 6	Standard 7, had repeated Standard 6
Kadzo	14	16	Mother and father	Mother and father	Christian	Muslim	Standard 5	Standard 7
Kanze	15	17	Mother, father passed away	Brother	Christian	Christian	Standard 7	Tailoring college
Mariam	14	16	Sister, mother lives in Garsen, father passed away	On her own, sister nearby	Muslim	Muslim	Standard 6	Standard 8
Mercy	16	18	Mother and father	Mother, separated from father, boarding in school	Christian	Christian	Standard 7	Form 1 secondary
Salma	14	16	Mother, father passed away	Mother, father passed away, boarding in school	Muslim	Muslim	Standard 7	Form 1 secondary

Appendix 7
The schedule

October 2005	Initial meetings with girls at 12 football clubs to introduce the Life Stories project and to recruit volunteers; 88 girls volunteered
November 2005	Individual interviews held with 21 girls; 9 girls selected to continue
January 2006	Individual interviews with the 9 girls in their schools and homes
May 2006	Individual interviews with the 9 girls in their schools and homes
September 2006	Individual interviews with the 9 girls in their schools and homes
December 2006	Individual interviews with the 9 girls in their schools and homes
June 2007	Individual interviews with the 9 girls in their schools and homes
August 2007	Meeting with 9 girls and 2 relatives of each girl
November 2007	Meeting with 9 girls and individual interviews
May 2008	Meeting with 9 girls to distribute final draft and discuss confidentiality
July 2008	Individual discussions with the 9 girls in their homes to discuss the final draft

Abbreviations and acronyms

AIDS	acquired immune deficiency syndrome
APHIA II Coast	AIDS, Population and Health Integrated Assistance II Coast
ART	antiretroviral treatment
CBO	community-based organisation
FIFA	Federation Internationale de Football Association
HIV	human immunodeficiency virus
KCPE	Kenya Certificate of Primary Education
KCSE	Kenya Certificate of Secondary Education
KEMRI	Kenya Medical Research Institute
MC	master of ceremonies
MDG	Millennium Development Goal
MTG	Moving the Goalposts
MYSA	Mathare Youth Sports Association
NACC	National AIDS Control Council
NGO	non-government organisation
TB	tuberculosis
SSR	social studies and religion
STI	sexually transmitted infection
UEFA	Union of European Football Associations
UNICEF	United Nations Children's Fund
VCT	voluntary counselling and testing for HIV

Kiswahili and local terms as used in this book

appo	a game played by three young girls where one girl stands in the middle and the other two throw a small ball, trying to hit the legs of the one in the middle. When she's hit, she swaps places with the girl who hit her
banghi	marijuana
barafu	small ice lollies
biriani	Swahili spicy rice and meat dish served mainly on Fridays and during Idd ul Fitr
bob	shilling
boda boda	bicycles used as a taxi with a seat for carrying passengers
boma	enclosed place for bathing in rural areas with makeshift walls and no roof. Also known as 'uwa'. 'Boma' is used for the whole homestead in other parts of Kenya
bui bui	burka, the loose, black, long garment worn by Muslim women
chapati	round, flat, pancake-like bread
chief	local administrative officer, employed by the government. Must be a member of the community. He or she (usually he) deals with local issues and disputes. Supported by subchiefs and village elders
half cakes	small round cakes cooked over a fire and sold for 1 shilling
hoteli	small local joint or cafe for tea and hot food
kanga	colourful rectangular piece of cotton cloth used as a wrap, to carry babies on the back, etc. Also called 'leso'.
kibanda	stall for selling things such as vegetables, peanuts, snacks
Kigiriama	one of the nine dialects of the Mijikenda; others include Kichonyi, Kiduruma
kikoi	Kenyan material used as a wrap

Kimasomaso	BBC World Service Swahili radio programme for adolescents on health and other issues
kusengenya	to gossip
kusengenywa	to be gossiped about
leso	colourful cotton rectangle of cloth used to wrap around clothes, carry babies, etc. A kanga.
mabuyu	sweets made from fruit, kernels found in baobab pods
madzaji	a local fruit, large, yellow-orange in colour, said to bring on a miscarriage
mahamri	sweet doughnuts
majembe	hoes
makuti	thatch for houses made of palm-tree leaves
mapanga	large knives, machetes for use in the shamba
marahaba	response to 'shikamoo'
matatu	public transport minibus
matufe	homemade footballs made of plastic, paper and string
mbaazi	pigeon peas, often cooked in coconut milk for breakfast
mchicha	leafy green vegetable
mganga	traditional healer
Mijikenda	group of nine tribes in Coast Province
mkilifi	neem tree; also known as 'mwarubaini' (literally 'of 40') because the leaves and bark are used as traditional treatments for over 40 illnesses
mnavu	bitter, leafy green vegetable
mnazi	palm wine
mshihiri	piece of material worn as a long skirt by men, in and around the home, and further afield, especially by Muslims to the mosque
murram	road surface of hard soil with impeded drainage
mzungu	white person
Ninja fresh	slang for woman wearing full bui bui with her face covered and only her eyes showing
omena	small dried fish
pepeta	juggling with a football
pilau	spicy rice and meat dish
posho mill	diesel-fuelled mill where maize is ground to make maize meal
sanduku	lockable metal box used by all secondary school

	boarding students for their personal belongings
sawa	OK
shamba	farm, plot of land for farming, which can be anything from 15 by 30 metres to 5 hectares or larger
shikamoo	greeting to an elder
sima or ugali	staple food cooked from maize meal and water
stage	a large bus station or simply the spot on the side of the road where you wait for the vehicle
sukuma wiki	kale, a leafy green vegetable, eaten with sima (ugali); literally 'push [through] the week'
tabia mbaya	bad behaviour
tarmacked	road surfaced with tar mixed with broken stone
tuk tuk	three-wheeled covered motorbike with seats behind for three passengers
tunaweza	we can do it, the MTG slogan
unga	maize flour
vibarua	casual work (singular kibarua)

Literature cited

Anyangu, S. 'Abortion forum turns chaotic.' *East African Standard,* June 27th 2007.

Chege, F. 'Researching gender: explorations into sexuality and HIV / AIDS in African contexts.' RECOUP Working Paper No. 7. University of Cambridge: DFID. August 2007.

Elimu Yetu Coalition. 'The challenge of educating girls in Kenya.' In Aikman, S. and Unterhalter, E., eds., *Beyond access: transforming policy and practice for gender equality in education.* Oxford: Oxfam, 2005.

Family Health International. 'Aphia II Baseline Behavioral Monitoring Survey Report Coast – Rift Valley 2007.' Nairobi: FHI, 2008.

Gollub, E. Choice is empowering: getting strategic about preventing HIV infection. *Women International Family Planning Perspectives* 32(4) (2006):209–212.

Head, J. Sexuality and HIV. Presentation in Understanding Human Sexuality Seminar Series (South Africa), African Regional Sexuality Resource Centre in collaboration with Health Systems Trust and Women's Health Resource Unit, University of Cape Town. 2005.

Jolly, S. Sexuality and development. *IDS Policy Briefing* 29, April 2006.

Kenya. Central Bureau of Statistics. *Kenya demographic and health survey 2003.* www.cbs.go.ke.

Kenya. Government. Adolescent reproductive health and development policy. 2005. http://www.ncapd-ke.org/publications

———. Adolescent reproductive health and development policy plan of action 2005–2015. http://www.ncapd-ke.org/publications.

———. Kilifi District strategic plan 2005–2010.

Kenya. Ministry of Finance and Planning. Second report on poverty in Kenya. Nairobi: Ministry of Finance and Planning, 2000.

Kenya. Ministry of Health. National AIDS and STI Control Programme (NASCOP). *Kenya AIDS indicator survey 2007: preliminary report.* Nairobi, Kenya, 2008.

Mbilinyi, M. Research methodologies in gender issues. In: Meena, R., ed., *Gender in southern Africa.* Harare: SAPES Books, 1992.

Mills, D., and Ssewakiryanga, R. No romance without finance: commodities, masculinities and relationships amongst Kampalan students. In: Cornwall, A., ed., *Readings in gender in Africa.* Bloomington, Indiana: Indiana University Press, 2005.

Mkhwanazi, N. Partial truths: representations of teenage pregnancy in research. *Anthropology Southern Africa* 29(3–4), 2006.

Mondoh, H.O., and Mujidi, J. The education of girls in Kenya: looking back and still looking forward. *CODESRIA Bulletin* 1–2 (2006):58–60.

Motsemme, N. The mute always speak: on women's silences at the Truth and Reconciliation Commission. *Current Sociology* 52(5) (2004):909–932.

Nyassy, D. Village teenagers learn bitterly not to experiment with love affairs. *Daily Nation*, January 16th 2007.

Odhiambo, A. Commentary: Opposition to abortion is a conspiracy by patriarchy. *East African Standard*, July 4th 2007.

Otoo-Oyortey, N., and Pobi, S. Early marriage and poverty: exploring links and key policy issues. *Gender and Development* 11(2), 2003.

Plummer, K. *Telling sexual stories: power, change and social worlds.* London and New York: Routledge, 1995.

Rani, M., and Lule, E. Exploring the socioeconomic dimension of adolescent reproductive health: a multicountry analysis. *International Family Planning Perspectives* 30(3), 2004.

Runganga, A.O., and Aggleton, P. Migration, the family, and the transformation of a sexual culture. *Sexualities* 1(1), 1998.

Silverman, D. *Qualitative methodology and sociology.* Gower, Aldershot, UK, 1985.

Sow, F. The social sciences in Africa and gender analysis. In: Iman, A., Mama, A., and Sow, F., eds., *Engendering African social sciences*. Dakar: CODESRIA Books, 1997.

Temple, B., and Edwards, R. Interpreters/translators and cross-language research: reflexivity and border crossings. *International Journal of Qualitative Methods* 1(2), 2002.

Tolman, D.L. *Dilemmas of desire: teenage girls talk about sexuality.* Cambridge, Massachusetts: Harvard University Press, 2002.

UNICEF. Adolescence: a time that matters. New York: UNICEF, 2002.

3399384

Made in the USA